1990 EDITION

46th ANNUAL SPORTS JOURNALISM AWARDS

BEST SPORTS STORIES

THE ANTHOLOGY THAT HONORS 1989's TOP SPORTS WRITING AND PHOTOGRAPHY

Edited and Published by

The Sporting News

Editor/Best Sports Stories 1990
DAVE SLOAN

President and Chief Executive Officer
THOMAS G. OSENTON

Book Publisher
GREGORY WILEY

Editorial Director of Books and Periodicals
RON SMITH

Published in the United States by THE SPORTING NEWS Publishing Co., 1212 North Lindbergh Boulevard, St. Louis, Missouri 63132.

Library of Congress Catalog Card Number: 45-35124

ISSN: 0067-6292
ISBN: 0-89204-353-9
10 9 8 7 6 5 4 3 2 1

First Edition

Table of Contents

The Prize-Winning Photographs

Other Photographs

The Prize-Winning Color Photograph
Speed!

by Bernard Brault of La Presse. The winning color photograph, which appears on the back cover, shows a marmot jumping into the air as Ricardo Patrese passes by during the Canadian Grand Prix in Montreal. Patrese finished second in the race, ahead of the marmot.

PREFACE

Historians will remember 1989 as the Year of Upheaval, both literally and figuratively. The national spotlight focused early in the year on the changing fortunes and misfortunes of five major sports figures and then, just when the country was settling into an interesting Bay Area World Series battle between the Oakland Athletics and San Francisco Giants, the biggest upheaval of all, an earthquake measuring 7.1 on the Richter scale, cast a pall over the nation's psyche as well as baseball's showcase event.

Two of the saddest stories of the year involved Cincinnati Reds Manager Pete Rose, baseball's all-time leader in hits, and baseball Commissioner A. Bartlett Giamatti. Following a long investigation that Rose attempted to block through a series of legal maneuvers, Giamatti finally suspended him from baseball for life for a "variety of acts which have stained the game," most notably gambling. Eight days after announcing his decision in the Rose matter, Giamatti died of a heart attack—five months after taking office.

Other shocking developments included the retirement of National Football League Commissioner Pete Rozelle, the man who had ushered the league into an era of unprecedented prosperity, the ouster of Tom Landry after 27 years as coach of the Dallas Cowboys and the resignation of Oklahoma football coach Barry Switzer in the midst of a drug scandal.

On the field, the A's went on to complete a four-game sweep of the Giants after an unprecedented 10-day delay in the fall classic, but the most noteworthy 1989 team victory belonged to the NFL's San Francisco 49ers. The 49ers crushed the Denver Broncos, 55-10, in Super Bowl XXIV to record their fourth championship in nine years while becoming the first team to win back-to-back Super Bowls in a decade.

Other title winners included the National Basketball Association's Detroit Pistons, who defeated the two-time defending-champion Los Angeles Lakers in the title series; the Michigan Wolverines, playing under interim Coach Steve Fisher, in the NCAA Tournament; the University of Miami in college football, and the Calgary Flames, winners of the 1989 Stanley Cup in hockey.

Wherever the action, *they* were there. "They" refers to the men and women who put as much effort into their pursuit of the perfect story or picture as athletes put into their search for excellence. The competition is fierce and the results gratifying. Those who chronicled the 1989 sports world for newspapers and magazines throughout the country continued to move toward the lofty goal of perfection, taking their readers behind the scenes for insight and perspective on the personalities and events that made the year memorable.

The Sporting News is proud to present a small sprinkling of those memories in the 46th edition of *Best Sports Stories,* the anthology that honors the year's top writers and photographers. TSN is editing and publishing its eighth edition of the anthology, which traces its roots to 1944 and the efforts of Irving Marsh and Edward Ehre. The contest to select winners and contributors attracted more than a thousand newspaper and magazine entries. It was open to writers and photographers throughout the country and accepted only stories and pictures that were published in 1989. Serving as judges for the eighth straight year was a panel of five professors from the University of Missouri, home of one of the world's most-respected journalism education programs. They are:

James D. Atwater, former dean of Missouri's School of Journalism and now a professor who teaches magazine writing.

Brian Brooks, associate professor of journalism at the University of Missouri and coordinator of the school's editing programs.

George Kennedy, Managing Editor of the *Columbia Missourian,* the daily newspaper produced by the School of Journalism that services the city of Columbia.

Bill Kuykendall, associate professor, director of the University of Missouri photojournalism sequence and director of the International Pictures of the Year competition.

Daryl Moen, professor of journalism and director of the School of Journalism's Professional Programs.

Those five judges can attest to the agonizing problems that arise when you sort through hundreds of creative, well-written stories in search of the *four* that deserve special recognition. Likewise, the selection process for *three* pictures. But, after painstakingly considering the merits of each entry, the judges chose the following winners, each of whom receives a $500 prize:

WRITING

Reporting	Angelo Cataldi, and Glen Macnow	Philadelphia Inquirer
Feature	Mitch Albom	Detroit Free Press
Magazine	Pat Jordan	Gentlemen's Quarterly
Commentary	Thomas Boswell	Washington Post

PHOTOGRAPHY

Color	Bernard Brault	La Presse
B&W Action	Stephen Morton	Gainesville Sun
B&W Feature	Greg Trott	Vacaville Reporter

It also was difficult to weed the selection list to the choice stories that would appear in this book. By no means are the stories and photos that follow the winning selections losers. They are, rather, a tribute to the sports journalism profession, which seems to get stronger every year. All of the *Best Sports Stories* contributors are providing an entertaining look at the 1989 sports year, as seen through the eyes and lenses of those who were there.

Best Commentary Story

Curse of Modern Sports: Me-Itis

GENERAL

By *THOMAS BOSWELL*

From the Washington Post

What ever happened to humble heroes? If Lou Gehrig were alive, would he wear a mohawk haircut? Or write a tell-all biography at age 22 about his former college team? Course not.

If Joe Louis were champ, would he deck himself in a dozen gold chains, then name himself Prime Time? No way.

If Jim Thorpe were in his heyday, would he do a TV commercial pretendeing to "know" all about sports in which he'd never accomplished anything?

If Walter Johnson won the final game of the World Series, would he kneel to say a public prayer? Then yell into a camera, "I'm going to Disney World?"

Would Bronko Nagurski sell himself as "The Refrigerator"? Would Sammy Baugh wear a headband in the Super Bowl criticizing the commissioner of his sport? Would Babe Ruth—yes, even The Babe, who'd do most anything—have a 900 number to make a buck off his fans by telling them what he ate for breakfast?

If Joe DiMaggio had somehow gotten himself banned from baseball, would he decline comment, saying he was saving his story to sweeten the book deal?

These days if a college football team isn't trying to run up a 100-point score, then a college basketball team is trying to full-court press its way to 100 points in a half against a pathetic foe.

All together now, everybody paint your face or chest in your team's colors, wear a Hog or a Dawg mask, chant an obscenity and hold up your bedsheet sign that says, "We're No. 1." Then unscrew your head and spike it in the nearest end zone.

Some of us who aren't old enough to remember the good old days are becoming nostalgic for them anyway.

What would Bobby Jones and Sugar Ray Robinson think of today's braggarts and blowhards? They loved celebrity and hobnobbed with the highest. The real Sugar Ray—now even nicknames get purloined in the interests of hype—drove a pink Cadillac. And Jones created a tournament to his own memory. But they didn't make fools of themselves. The combined personal style with class.

Once modesty was the norm. For every Dizzy Dean, there were countless Babe Didriksons and Bill Tildens. Now we cling to athletes who see themselves as the last examples of some noble endangered species. People such as Chris Evert or Michael Jordan or Cal Ripken Jr., who have an innate sense of reserve, seem like treasures. You can do a zillion ads like Evert, or wear fur coats and invent new dunks like Jordan, or sell milk like Ripken and still remain essentially unpretentious. Granted the difference between self-expression and self-glorification is a knack, a gift.

But once upon a time, it was far from a rare ability. The current vogue of "Home Run Derby" (a '50s TV show now being replayed on ESPN) is not primarily due to curiosity about the batting stances of Hank Aaron or Mickey Mantle or Willie Mays. Rather it's the corny interviews we love. Why? Because those players were unfailingly modest—even a little bashful. Their answers were not rehearsed or self-promoting. Common decency and a common touch were expected of them. And they demanded it of themselves. If in private some of them were louts, at least they'd been trained to hide it.

As recently as 25 years ago, no one gave a high-five after a homer, much less a low-five or elbow bash. A curtain call was reserved for a 500th home run—maybe. A tip of the cap was a big deal. Self-congratulation was viewed, as it should be, as beneath a person of real talent or character. The act was self-evident, self-explanatory, to those capable of grasping it.

In sports, humility was enforced rather than encouraged. An athlete's dignity, not his salary, was his calling card. If you "showed up" your foe, you got a fastball in the ear or a blindside block.

Wilt Chamberlain never smashed a backboard because nobody doubted that he could. Bill Russell didn't have to talk trash at his foes. He just stared at them. He didn't *try* to scare them; he *did* scare them. Jackie Robinson never wore a day-glo lime-green batting glove. He concentrated on stealing home, not headlines. Bob Cousy never dribbled between his legs as he came up court unguarded, although he might dribble between your legs once you tried to cover him. One is showboating, the other is art.

To what do we owe our current glut of athletic hubris?

The easy obvious answers might be TV and money. Lots of exposure and lots of wealth can swell your head.

But how much more famous can you be than Rocky Marciano or Jesse Owens? Athletes were joking about making more money than the President of the United States in the 1920s.

Instead of blaming TV or million-dollar deals, perhaps we should also give sarcastic thanks to the radical '60s and the conservative '80s.

The first begat an unreflective worship of freedom. Truly gifted athletes such as Muhammad Ali and Joe Namath mirrored the times with their poetry and predictions, hairstyles and hip fashions, tassled shoes or white spats. Thanks largely to them, a pernicious cliche took root: "It's not bragging if you back it up." Oh? Who says? Bragging is bragging—period.

Gradually the message of the athletic Age of Aquarius became clear: if you're good and also gauche, you'll be even richer, even more famous.

Unfortunately, unfettered expression is a curse when you have nothing to say. Now a million imitation Broadway Joes later, we have a generation of jocks who think that greatness isn't certified until there's a candy bar named "Reggie" or a chocolate soda called "Pete." The end result is someone like Deion Sanders, who actually believes he's speaking an undeniable truth when he says: "They don't pay nobody to be humble."

The '80s have given us an equally unreflective worship of personal wealth. When we respect what a person has, rather than how he got it, it's no wonder many athletes consider it a crime not to capitalize on every "opportunity."

In sports, as in much of a modern consumer society, the real thing begets the knockoff. The genuine article degenerates into the copy. Ali was a unique self-creation. But what can we say about The Boz, The Fridge and Neon Deion? Imitation may be the sincerest form of flattery, but it's a poor substitute for identity.

Luckily, tastes and trends tend to go in cycles. Maybe the farewell tours of Kareem Abdul-Jabbar and Julius Erving were a good sign. Perhaps the children who've grown up in the '80s have had keen eyes. Somehow between Wrestlemania VII and Halftime At The Super Bowl, perhaps they've noticed the real athletic iconoclasts of the last decade: Wayne Gretzky, Larry Bird, Joe Montana, Walter Payton, Nancy Lopez, James Worthy, Don Mattingly and Dave Stewart.

Here's hoping.

Judge's Comments

Almost all 1,600 newspapers in the country offer commentary on the sports pages. We have come to expect it. Just as we look for movie reviews, we look for evaluations of the athletes and teams we follow. Perhaps more than anything else, that certifies sports as entertainment.

Just because there is a lot of commentary available, however, doesn't mean that there is a lot of good commentary. Too much of it rambles, lacks specifics and offers little context or solutions.

Not so with Tom Boswell's commentary on the ego-driven braggarts that so often dominate our pages and television screens. Boswell offers us a wonderful trip down memory lane to recall the "real" heroes, the athletes from the days when it was OK to be humble, when they didn't use every interview as an opportunity to promote themselves. By invoking these athletes from the past by name, he is specific and thus more convincing.

By listing specific transgressions of so many modern athletes, he piles up the evidence. He does this with a light hand. He doesn't name any modern athlete, but those of us who follow sports know whom he is talking about: the player who wore a mohawk, the player who kneeled in prayer before the cameras and then yelled into the microphone, "I'm going to Disney World!" The player who marketed himself as "The Refrigerator."

We know them, and Boswell knows we know them. On the other hand, he names names when he wants to honor those who have both unusual ability and unusual (for this age) modesty.

Agree or disagree, you must react. The issue is significant, the evidence is substantial. Most commentators on sports hope to get you to think about what you are watching. Perhaps even sometimes to register your protests.

Best Magazine Story

War of the Roses

BASEBALL

By *PAT JORDAN*

From Gentlemen's Quarterly

"What'd I learn from my dad?" he says. "You mean, like a father-and-son talk?" He tugs on the bill of his baseball cap and sprawls back on the sofa. A nice-looking boy of 19. With a red crew cut, brown eyes and freckles. He is dressed in a gray T-shirt, jeans and high-top sneakers. A perfectly ordinary boy of his time. Born and raised near a river in the Midwest, he could pass for the Tom Sawyer of his age, if, like Tom, he still had boyhood illusions. . . . *He tosses a scuffed baseball to his dad. His dog leaps at the ball suspended for eternity in a cloudless sky. His dad looks up with his kind face. His sister, pouting on the porch, dresses her doll. His mom, smiling at her boys, stands at the screen door with two glasses of cold lemonade.*

He stops fidgeting with his cap and stares at the ceiling. Finally he says, "My dad told me to hit the ball where it's pitched." That's it. In a flat voice, devoid of emotion. He knows precisely what he's saying. The nuance of it. "That's all I remember," he says and sits up on the sofa in a barren room in a West Palm Beach, Fla., apartment complex. A minor-league-baseball player's apartment. A few pieces of cheap Danish-modern furniture. A half-eaten bowl of Froot Loops on the table. A crumpled Fritos bag on the sofa. A pair of baseball spikes and sweat socks on the floor. A copy of *Playboy.* A new, leathery-smelling glove in an open box. A photograph of his girlfriend beside an unmade bed.

"We don't talk like that," he says. "You know what I mean? I never hugged or kissed my dad. If I did, he'd think I was a sissy. You know, queer. My relationship with him is more player-manager. Sometimes he gives me a high-five."

He is at that age when most boys lose their illusions, against their will. It is a scary time for boys who want desperately to hang on to the fathomable verities of their boyhood, even as they are about to become men. "If I work hard, then everything will fall into place," he says. . . . "I never thought, What if I make the big leagues? It never crossed my mind I wouldn't. . . . I hope I room with two blacks, so people won't think I'm a rich kid. . . . My dream is to have my mom and dad in the stands watching me play. . . . I see myself at bat in a Cincinnati uniform in the ninth inning of a playoff game, with a runner on third and the score tied. . . ."

He looks down at the rug as he speaks. A curiously passionless boy for his age. Without conviction even for the illusions he mouths. Which is why he's no Tom Sawyer. He is, rather, a Huck Finn who's seen the world earlier than most and found it wanting. The loss of his illusions at such an early age was a kind of premature theft of his boyhood. It has left him partially empty, filled only with a vague sadness, suspicion and fear. Even when he smiles or laughs, it always comes from his mouth and never his eyes. Still, like Huck, he has not lost his generous heart.

"I'm a lot like my dad," he says. "I like fast cars, the ponies, clothes and baseball. I hustle like him. I'm a better fielder than he is, but I'm not as good a hitter yet. If he's got size-16 shoes, then I'm only a size 4 now. It'll be tough to fill them, but I'm gonna try to be better than my dad. It's hard for me, though. People never see me. When they come to see me play, they expect to see my dad. That's why I never run to first base on a walk. I want to be my own person.

"In some ways, I guess, I'm not much like my dad. We're not alike inside. I show more emotion than he does. When he used to kiss my mom or my sister, it hurt me. I wish he could kiss me. I wish he'd made time for me when I was growing up. If he'd been around, I'd be a lot like him now. But he wasn't, so I'm not. I don't see him much now. He said he'd try to see me play here in West Palm, but I know that means he won't come. Even if I wanted to call him, I don't have his telephone number. I have to call his agent, and he tells my dad I want to talk to him. We don't get in touch unless my dad wants to. Still, I love him. He's my dad."

★ ★ ★

His dad, Peter Edward Rose, currently the manager of the Cincinnati Reds, is the greatest singles hitter in the history of baseball. "I *live* for 200 hits a year," he once said. He became one of only a handful of modern players to surpass the achievements of time-honored legend Ty Cobb, when he got his 4,192nd hit on September 11, 1985. He holds a .303 lifetime batting average and more than 30 major and National League records; has played in 16 All-Star games and 34 World Series games; was named Sportsman of the Year (1975) by *Sports Illustrated* and National League Player of the Decade for the 1970s by *The Sporting News.* He accepted that accolade as his right, saying, "*I'm* the Player of the Decade, not (Hank) Aaron."

He is a guaranteed first-round selection to the Hall of Fame, his last and greatest achievement, when he becomes eligible for that honor five years after his retirement from the game he has played so much longer than most. Forty-eight years old this month, he has yet to officially retire from baseball, although he has not played in two years. He prefers, instead, a state of limbo from which, at any moment, he might rouse himself to play again, to continue his avaricious pursuit of hits, games, wins, awards, honors. Despite his pride in his achievements ("I'm the biggest winner in history," he has said), they seem to have left him unsatiated. He still has that glutton's gleam in his eye for more and more and more of what he has devoted his life to at great cost, not necessarily to himself but to those who love him. His daughter once said, "We'll all be happy when he becomes the best of all time, because he sure had to give up a lot to get it."

His accomplishments in his game have rewarded him handsomely. He has made millions of dollars from his salaries as player and manager—$500,000 a year now ("And I never even went to college," he's said); from an as-told-to autobiography he coauthored, called, simply, "The Pete Rose Story" ("I never read it"); and from the dozens of products he has endorsed over the years: Aqua Velva, Jockey, Geritol, Swanson TV dinners, Gekimen noodles, Mountain Dew, Zenith, Mizuno, Grecian Formula and his own soft drink called, again, simply, Pete. He has also merchandised, at various times, T-shirts, key chains, hats, posters and gold and silver coins, all with either his name or his likeness on them. Most of the money he has made, it seems, he has spent on himself. He buys expensive clothes and even more expensive cars. He owns three Porsches, a Rolls-Royce and several other fine machines. He has also been known to indulge his gambling appetite at dog and horse tracks around the country. He was once rumored to have lost $13,000 in a single day at the track, and on another occasion he received a dead fish in the mail as a warning to pay a gambling debt he was refusing to acknowledge. "He said he was Pete Rose, and he didn't have to pay no gambling debts," his ex-wife says. But the wise guys he owed didn't see it that way.

He has been married twice and fathered three children (possibly four, according to a Tampa woman, who filed a paternity suit against him in 1979; Rose didn't contest the suit), and he has a reputation as a ladies' man. His attitude toward his women is not much different from that toward his gambling debts, and he is notoriously cavalier about his adulteries.

His present wife, Carol, 34, is a former barmaid and Philadelphia Eagles cheerleader who tends to dress in leopard-skin Capri pants and was once described by a friend as "looking like a lonely go-go dancer." He was attracted to her because she had, according to another friend, "the prettiest butt in Cincinnati," and also because she was almost 15 years younger than him. He likes young women, he's said, "because they make me feel young." He feels the same about baseball and money, which may explain his avaricious pursuit of all three.

Of all the products he has endorsed over the years, the one people most identify him with is Wheaties, "The Breakfast of Champions." It perfectly fits his fans' perception of him. The athlete from an ordinary background, who achieved great success not from an abundance of talent but from an abundance of boyish desire and hard work. He played his game the way young boys played it when Norman Rockwell was painting covers for *The Saturday Evening Post.* He slid headfirst into third base. He ran to first on a walk. His uniform was perpetually caked with dirt and ripped from his fearless style of play. His fans read into that style of play a host of qualities—courage, discipline, desire, perseverance—that have little to do with him or his success. The secret is much simpler than that. He devoted his life to one thing—baseball—at the exclusion of almost everything else.

"All I am is an American boy," he said in his 40s, "who knew what he could do and what he couldn't do and did it for a long, long period of time."

"Pete hits the ball on the ground more consistently than any player I ever saw," explains Tom Seaver. "Some of those ground balls are bound to get through for hits."

★ ★ ★

"What would I do in that situation?" the son says. "With a runner on third in the playoffs?" He does not hesitate. "I'd hit a single to center field."

In the summer of 1988, Peter Edward Rose II, "Little Pete," "Petey," led his Cincinnati American Legion team to the Legion World Series Championship. Around the same time, he was drafted in the 12th round by the Baltimore Orioles as a third baseman. Petey was crushed. He thought he should have been drafted higher, but most of all, he had dreamed of being drafted by his father's team, the Reds. On the night of the draft, Petey and his mother, Karolyn, sat in their living room with 26 baseball caps, one for each major-league team, and waited to see which one Petey would wear. Their celebration turned to despair as Petey was bypassed in round after round. Finally, he fled the house in anger, only to discover the next day he had been drafted 295th overall.

Petey claimed most teams bypassed him in deference to his father's team, which they assumed would draft him. John Cox, the Reds' director of scouting, said that was foolish speculation. In the opinion of most clubs, he said, Petey was a 12th-round choice. The scouts' criticisms of the son were the same as those leveled against his father years ago. He was slow afoot, his throwing arm was only adequate, and he didn't hit for power. But according to Len Johnston, the Orioles' scouting coordinator, "We waited to see what Cincinnati would do. I don't think Pete's old man had enough balls to sign his own kid. If it was my kid, I'd break my neck to sign him for my team. I don't think the old man wanted to."

(Despite repeated requests, Pete Rose declined to be interviewed about this or anything else in this article.)

When Petey finally overcame his disillusionment, he signed with the Orioles, received a $21,000 bonus and in early fall was promptly dispatched to the team's winter-league club in West Palm Beach. There he would get special instruction with other young prospects in preparation for his first spring training in March. He arrived at West Palm Beach boyishly happy. Reporters clustered around him constantly. He told them that he "loved the game because it's fun" and that he was happy with his famous name, even if it did put extra pressure on him. "It'd be a lot easier for me if my name was Smith," he said. When he walked into his clubhouse, he said, "I got a big cold chill when I saw a locker with my name on it . . . my *own* locker."

For someone so young, he handled himself remarkably well in interviews. He had spent a lifetime watching his father be interviewed and, on occasion, being interviewed himself. ("I'll bet your friends envy you having such a famous dad, eh, Petey?") Now it was his turn to talk solely about himself, but nobody seemed to be listening. When he appeared on a Fort Lauderdale TV sports show one night, the host, smiling, said he guessed Petey owed a lot of his talent to his famous dad. Petey said, "My mom has been the main influence in my career." The host, still smiling, continued to talk about his famous dad while Petey, flushed, stared at his hands in his lap.

The father never did come to West Palm to see his son play, although he indicated he was proud of his son for following in his footsteps. "He and I put a lot of hours into preparation," the father said. "I'll live and die with every at-bat he takes in the minors. That's my blood."

★ ★ ★

When Little Pete was a boy, he says, he had no sense of growing up with a famous father, except on those rare occasions when his father took him to the stadium. They were usually Father and Son Days, or All-Star or World Series games, when there would be a host of reporters and photographers present. Petey would be dressed in a fitted uniform, with hat, spikes and glove, a miniature of his father. "I went first-class from the age of 5," he says. He would be photographed playing pepper with his dad, swinging a too-heavy bat at his dad's underhand tosses and sitting beside him on the dugout bench. He was a silent little boy, with scared eyes that squinted into the photographers' flashbulbs. After the game, still in his uniform, Petey would get into his father's black limousine for the ride home. His face was barely visible pressed against the limo's blacked-out window.

At home, his father rarely played catch with him on the lawn. And even when he did, those catches bore not the slightest resemblance to the kinds Norman Rockwell captured on his *Saturday Evening Post* covers. The leaping dog. The sister pouting. The mom with lemonade. They were less "catches" between a father and son on a sunny afternoon than they were fierce "workouts." Baseball for an adult, not a child. Pete rarely praised his small son's efforts to please him, to be like him, because he always assumed a certain adult level of competency from Petey that he could never deliver. Pete did not understand how to "play" with children, nor did he bother to try. He did not take a father's delight in his children, because his mind was always on his concerns. *His* career, *his* desires, *his* single-minded pursuit of *his* boyhood dreams. He sustained those dreams over the years of his son's childhood. Ultimately, they are what robbed his son of his own dreams.

Pete Rose took even less interest in his daughter's attempts to please him. He tried to discourage her from playing baseball, even though Fawn, five years older than Petey, was a better ballplayer than her brother. "Some people don't even know I have a sister," Petey says. "But Fawn was a bitch in baseball. Dad didn't want her to play, because she was better than the boys. One day, he hit a pop fly that hit a tree branch and came down and broke Fawn's nose. When she cried, Dad called her a sissy."

Pete had trouble relating to his daughter for a number of reasons, not the least of which was that she is a girl. (An irony is that Pete now has to work for a very tough-minded woman, Reds owner Marge Schott.) Fawn is also very bright, honest and, like him, stubborn. Karolyn likes to say that "Fawn always did favor Big Pete," but that description doesn't sit well with Fawn. "I love my dad," she says, "but I don't respect him." Fawn's relationship with her father has always been confrontational, in contrast to Petey's worshipful childhood view of his father. She was never afraid to question him to his face on his lack of interest in her and her brother. She was probably one of the few people in his life who ever had the courage to question him. But he had trouble dealing with her for another reason, too. Fawn has always had a serious weight problem. It embarrassed Pete. When he was taking his son to the track one day, Karolyn asked why he wasn't taking Fawn, too. Pete said she was too fat and he would be ashamed to be seen with her. Fawn heard him from another room.

Karolyn Engelhardt Rose was the perfect baseball wife. Not only did she subordinate her life to her husband's career but she actually seemed to relish that subordination. Whenever Karolyn asked her husband to do some small chore around the house, to mow the lawn, say, his response was always the same: "What if I get hurt?" Then he would go to his room, where he spent long hours watching sporting events on television. His wife would bring him sodas and chips throughout the day.

When he spent lavishly on himself, on his clothes and cars ("It's *my* money, not yours," he would tell her), she did not question him. She merely saved pennies by shopping for the rest of the family at K mart. It was not only her wifely duty, it was her higher calling, because Karolyn was her husband's biggest fan. When he came home depressed by a hitting slump, she would console him with advice. "I think you're crouching too much," she said once. His response: "How many home runs have you hit, anyway?" At the ballpark, she was his most visible fan. Whenever Pete Rose came to bat at Riverfront Stadium, the television cameras would immediately pan to his wife in the stands. Karolyn was a beautiful woman, with luxuriant chestnut-colored hair, a raspy cigarette smoker's voice and a body so voluptuous she was once detained at the stadium gate by a security cop who thought she was Morganna Roberts, the Kissing Bandit. Eventually the Reds' camera crew was given instructions not to focus in on Karolyn so often, because some of the team's more straitlaced fans were complaining about her heaving breasts.

Karolyn had a kind of celebrity of her own in Cincinnati (she had her own radio program), attributable not only to her husband's fame but also to her own goodnatured, vivacious personality. She drew people to her, especially men, in the same way tough-talking waitresses at truck stops have their legions of fans. She was honest and earthy, and more than one man had a crush on her, even if she did not see any man but her husband. When Karolyn and Pete went to parties, which they rarely did, Karolyn, as much as Pete, would be surrounded by admirers. That annoyed her husband, and soon he would drag her home.

Still, Karolyn Rose accepted her subservient role because she was proud to be part of her husband's career. She even accepted the fact of her husband's many girlfriends. She had known about them almost from the first year of their marriage, in 1964. She conceded them as part of the lot of a baseball wife—*if* Pete followed the rules of that game. He could have his girls while on the road and if he was discreet about them. When the Tampa woman filed the paternity suit against Pete, Karolyn described it as "nothing." "It happens," she says. "I handled it." Nor did Karolyn complain when she was hospitalized with a blood clot and Pete never bothered to visit her. "I didn't get flowers, and I didn't get a call or anything," she once said. "But I accepted it because he was busy playing baseball, and they were trying to win a pennant." But his teammates' wives became furious, for by then Pete had begun to flaunt his affairs in a way that even Karolyn could no longer ignore. He started giving Karolyn's game tickets to his girlfriends. He flew them with him on the team plane and began to squire them around openly in Cincinnati. He acted as if now that he was Pete Rose, the greatest singles hitter in baseball, the conventional rules of morality, even of baseball morality, did not apply to him.

One time, Karolyn was driving home when she saw her own red Porsche being driven by Carol Woliung, who would become Pete's second wife. She turned around and followed the Porsche until she caught up with it at a stoplight. She jumped out of her car, tapped on the window of the Porsche and, when Carol rolled it down, punched her in the face. When the police arrived, Carol claimed the car was a gift from her fiance, the famous baseball player Pete Rose. Karolyn, who was still married to Pete, told the officer to check the car's registration. It was registered to Karolyn Rose. While Carol found another way home, Karolyn drove to the stadium to confront her husband. He refused to come out of the clubhouse.

Another time, when Fawn and Petey were old enough to understand their father's affairs, and be crushed by them, Karolyn took them to a banquet in Cincinnati honoring their father. The children burst into tears when they saw Pete's brother escorting Carol to a table.

Petey was 9 when his father asked him one day if he wanted to go to the track with him. Pete left the house thrilled to be out with his father. When he returned home, he was curiously silent, until his mother asked him if he'd had a good time. Petey, with the innocence of a child, responded, "We had lunch with Dad's girlfriend." Even today Petey refuses to talk about that moment when he lost his boyhood innocence. He just shakes his head and says, "I don't want to say nothing about Carol."

Karolyn Rose filed for divorce a few months later, in 1979. "I divorced Big Pete because he was flaunting his women, and I had to protect the kids," she says, "not because I didn't love him anymore."

The divorce didn't seem to bother Big Pete much. He got four hits in one game against the Mets soon after the couple separated. He justified his adulteries by saying, "If a guy doesn't like women, he's queer, so if you want to say, no, I'm not queer, then I'm not queer." He justified his divorce by saying, "I guess if I have an All-American image, I should go through a divorce, because that's what all Americans do." Then he said that he had no sympathy for his wife of 16 years, because "she ain't a ballplayer's wife anymore, is she? . . . I'm happy the way it is. What do I need a wife for? As far as being lonely, baseball is my substitute." Finally, he said, jokingly, that the secret to dispatching wives was simple: "Hey, just give her a million dollars and tell her to hit the road."

After their divorce, as parents often do, Pete and Karolyn used their son as a conduit for their frustrations with each other. Petey was the go-between for communicating anger, in Pete's case, and heartbreak, in Karolyn's. She sent her son off to visit his father with the hope that seeing him would remind Pete of the family life he was missing. Karolyn always harbored fantasies that Pete would return to her one day. Almost a decade later, she still does. "Every January 25, our wedding anniversary, I set an extra plate for Big Pete," she says. "I still believe he'll come home someday. Is that stupid?"

But Pete didn't miss family life with Karolyn. The only thing Pete was reminded of when he saw his son was his ex-wife. He cut short his son's visits, never asked him to sleep overnight and finally made those visits fewer and farther between. "I see my son as much as I want," Pete said. Petey was confused and hurt and angry. He blamed his mother for the loss of his father.

"I got mad at Mom 'cause Dad was gone," Petey says. "Then one day she sat me down and told me that me and Fawn were her whole life now. Since then, she's been Mom and Dad for me."

Petey grew so attached to his mother (he was almost a mama's boy, says Fawn) that he would cry when she left the house. He was terrified that she would leave him, too. When she got a job as a barmaid at a shot-and-a-beer bar in Cincinnati called the Wagon Wheel, Petey would call her, crying, late at night to make sure she was going to come home.

Petey grew up over the next decade in the new house his mother bought after the divorce. They moved their things in the Rolls-Royce Karolyn got in the divorce settlement. ("Just like the Beverly Hillbillies," she says.) "I hate that car," says Fawn. Karolyn rarely drives the Rolls anymore. She keeps it in storage. Still, she can't bear to sell it, since it's one of the few reminders she has left of her days as Mrs. Pete Rose. (She may have to sell the car eventually, though, since her $50,000 a year alimony will expire in 1995.)

The house is big and empty, except for furniture and necessities. It is virtually devoid of family mementos, since the only ones Karolyn ever had in her houses were her husband's plaques and trophies. She seems not to know how to fill her house with signs of a new life. Or maybe she is simply disinclined to, until her husband comes home. She fills that house, instead, with people. It has become a kind of way station for the troubled in Cincinnati. Throughout the day and night, her house is filled with boys and girls moving about, rummaging through the refrigerator, watching TV, sleeping in one of the spare bedrooms, while Karolyn labors in the kitchen, cooking a 20-pound turkey for whoever appears at the dinner table.

She "adopted" a black high-school friend of Petey's after his parents split up. Petey likes to tell people he has "a brother who's a lot smarter than me. He's gonna get a college scholarship." Then he adds, with a grin, "He's black." Pete and Larry Canady are a lot alike, except that Larry doesn't play sports. They both like to spend long hours watching movies on television in their room. Often, they entertain Karolyn by acting out parts from such movies as "Slap Shot" and "Used Cars," or, in Petey's case, doing a parody of his father. It is a good imitation, especially when he acts out his father's middle-aged attempt to spike his hair with gel or wear his double-knit suit with flared-legged trousers. "You know the kind I mean," he'll say, "with the real tight pants, so you can see Dad's wad of bills bulging in the front pocket." Petey struggles, mimicking his father, to get his hand into his front pocket while Larry laughs.

Karolyn also took in a local doctor and his family for a few months while they were waiting for their home to be built. And she took in the wife and two sons of Pete's old Reds teammate Tommy Helms after their marriage broke up. Karolyn gave up her own bedroom to Rita Helms, while she slept on the sofa in the family room.

Rita and her sons stayed for six months.

Karolyn thinks nothing of giving up her bed to guests. She will work all night at the Wagon Wheel, where she fancies herself a kind of Carla on "Cheers," and arrive home exhausted at 4 a.m. She will flop down on the couch and then bolt awake two hours later to take her guest to the airport on a freezing winter's morning. Before she lets them into her car, she warms it up for them. She drives in darkness, talking herself awake until they get to the Ohio River, where they have to wait for the ferry to transport the car to the other side. Karolyn sees a flock of ducks on the river. She castigates herself for being thoughtless. "Oh, I should have remembered to bring them bread," she says.

During the years when Petey's relationship with his father grew more and more strained, Pete and Carol had a son, Tyler, now 4. (The boy is named for the object of Rose's great quest, Ty Cobb.) Petey became jealous of the attention his father bestowed on his new son. "He took Tyler to Kings Island amusement park," Petey says, "so I asked him why he never took us when we were kids."

Petey thought that now that he was becoming a man, his father would want to get closer to him, but just the opposite happened. Pete seemed to feel threatened by Petey's emerging manhood in the face of his own fading career. As Petey forged his own identity as an athlete (despite heavy abuse from fans, who reminded him constantly he was not his father), Pete tried to undermine his son's achievements. When Petey had trouble making his team one year, his father told him to quit baseball. "I thought that was kind of strange," says Karolyn, "since Big Pete never quit anything in his life." Another time, Pete told his son that when Tyler grew up, he would be a better baseball player than Petey. And finally, just before Petey was drafted, his father told him that maybe it would be better for him to go to college than to play professional baseball. When Petey insisted on giving pro ball a try, his father then suggested that he change his name to make it easier on him.

"That really hurt Petey," says Fawn. "I've always thought Dad was jealous of Petey. He doesn't want another Pete Rose in baseball. Besides, Dad's not playing anymore and Petey is. Petey has the only thing Dad doesn't have now. Youth."

Fawn is sitting at a table at the Wagon Wheel late at night while her mother works. The Wheel is filled with blue-collar couples drinking their shots and beers while listening to 50s rock-and-roll songs played by a disc jockey. There is a poster of Pete Rose II, in an Orioles uniform, on the wall behind Fawn. She glances over her shoulder at her mother, who is smoking a long cigar, tossing back drinks and laughing with her customers. At 47, Karolyn Rose doesn't look much like that curvy woman in the "Big Red Machine" T-shirt anymore. She has gained a lot of weight in the years since her divorce. Pete told her she was eating herself to death.

"I wish Mom wouldn't smoke," Fawn says. "Or drink. She

doesn't need to be here. The owners take advantage of her because she's so good-hearted. They don't pay her hardly anything. People use her. All those people around our house. It bothers me. She just does it to take the place of Dad."

Fawn Rose is 24 now, and recently got her degree in psychology at Thomas More College in Kentucky. She says the first person she wants to psychoanalyze is her father. "He's unique," she says. "My father is the world's worst father."

Fawn is a pretty girl, but vastly overweight. In a way, she is trapped in her body. It defines her in the eyes of people who cannot see the woman beyond it. Friends of her mother's are always asking writers doing stories on Petey to "mention Fawny in the story, won't you? Nobody ever mentions poor Fawny."

"Petey was kind of a brat when he was a boy," Fawn says. "He got more attention from Dad than I did. Dad never took me anywhere. He was more comfortable with Petey. He only talked sports with us. He talked down to Petey a lot, and it hurt Petey. He's very sensitive. Still, sometimes I wish Dad was hard on me like he was on Petey."

Karolyn Rose is dancing now. Her face is flushed as she works up a sweat on the dance floor. The long cigar is still clenched between her teeth.

"Mom's not healthy about Petey's baseball career," Fawn says. "Baseball is an obsession with her. Sometimes I think she's ignorant about it. I think she uses Petey to show up Dad, now that he's not playing and Petey is. The only thing Petey has is baseball. He'll never get away from it. But I don't know if he's driven toward it like Dad. He used to look up to Dad, but not anymore. When Dad's agent, Reuven Katz, found out that Petey was being interviewed for an article, he warned him not to say anything bad about his father. Petey told him that he was going to tell the truth, like his dad had taught him.

"We never thought of ourselves as children of a famous man. He was just Dad. Sometimes I even denied I was Pete Rose's daughter when people asked me. But then I felt guilty. I would still like to have a normal father-daughter relationship with him, if there is such a thing. I want him to give me away some day when I get married. I will never understand why he never had any time for us. We didn't expect anything from him, except to just like us. All we ever did was love him and want him to love us back. Sometimes I think he will come back some day, and when I do, I hope Mom won't take him back. She devoted her whole life to him, and all he ever did was shit on her."

★ ★ ★

Karolyn Rose is sitting high up in the stands behind home plate a few minutes before her son will take the field for his first professional baseball game. It is a cool, sunny fall day in West Palm Beach. The stadium is almost deserted, except for a few older men, scouts, with radar guns behind the home-plate screen, and a few young girls higher up, the girlfriends of players.

Petey, in his Orioles uniform, stands beside the dugout squinting up into the bright sunlight. He scans the home-plate bleachers for his mother, as he always does. "The hardest thing in the world for me," he says, "will be to look into the stands someday and not see Mom there. She's always come to my games, cheering me on, picking me up when I'm down, yelling at me to keep my ass down on the grounders."

When he spots his mother, he smiles and waves. Karolyn waves back and yells, "Go get 'em Goog!" just before he runs onto the field with his teammates.

"That's always been his nickname," Karolyn says, without taking her eyes from her son at third base. "So people won't know who his father is."

Karolyn is dressed in Bermuda shorts and a sweater she hugs to herself. She is heavily made up, with long red fingernails and lots of gold jewelry dangling from her wrists and on her fingers. She is compulsively popping sunflower seeds into her mouth, shelling them with her teeth and spitting out the shells while she talks.

"I look at Little Pete and I can't believe it," she says. He is hunched over at third base in that simian pose of his father's, waiting for the batter to swing. "It's funny how time repeats itself," Karolyn says. "Except now I'm a mother, not a wife. You know, baseball must be a calling from God, I think. Little Pete has it in his blood just like his father. Big Pete's first love was always baseball. He used to say he had this much ability (she holds the thumb and forefinger of her left hand about an inch apart) and this much desire (now she spreads both arms wide)." She keeps her arms spread wide and adds, "I think Petey has the same desire as Big Pete, only more ability. He has more compassion for people, too."

All the while Karolyn is talking, she keeps her eyes glued to her son in the field. When he handles a routine grounder and throws the runner out, she starts tapping the arm of the man besides her. "See that!" she says. "See that!"

The game unfolds on this lazy day while Karolyn rocks nervously in her seat, popping the sunflower seeds into her mouth, rummaging through her purse for Kleenex, sipping from a can of Coke, and talking. "Big Pete had to fight for respect in baseball," she says. "Baseball never thought he was that great. Now Big Pete is the greatest. He doesn't think anyone will ever break his records. It's an awful pressure on Little Pete. I told him he can't live through his father any more than his father can live through him. It's over."

When Petey steps up to hit, his mother stops talking for a moment. Unlike his switch-hitting father, Petey bats lefthanded and, at 6-foot-1 and 190 pounds, is taller and slighter. He stands at the plate with his feet primly close together and his bat held high above his head. He holds the bat very still, almost delicately. His stance is almost the exact opposite of his father's squat, spread-out attack. Big Pete was intense, coiled anger, at the plate. He used to grind the bat handle in his hands until his knuckles were white, and wave the barrel menacingly at the pitcher.

Petey hits a soft curving liner to the left fielder to retire the side. Karolyn begins to talk again, now about the good old days when she was a ballplayer's wife and Pete was struggling to make the major leagues in his rookie year, and how he came home from practice with blisters on all his fingers, and later when pennants were won or lost and her husband had batting streaks or slumps, and how once a broken thumb kept him out of the lineup for so long that she had to hide his uniform to keep him from playing.

"I miss those days," she says. "It's the one thing I have that no one can take away from me. Going to spring training with Little Pete will bring back memories."

Len Johnston, the Orioles' scouting coordinator, stops by to say hello to Karolyn. He tells her Petey is looking good, progressing nicely. He's slotted to play in Frederick, Md., in the Carolina League come spring '89. Karolyn thanks him and then says, "Big Pete will be coming to see Petey play soon. He'll want all his stats." Johnston tells her they don't keep statistics in the winter league. Karolyn just shakes her head and says, "Big Pete'll want to see 'em."

(At the end of the season, Johnston offers this assessment of Petey as a ballplayer: "He played against three- and four-year minor-league veterans, and at first the pitching was too hard for him. It affected his fielding. He got down on himself. But he came on strong near the end. Made a little bat contact, and his fielding improved. His running is still below average, and so is his throwing, and he needs a quicker bat. His strength is that he always hustles and wants extra work. Nothing about him reminded us of his father, except he wants to play.")

When Johnston leaves, Karolyn says, "It'll really hit Big Pete when he sees his son in uniform. I still love him, you know. I've never dated since our divorce. I refused to accept the annulment papers from the priest. I told him, in my eyes and the eyes of the Church, I'll always be married to Pete Rose. I just don't know him anymore."

The batter hits a sharp grounder to Pete Rose II at third base. He bobbles the ball for a split second, then throws it to first on a bounce. The runner is safe. Petey hangs his head and kicks the dirt.

"Don't get disgusted with yourself, Goog!" his mother yells.

It is an attitude, self-disgust, his father was not familiar with. They are not much alike, father and son. The son has more talent than his father did at the same age. But that is not saying much. His father didn't become the greatest singles hitter in baseball history because of natural talent. He succeeded because he had an angry intensity and a chest-puffing arrogance, both of which are defined in baseball by the word "heart." The son lacks his father's heart, in a baseball sense, but in another sense he has his own heart, which, although admirable in life, doesn't count for much in the game he's playing.

★ ★ ★

"It's time to go to the yard," he says, sitting on the sofa in his minor-league-baseball player's apartment. An ordinary-looking boy of his time. But before he goes, he says, "You know, I love my dad. I just don't want to be like him. Whatever money I make is gonna be my wife's, too. I'm gonna take my sons to the stadium all the time. I'd like to get up to the point in my career when people will just see me as Pete Rose, not Pete Rose's son. And then, after I retire, they'll come to see my son play, too. They'll say, 'Oh, shit, here's Pete Rose at the plate. Ya know, his father played ball, too.' "

Judge's Comments

We've known for years that Pete Rose was obsessed with getting base hits and obsessed with himself—not necessarily in that order. But until Pat Jordan looked at what Rose had done to his family in his head-long, head-first pursuit of Ty Cobb, we never knew the full measure of the man. It is pretty small.

Jordan is one of the growing number of sensitive reporters covering sports who is not a sportswriter at all; that description is far too limiting. Jordan is a writer who happens to be interested in sports, perhaps because of what they do to people. Big-time athletics (is there any other kind these days?) do little if anything to build character, despite what the Old Coach used to say. But the pain and the glory and the scent of money can bring out the best and, far more often, the worst in the stars.

There's a morality play going on out there around second base, if only we could cut through the flim-flam and the flackery to see it. Jordan succeeds by describing the desolation that Rose left behind at home. The daughter of his first marriage, who once was spurned by him because she was too plump, says flatly: "*My father is the world's worst father.*" Son Petey, doomed to be a baseball player without his father's egotism, is blunter still. When Jordan asks him what he'd learned from his dad, Petey thinks a while and then says—knowing full well the import of what he is saying: "*My dad told me to hit the ball where it's pitched.*"

It is no coincidence that most of this year's crop of outstanding sports stories in magazines are profiles of strong-minded athletes or coaches, good or bad, that seldom mention the competition on the field. Perhaps this is one of the benefits of television. These days we see, and see again and again, the action so vividly that we become impatient with a written narrative of a game, although, to be sure, there are times when we do want to read all about it.

But television cannot get us inside the mind, let alone inside the soul, of an athlete as well as a writer with a sense of compassion and the flare of anger, and a notebook full of good quotes. That's what Pat Jordan has. So do his peers, who are growing in number. May they all flourish.

Best Feature Story

Mark Messner

PRO FOOTBALL

By *MITCH ALBOM*

From the Detroit Free Press

Isn't life funny, Mark Messner thought. He held a spoonful of malted shake up to his father's lips, which were black and peeling, burned from the chemotherapy. "Here you go, Dad," he said. His father rolled his eyes and made a "mmm" sound, like a child. Mark smiled, pulled the spoon out and dug it back into the cup.

Isn't life funny? A few weeks ago, Messner, 22, was a rookie linebacker for the Los Angeles Rams. He was getting paid to play football. He was living in sunny southern California. Then the phone rang. "You'd better come home," his sister said. He knew what that meant. He left the team, without pay, and boarded a plane for Detroit.

When he first saw his father, lying in the hospital bed, Mark bit his lip. Then he went out in the hall and began to sob. He showed the nurse an old photo, before the disease, and she said, "Oh, my God."

Now he sat by the bed and fed his father, the way Del Pretty had done for him when he was an infant. Of course, technically, Del was his stepfather, but Mark never cared for that phrase. He figured if the man raised me, fed me, spanked me, hugged me, took me to school, wrote me poems, came to all my football games and made me feel like the most important person in the world, well, the hell with it. He is my father.

And I am his son.

"Have some more, Dad" he whispered. He looked at the blotches of red along Del's arms and legs. He saw the blood stains on the sheets where the skin had peeled away. He thought back to a year ago, when life seemed so carefree. He was heading to the Rose Bowl with the Michigan Wolverines. There would be Hawaii after that and

Japan after that. And then came the NFL draft. The Rams took him with a low-round pick. Then in training camp they had him carrying the red cones up and down the field, like some equipment boy.

"Dad," Mark said one night in a phone call home. "You'd better pull my resume off my computer. I can't compete on this level."

"Just keep plugging," Del said.

"But they got me *moving cones!*"

"They didn't draft you to move cones."

What does he know? Mark thought. He's never been in the NFL. He owns a piano store, for pete's sake. But eventually the Rams did come around. He stopped moving cones. He played in the exhibition games. He made the team. His father had been right. Again.

Mark looked at him. The room was quiet. He dug the spoon into the melting chocolate.

★ ★ ★

Take the chemo, they had told him.

"No," he had said.

"There's no alternative."

"There's got to be an alternative."

Del Pretty had been diagnosed as having lymph node cancer in 1980. He fought the very idea, as if it had somehow insulted his pride. He scorned chemotherapy, because he felt it would deteriorate him. Instead he searched for other methods. He tried special diets and experimental drugs. And eventually he beat the illness into remission. Who had time to be sick? There was the business. The family. And Mark's football games.

"He never missed one," Mark recalls. "He came to all the home games at Michigan and a lot of the road ones, too. There was this game in Indiana where the weather was horrible. He sat there in the rain the whole time."

Not that he was one of those jock-hungry fathers. On the contrary, Del Pretty was *not* a very athletic man. Silver-haired, dapper, with glasses and a gentle but disciplined expression, he looked more like a well-placed accountant. Which he was. But he loved his children. He would show his feelings quietly, in notes that Mark found in his college mailbox: *"Dear Mark, I want you to know how proud you make me feel."*

Mark's friends would tease him sometimes about how close he was with Del. It was almost corny. He had chosen Michigan over UCLA because he wanted Del to be able to see him play. Before he left for the Rams, Mark gave his Dad a record. "Wind Beneath My Wings" by Bette Midler. He told him to listen to the words, because that's how he felt. *"Did I ever tell you you're my hero. You're everything I wish I could be."*

It was the stuff of sappy movies. Unless you know the whole story. Mark was the son of divorce, several times, his mother married and remarried. His natural father (Max Messner, a former NFL player) also remarried. The one constant in his life was Del. He was there when Mark had problems. He was there when Mark wanted to talk about life, or girls, or football. He gave honest answers. Strict, but from the heart.

When Del and Mark's mother divorced, it tore Mark apart. His Dad had to live alone in some apartment in Northville. Why? It's not fair.

And then the cancer came back.

★ ★ ★

Take the chemo, they told him.

"No," he said.

Once again he tried experimental drugs. He flew to Houston for a new pill. He flew to California for a procedure in which animals are injected with samples from the patient's tumors, then the antibodies formed are injected into the patient.

"I'm sorry," the doctor said. "The process takes six to eight months."

"Yes?" said Del.

"Well, quite frankly, I don't think you have that long."

What do you do when a doctor tells you that? Already the disease had changed him physically. The tumors were stealing nutrients from his food and releasing lymph fluid instead into his abdomen. He was bloated like a pregnant woman.

"He couldn't sleep in a bed anymore," says Messner. "His stomach was so large. But meanwhile, the rest of his body was suffering from malnutrition."

Alone, out of options, he went to doctors in Ann Arbor. "Chemotherapy," they said. It was early fall. Football season. Mark was in L.A., getting paid. It was as if Del had held out all this time, just to make sure his son could handle adulthood.

"All right," Del said, finally. "I'll try the chemotherapy."

They put the needle in his arm.

★ ★ ★

The blotches began after the second treatment, they looked like a rash. He asked his doctors. "Must be a skin condition," they said. "Have you changed your soap recently?"

His soap?

Another round of chemo, an increased dosage. Now the skin began to puss and fester. Like a horrible sunburn, it would die and peel away. His back. His legs. Around his mouth. Without so much as a match's flame, he was burnt all over.

"It was the chemo," says Mark now. "And what was happening outside was happening inside him as well. The organs were being destroyed." How could this be? Wasn't chemo supposed to help him? You would touch his back and the skin would come off in your hands. One time, a nurse tried rubbing ointment on the sores. Del began to moan in pain. Mark came running in.

"What's wrong, what's he saying?" the nurse asked.

"He's saying don't rub, don't rub," said Mark. "It hurts too much."

This was the horrible reality: Del Pretty was dying, one layer at a time. Few of us could witness such a thing.

But the love between son and father is like God's muscle. So while his teammates worked out back in Los Angeles, Mark Messner came to Harper Grace hospital every morning, 10 a.m., two hours before visiting time, to bathe his father.

He would lift him with his powerful arms and slide him gently into the tub. Sheets of bloody skin would stick to his hands, get under his fingernails. He did not flinch. He poured cool water over his father's body and comforted him. While Del could still speak, Mark held the phone to his ear and let him talk to the office at Hammell Music, the piano store which he owned in Livonia. Together they went over the books of the church, where Del was treasurer.

When Del's vocal cords no longer worked, Mark did the talking. When Del's eyesight went, Mark would tell him what he was missing.

On November 25, they put the Michigan-Ohio State game on TV. Del stayed awake for the entire thing. When the final gun sounded, Mark said "Hey, Dad! How about that? They're going to the Rose Bowl!"

Del raised his arm and made a soft fist. He shook it once.

Two days later, he died.

Mark knew as soon as the phone rang. It was 4 a.m. His mother was crying in the other room. "Mom," he whispered, "they said Dad expired."

He paused.

"It makes him sound like a license plate."

At the funeral, Mark read a poem Del had sent him this fall. And when they closed the casket, Mark's Rose Bowl watch was around his father's wrist. Before it was always Del taking care of business matters, but now Mark handled the arrangements. He signed the papers. He went through the bills. He re-read the old letters and thought about their final moments together in the hospital, the feeding, the bathing. The circle was complete. The child had become father to the man.

"You know," Messner says now. "I was never embarrassed in the hospital. All that blood and skin, that was just his body. It was his heart that I was dealing with. I would have done anything for him. Anything."

* * *

Today, Mark will play a football game for the Rams, the regular season finale.

When it is over he will go to call his father, as he always did. And instead, he will have to close his eyes and imagine. "I know he's watching," he says without sadness. "He used to joke about having a beer with God. I'll bet he's doing it now."

You hear about the decline of the American family, how the old are tossed aside by the young. And then you hear of a kid who left pro football to tend to his dying father. These are the last words of the poem Del wrote, which Mark read at his funeral:

"If all else in a man's life added to zero, no greater success than to be counted his son's hero."

Isn't life funny? It takes us and leaves us. And love endures. Monday is Christmas, and that means this: Count your blessings, everybody, count them all very carefully. One precious person at a time.

Judge's Comments

It's easy for one to get caught up in the games of sport, and increasingly we also are subjected to the crimes of sport. It's refreshing, then, to find a first-rate article that focuses on the humanity of sports figures.

Mitch Albom's gripping story of the Los Angeles Rams' Mark Messner and how he cared for his dying stepfather is graphic at times, rich in detail and a real tear-jerker. That's a lot to ask in one story, but Albom delivers.

The graphic nature of the article (and an example of the richness of detail) comes as Albom describes Messner's attempt to bathe Del Pretty, his dying stepfather, in the hospital: *"He would lift him with his powerful arms and slide him gently into the tub. Sheets of body skin would stick to his hands, get under his fingernails."*

Albom's ability to turn a phrase is what really makes this article a delight:

"This was the horrible reality: Del Pretty was dying, one layer at a time. Few of us could witness such a thing. But the love between son and father is like God's muscle . . ."

Albom has given his readers a first-rate story to show them that National Football League stars, like the rest of us, are subject to the frailties of life. He does an extraordinary job in a category with plenty of top-notch competition.

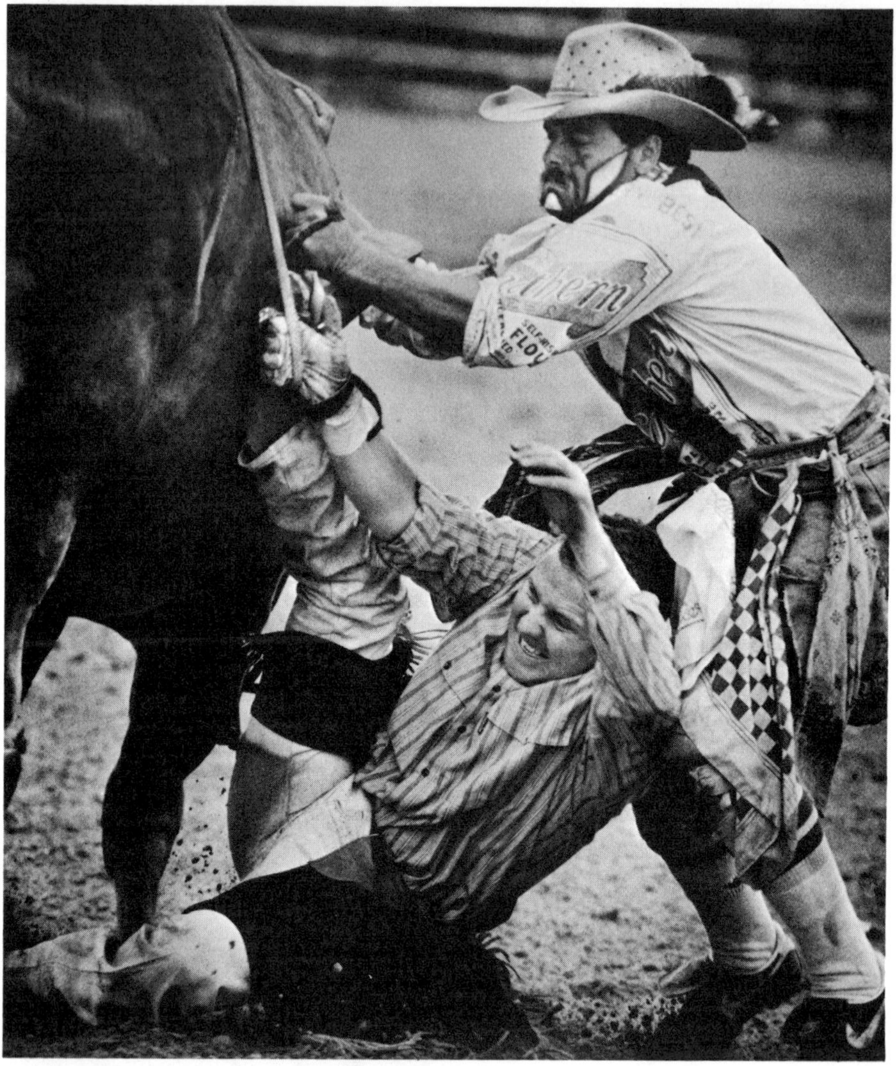

Best Action Photo

A Bunch of Bull

by Stephen Morton of The Gainesville Sun. Morton had the perfect angle and timing to capture this critical moment in the life of rodeo bull rider Joel Welch. The picture's composition is nearly flawless. Details of the rider's trapped hand and foot and rodeo clown Joey Herbert's efforts to free him are as clear as the expressions on both men's faces. Tight cropping emphasizes the drama, as does the selective focus produced by the long lens. Welch walked away from the event without injury. Copyright © 1989, Stephen Morton/The Gainesville Sun.

Best Feature Photo

Ump Grump

by Greg Trott of the Vacaville (Calif.) Reporter. Trott exploited dramatic lighting to emphasize the painful expression of San Jose Giants Manager Duane Espy and the umpire whose call he violently disputes. The legs of running figures in the background suggest that the controversial play either ended an inning or added to the score of the Giants' opponent during a Class A California League game. Espy's body language suggests anguish of the highest order.

Best Reporting Story

Team Doctors: A Crisis in Ethics

GENERAL

By *ANGELO CATALDI & GLEN MACNOW*

(First of three parts)

Charlie Krueger spent 15 years climbing to the top of his profession in the National Football League. Today, he can't climb a flight of stairs.

The blood and grime that stained his uniform at the end of each game were badges of honor. So were his ailments—broken noses and fingers, separated shoulders, torn muscles, back spasms, bleeding ulcers, sprained ankles, fractured arms.

Through it all, Charlie Krueger always followed doctors' orders. With the help of 150 numbing injections, he missed just one of 211 games. And he limped away a hero.

Years later, court testimony showed, Krueger learned that the San Francisco 49ers, in their desire to keep him playing, never told him about serious injuries he incurred on the field—injuries that now cause intense daily suffering. He wasn't even told that a surgeon had removed part of his knee early in his career.

In a landmark ruling last June, a California Superior Court judge agreed with Krueger that the 49ers and their team doctor had "fraudulently concealed" medical information and sacrificed his body for the short-term good of the team. The judge ordered the club to pay Krueger $2.36 million, an amount that was reduced to about $1.5 million in a settlement.

Now, after eight operations, Krueger can't squat, kneel, lift, stoop or even walk for more than a few minutes before the pain becomes unbearable. The injections he took during his career destroyed his joints.

For Charlie Krueger, the greatest anguish comes when he ponders what lies ahead, a bone-fusion operation that will eliminate his knee joint and permanently lock his left leg ramrod straight.

"I've only got so many steps left," Krueger said. ". . . They said they would fix me. They fixed me, all right."

Krueger's story underscores a dilemma team physicians face every day in professional and college sports. They are trapped in an ethical quandary, a classic conflict of interest between serving their employer, the team, and fulfilling their medical responsibilities to their patient, the athlete.

Team doctors regularly face pressure—from coaches, whose own future rests on winning; from owners, who invest millions in certain players; and from players themselves, whose job security depends on their ability to perform.

Every day, injured athletes are carried off the field and cared for by team doctors. Usually, the treatment and rehabilitation proceed without problems.

But when the system breaks down, the consequences are often devastating:

- Players retire from professional sports each year with permanent injuries caused by the maltreatment or neglect of team doctors. Former National Hockey League defenseman Mike Robitaille suffered such severe spinal damage that he could not take the pressure of a feather against his skin. The team doctor's prescription, according to Robitaille's wife, was "Put him to bed and give him a shot of Courvoisier." NFL linebacker Bill Enyart had to retire at 25 after the team doctor rushed him back into action with torn knee ligaments and cartilage. Another physician who examined Enyart told him, "They let you heal like a caveman."
- Coaches and franchise owners pressure team doctors to persuade athletes to play despite serious injuries. A former Washington Redskins physician said he was about to explain a hip injury to a young player when an assistant coach called him aside and said, "You don't want to tell him what's really wrong, now do you?' " The head trainer at The Citadel testified in a court case that "hard-nosed" football coaches sometimes tried to override the medical staff's decisions to prevent injured athletes from playing. The coaches, Andy Clawson said, "are totally interested in the game, the wins and losses. . . . They obviously want them always to play."
- Painkilling injections remain an accepted practice in sports medicine, despite their long-term health implications. Dan Colchico of the 49ers said he received 150 shots per year, leaving him with permanently damaged joints and bones. Former Villanova and Oakland Raiders star Mike Siani documented 16 episodes one season in which he had cortisone or Novocain injected into his broken toes. His joints, he said, "just melted," necessitating the surgical removal of the bones from two toes.
- Although they profess to place the individual needs of players above the concerns of the team, doctors always side with the club in lawsuits and board hearings. In an estimated 110 cases to come be-

fore the NFL's injury grievance board over the last four years, team doctors testified every time against the players they treated—making arguments that saved their employers millions. Injured Miami Dolphins star Bill Stanfill won a $245,000 award by proving that the team physician had cleared him to play even after five neutral doctors agreed that Stanfill risked paralysis and death on the football field.

• Athletes themselves pressure team doctors to compromise their ethics and allow injured players back onto the field. Former Denver Broncos running back Otis Armstrong persuaded the team doctor to let him play even though his limbs became momentarily paralyzed after almost every tackle. Bob Moore, a former tight end for four NFL clubs, recalled once grabbing and threatening to punch a team doctor who had balked at giving Moore a painkilling shot. The doctor relented.

These days, more players are taking formal action against the team doctors. According to a recent NFL Players Association survey, injury grievances filed by players (discounting the 1987 strike season) went from 43 in 1985 to 59 in '86 to 68 last season. In virtually every case, the diagnosis of the team doctor was challenged.

More and more, those challenging are heading into the courtrooms. In addition to Krueger's landmark case, some of the biggest stars in sports—Dick Butkus in football, Bill Walton in basketball and Rick Martin in hockey—have sued their teams over medical treatment. In April, former All-Pro defensive back Kenny Easley sued the NFL Seattle Seahawks and their two team physicians, saying that his kidneys and career were ruined by large doses of the pain killer ibuprofen.

The rising number of grievances and lawsuits reflects a declining trust between players and team physicians. A 1988 *Los Angeles Times* survey of former NFL players found that 53 percent believed that their best health interests were compromised by a team physician during the course of their pro careers.

Earlier this year, Danny Manning, a rookie forward for the NBA Los Angeles Clippers, refused to allow the team doctor to treat his knee injury. Cris Collinsworth, a wide receiver for the NFL Cincinnati Bengals, contended that his team doctor misdiagnosed a knee problem, thereby placing his career in jeopardy.

Doctors from each Philadelphia professional team have become embroiled in controversies involving some top players—Tim Kerr of the Flyers, Andrew Toney and Jeff Ruland of the 76ers, Ron Solt of the Eagles and Mike Schmidt of the Phillies. Most recently, Sixers guard David Wingate had an operation on his injured right knee against the advice of the team's medical staff.

"The way the system is now, it borders on illegal," said Clark Leslie, lawyer for Krueger. "It almost certainly guarantees that, at some point, a conflict is going to arise that never should exist. How can you keep two competing interests happy?

"Sometimes, they're both asking you to look away from your duties. The rookie is saying, 'Let me get out there. I'll lose my job. I've got a wife and two kids. Just do what you've got to do.'

"Meanwhile, the management is saying, 'Get him out there.' The coach is saying, 'I need him.' If the doctor does what's right—and that would be to bench the player or put him in the hospital—he won't be back next year."

★ ★ ★

Charlie Krueger had a reputation for playing with pain that was almost unrivaled in professional sports. Toward the end of his career, his teammates called him "Old Leather," because he was so tough, so durable.

One time, on a camping trip with his wife, he decided to see a doctor because he was feeling "a little discomfort." It turned out that his appendix had ruptured.

But wrestling each Sunday with younger, stronger opponents became an increasing physical burden as Krueger's joints began to weaken. Team doctor Lloyd Milburn made the pain more bearable with shots and pills: Novocain and cortisone; amphetamines and codeine; DMSO and Butazolidan, painkillers designed for horses.

"From 1964 until he retired in 1973, Krueger endured as many as 50 Kepplemann treatments each year, whereby bloody fluid was removed from his swollen knee and replaced with steroid compounds," wrote one of the judges who heard Krueger's case. "He became more and more dependent upon the use of dangerous and addictive drugs to mask his acute pain. He continued to play."

During his deposition, Milburn described a month-long pattern late in Krueger's career, when Krueger was admitted to the hospital with severe back spasms after each game, placed in traction until Friday and released each Sunday from the hospital room straight to the playing field.

"That was the most I ever hurt in my life," Krueger said. He contended that he wanted Milburn to hold him out of games, but when Milburn cleared him for action, "I didn't have enough sense not to play."

Krueger was 36 in his final season, challenging the skills and strength of men 10 to 15 years younger. He announced his retirement in 1973, and the club held a day in his honor, parading him out to the 50-yard line for some flowery speeches and awarding him the ultimate accolade by retiring his gold-and-red No. 70 jersey.

"They spoke of what a credit I had been to the franchise, praised my 15 years of loyal service," Krueger recalled.

At the end, Old Leather embodied his nickname—cracked and battered beyond repair. His knee and his back throbbed constantly. His nose was so out of joint, bones had to be removed through his nasal passage to allow him to breathe.

Even now, 16 years after his final game, Krueger vividly recalls the highlights of a bittersweet career. Frozen in his memory are the punishing tackles that won him distinction as one of the game's most feared defensive linemen, and the stabbing pain that often followed those collisions.

But his mind is occupied no longer solely by thoughts of football. He can quote Byron and Melville just as easily as he can Lombardi and Landry. He can recite details about Mexican songbirds and distant constellations in the same authoritative way he once discussed quarterback sacks and offensive formations.

All of his information is packed inside a head that resembles a sackful of nails. His nose—broken five times—takes more turns than San Francisco's famous Lombard Street. His skin has the consistency of burlap. His white crewcut is translucent.

He still has the upper body of a football player—broad-shouldered and thick-armed. But his lower body is that of a former player —scarred and brittle.

Football is part of his life now only in a historic sense. He does not attend 49ers old-timers' reunions and only rarely watches the game on television. When the 49ers played in the Super Bowl in January, Krueger spent the day watching birds.

"Do you think these guys that worked for Johns Manville would like to go back and watch other people hang asbestos?" he said, referring to the company found to have exposed its workers to life-threatening fibers. "The guys who are sick with cancer and emphysema, do you think they'd like to watch some guys hang asbestos?

"Every time I see these players with their legs getting twisted and hit and hurt, I realize that those guys, if they play long enough, they're going to wind up in the same goddamned boat that I'm in."

★ ★ ★

Krueger joined the 49ers as a first-round draft pick in 1958, an All-America who studied under legendary coach Bear Bryant at Texas A&M. As a pro, he was so strong that other teams usually assigned two players to block him.

He had already undergone cartilage surgery on his left knee as a college freshman and, as a rookie in the NFL, broke his arm making a tackle.

Somehow, he played through those injuries, and numerous others. Indeed, later in his career, Krueger played a half-season after pieces of his left femur and tibia broke off during a game. Playing with pain comes with the job in college and professional sports. It is part of an unwritten code under which an athlete can honor himself in the eyes of coaches, teammates, fans and media.

"When I had an injury, I presented myself to the doctor and I did what he told me to do," Krueger recalled. "There were times when I really wanted to sit, but he didn't say anything. The coach is standing there, the doctor is standing there, the trainer is standing there, I'm standing there and they're all saying I can play. I thought, 'If the doctor doesn't tell me no, well, I'll go out there and try.' "

That blind trust betrayed him in 1963, when he underwent surgery to tie together the shredded ligament in his left knee. The procedure was unsuccessful, and Krueger ended up with no anterior cruciate ligament in the leg.

Testimony later in court showed that Milburn and the 49ers' management knew that playing on a knee with a missing ligament could leave a man crippled. It also showed that no one had ever warned Charlie Krueger; no one even told him that his ligament was gone. The team doctor gave Krueger at least 11 physical exams through the rest of his career—passing him each time.

When asked to discuss the Krueger case, a 49ers spokesman said club officials would not comment. A spokeswoman for Milburn said the physician was on sabbatical overseas and could not be reached for the next year. She said he had previously declined to discuss the Krueger lawsuit.

In his court deposition, Milburn said he was "apprehensive" about Krueger's condition but could not cite a specific conversation in which he explained the future implications of playing with an injury. He praised Krueger as "a real professional" for playing through increasingly serious pain.

Other 49ers played through similar pain. Dan Colchico, a lineman with chronic problems in both knees and ankles, testified at the Krueger trial that he received up to four shots of a steroid compound into each of his knees every week. He estimated taking 300 shots in two seasons, without ever questioning the doctor.

"It's a wonderful thing they do with cortisone," Krueger said recently of his own treatment. "It's a great healer on a short-term basis because you can have a bad knee on Wednesday and it feels pretty good on Sunday.

"But they didn't say, 'This is cortisone, and if I give you more than a half a dozen of these shots, it may just melt your joint.' They would never say that. They just said, 'Get on the table. What have we got here? We'll take care of it.' "

Once the problem with Krueger's knee developed, the only way to escape permanent damage was retirement. On the other hand, the only way to keep playing was to take the shots. Had he realized the high risk of permanent damage—had Milburn informed him of the long-term dangers—Krueger said he would have quit after first injuring his knee. But ignorant of the implications, he played on.

For 15 years, he had always assumed that the pain would go away when he stopped playing. For 15 years, he had accepted every pill, every shot, every treatment from the team doctor without challenge or question. For 15 years, he had been deceived.

"It hurts me to talk about it now," said Krueger. ". . . My buddy once said to me, 'For a fast learner, you sure are slow.' "

★ ★ ★

Although he had spent most of his life playing football, Krueger made the transition to private life with relative ease. He bought a liquor store near his home in Concord, Calif., and settled down to a quiet existence with his wife, Kris, running the business and pursuing his favorite hobbies of bird-watching and stargazing.

The only problem was his knee. As he grew older, it became increasingly difficult for him to walk long distances and increasingly troublesome to push his left leg up a staircase.

In 1978, while planning a grueling raft trip down the Colorado River, Krueger decided to see a private physician about his knee. It was then, for the first time, that he learned the full extent of his problem. The doctor—a specialist recommended by Milburn—removed a wedge of bone from Krueger's tibia in 1979 to allow freer movement in the damaged joint.

Three months after the surgery, complications developed, prompting a second operation in which rods were inserted to hold Krueger's leg together. When the cast was removed after eight months, his knee was worse than ever. He could no longer even work a full day at the liquor store.

Around that time, he ran into an old teammate, Tom Keating, who was active in the NFL Players Association. When Keating heard the story of Krueger's medical problems, his first words were, 'Damn, you ought to see a lawyer.' " Until then, Krueger said, he had never entertained the possibility.

Reluctantly, Krueger hired Clark Leslie of San Mateo, Calif., to handle his case, but only in petitioning the NFL's Bert Bell Pension Plan for $65,000 in disability pay to help defray his medical costs. At that point, there was no thought of a lawsuit.

It wasn't until after the league's six-member disability panel twice deadlocked on Krueger's request that his frustration turned to anger. Krueger was especially upset that the panel split right down labor and management lines—the three player representatives voted for him. In fact, until the system was changed recently, every vote before that panel for years ended in a 3-3 tie. And under NFL rules, a tie vote went to the owners.

Krueger was infuriated that the board's management representatives refused to discuss the seriousness of his injury. They argued solely that he had not applied for the money by the deadline, 36 months after retirement. His contention that the most severe symptoms did not surface until after that deadline did not sway the three management representatives.

"I remember standing in a phone booth after they turned me down the second time," he said. "I had a cast up to my ass, and it hurt. . . . If they had paid me 65 grand then, that day, we wouldn't be here (talking about it) now. I would have felt that I had been decently dealt with.

"But by the time I got through the Bert Bell Pension Plan, I had a well-developed case of hatred for the National Football League."

In 1982, Leslie filed two lawsuits, one challenging the pension plan and one charging the 49ers and Milburn with "fraudulent concealment" of Krueger's injuries. Eventually, Krueger's disability application was approved unanimously, but by then, he had committed himself to the long and bitter legal battle.

His lawsuit against Milburn and the 49ers took two years to get inside a courtroom. When it finally did, he lost, largely because the judge ruled that the doctor was an official agent of the club, whose role was to represent the team's interest, not the player's.

"The doctor works for the team," Krueger said, "and he doesn't know what the Hippocratic oath means as it pertains to you."

Krueger appealed, and in June 1988, Judge John Dearman of the California Superior Court awarded him damages of $2.36 million. Dearman wrote: "In 1979, (Krueger) underwent a difficult and unsuccessful knee surgery. . . . He came to realize the root causes of his unnecessary anguish. Since then he has been forced to live not only with the physical pain, but also with the grievous knowledge that he was betrayed by the very people for whom he sacrificed so much."

The 49ers appealed Krueger's victory, and a second judge increased his award to $2.66 million. The club then moved to file another appeal, and Krueger—after close to a decade of board meetings and court hearings—agreed last October to settle for about $1.5 million.

Just this month, the 49ers filed court papers asking that the settlement costs be shifted to Milburn. According to club attorney Carlos Bea, "The Court of Appeal in the 1987 decision said that it was Dr. Milburn who failed to disclose to Krueger what the condition of his knee was and what the effects of further playing on the knee would be. We'd like to get our money back from Lloyd Milburn."

Milburn's attorney, James Penrod, countered that the 49ers might be wise not to explore the issue of "who does or doesn't benefit from people playing injured."

Krueger plans to stay out of the debate over who should pay.

"It was strictly pure luck that I won," Krueger said. "If I had gotten a wrong judge or the judge got sick that day and I got another judge, or my lawyer said, 'I don't think this case is going to make it,' I'm out in the cold."

What did he do with his windfall? He painted his truck, bought his wife a few dresses and carpeted the living room. Money clearly has not changed Charlie Krueger's lifestyle.

Another thing the money hasn't changed is the daily pain Krueger must endure. He carries a pocketful of Super-Tylenols and Darvocets at all times but finds that more pills he takes, the less effective they are.

"It hurts all the time," he said. "If I stop taking medicine tonight, tomorrow night I'll be hobbling. What I'd like to do is take those pills all day long."

These days, walking on anything but the flattest surfaces is nearly impossible. He cannot push a cart through a supermarket, cannot bend down to pick up a dropped coin.

The next step, doctors have told him, is the fusion operation that would eliminate the pain by removing his knee joint. He fears the procedure, which would make it awkward even to sit, but he knows that it may be only a few years before it becomes unavoidable.

And so now, Charlie Krueger looks back at his long and distinguished football career and reconsiders the meaning of words like *honor* and *courage* and *trust*. He tries to explain why players were then—and remain even today—willing to risk permanent injury for the sake of temporary glory.

"You've got to realize that players have their values, their standards and their ethics set for them by football coaches," he said. "And the only thing football coaches are concerned with is their job.

"We just didn't doubt the doctor. We thought our best bet was to go along with him. It took time to go outside and get another opinion. Also, we all knew that if we went outside to get another opinion, first we were going to be in dutch with the doctor, and then we were going to be in dutch with the coaches.

"The environment breeds a compliant, willing person. That's America—the home of the free and the land of the brave and justice for all. Well, we all know that a lot that we learn in school and in our ethics is B.S. And a lot that you learn about football is B.S.

"If I had it to do all over again, I would not play football at all."

It's a Question of Trust

(Second of three parts)

Every time he swallowed, Mike Robitaille felt an electric shock surge down his throat. He had sustained dozens of injuries during his eight-year National Hockey League career, but nothing as strange as this.

Although Robitaille feared that something was terribly wrong, the Vancouver Canucks' team doctor dismissed his symptoms. Robitaille had played with pain for so many seasons, he figured he could endure this problem, too.

But then he crashed into the boards a few days later and felt an electric charge race through his body. For 20 seconds, his right arm and leg quivered. Don't worry, the team doctor said. Keep playing, the coach said.

So he did. In the next game, Robitaille took a hard check from behind and crumbled to the ice, his arms and legs flailing wildly. Witnesses recalled a loud crack reverberating through the arena at the moment of impact. Others who saw him later said Robitaille's body hair was standing on end.

As it turned out, Robitaille had sustained a spinal contusion, ending his career and causing permanent disability.

According to a lawsuit Robitaille later filed, the team doctor examined him in the locker room and made this prognosis:

"Take him home," Dr. Michael Piper told Robitaille's wife. "Put him to bed and give him a shot of Courvoisier."

Even after Robitaille ended up in a hospital bed, unable to take the pressure of a feather against his skin, Piper described his symptoms as "conversion hysteria," a physical paralysis caused by emotional troubles, the suit said. The team's general manager told the media that Robitaille was having a nervous breakdown. The coach threatened to suspend him or send him to the minors. The assistant general manager called him a "con artist."

Robitaille's case emphasizes what more and more athletes are now suggesting: that they cannot trust the team physician hired to care for them.

Whereas a private patient chooses his own doctor, an athlete's physician is hired and paid by team management. The club gets to share in information that traditionally would be confidential, sometimes even imposing its own ideas about treatment.

This arrangement ultimately forces team doctors to serve two masters, and it leaves them vulnerable to pressure—from coaches, whose futures rest on winning; from owners, who invest millions in players; from agents, whose earnings come out of players' paychecks; from fans, who care only about winning, and from players themselves, whose job security depends on their ability to perform.

Meanwhile, team doctors are asked both to guide players toward full recovery and to return them to the playing field as soon as possible. It is a tightrope not easily walked.

"That's the problem most football players have with team doctors," said Cris Collinsworth, veteran wide receiver for the Cincinnati Bengals. "They're hired by management, so their main concern is getting you back on the football field. The doctor who is paid by them, he reports back to them. There is always that question of doubt whether he is telling you the whole story."

★ ★ ★

Collinsworth was recently at odds with the Bengals' team doctor, Robert Heidt Jr., who diagnosed his recurring leg pain in 1988 as a stretched hamstring tendon and told him that he could safely play. After the team's Super Bowl loss, Collinsworth independently went for a bone scan, which revealed a stress fracture in his knee—an injury best treated by several months of inactivity. Collinsworth says he believes that the Bengals' doctor's diagnosis jeopardized his career. He has since signed a new contract with the Bengals and has decided not to pursue the issue.

Heidt declined to comment, except to say that he left the decision to play up to Collinsworth.

"My question to team doctors is this," Collinsworth said. "Are you looking out for the best interest of the person who's paying you, or of the person you're examining? Because sometimes you can't look out for both."

Team doctors insist that they would never abandon their Hippocratic oath for the sake of a club's won-lost record, but the players apparently don't agree. In a 1988 *Los Angeles Times* survey of 440 former NFL players—the only such survey ever taken of professional athletes—53 percent said their best health interests were compromised by a team physician during the course of their pro careers. Some players said their injuries were misdiagnosed or treated incorrectly; others accused team doctors of tailoring their decisions to the wishes of management.

In recent years, more than a dozen players—led by stars such as football's Dick Butkus, basketball's Bill Walton and hockey's Richard Martin—have sued teams and doctors over issues of malpractice and negligence.

Former All-Pro safety Kenny Easley of the NFL Seattle Seahawks became the latest player to seek judicial relief, filing a suit in April that said his kidneys and career were destroyed by massive doses of an anti-inflammatory drug. Several other players have cases awaiting trial.

Some athletes who challenged their team doctors won damages; many more received settlements. In virtually every case, the process was fraught with delays and frustration. Robitaille spent more than four years in the Canadian Courts before receiving $355,000 in damages. Former Oakland Raiders receiver Mike Siani fought five years to win a settlement with the team doctor after documenting 16 episodes one season in which he had drugs injected into his broken toes.

★ ★ ★

Most disputes, however, are played out in the locker room, not the courtroom. 76ers guard David Wingate recently rejected team doctor Raymond Moyer's prognosis of his knee injury and hired his own physician to perform surgery—against the advice of the 76ers. New York Yankees shortstop Rafael Santana said in March that the team doctor's earlier misdiagnosis of his elbow injury forced him to undergo preseason surgery and will cost him the entire 1989 season.

And Los Angeles Clippers rookie forward Danny Manning chose not to let the club doctor operate on his torn knee ligaments after that doctor and Manning's agent, Ron Grinker, battled over treatment of another of Grinker's clients, Clippers guard Derek Smith. Smith now plays for the 76ers.

"There very clearly could be a conflict between the team and the player, and the team doctor is in the middle," said Grinker. "My problem with it is that the team doctor is not always the person who makes the decision. Sometimes, there may be pressure from above."

Robitaille knows about pressure from above. He said he played through intense pain in 1977 because Canucks management threatened to trade or suspend him, and because the team doctor dismissed his ailments as insignificant.

Only four years later were Robitaille's initial suspicions confirmed, when a judge ruled that he had exposed himself to permanent injury by playing after he was first hurt.

The final body check that night in Vancouver caused his already damaged spinal cord to be pinched between the vertebrae in his neck. And that created a condition that leads to numbness and involuntary jerking of his arms and legs; causes his right hand to clutch up when he becomes tired or cold, and impairs his sex life, his ability to drive and his job prospects.

Just as the injury scarred Robitaille's spinal cord, his treatment by the Canucks and the club doctor scarred his psyche. For several years, he suffered from panic attacks and agoraphobia—fear of leaving the house.

"When the doctor keeps telling you you're OK, that it's all in your head, you get brainwashed into believing it," he said. "I actually started to doubt myself."

But as his condition worsened, he decided to sue the Canucks for negligence. In 1981, British Columbia Supreme Court Justice William Esson ruled that "in carrying through their chosen treatment, (the Canucks') management and medical team displayed a reckless disregard for (Robitaille's) feelings and his well-being—they ignored the dictates of common decency as well as common sense."

Esson ordered the Canucks to pay Robitaille $355,000.

Piper, who is no longer team physician, now calls that ruling "a travesty of justice." He insists that he was not even at the game at which Robitaille was injured and that he never called Robitaille's injuries psychosomatic. He chides the Canucks for presenting a "nice guy" defense and for not appealing the case to the Canadian Supreme Court.

For Robitaille, the verdict served as vindication, but it has done nothing to bring back his health. Twelve years later, he said, "I can't work an eight-hour day. Even if I'm just bearing down on a book or doing some mental work for an hour or two, my knee will start quivering. Or my hand will start turning inward. I'll need to take a rest."

Robitaille, now 41, is back in hockey as a television announcer for the Buffalo Sabres, a team he once played for. He leads a quiet suburban life with his wife and two daughters, but he faces restrictions.

"I've been told that one more jolt to my neck might lead to permanent paralysis," he said. "So I can't do anything physical—from golfing to skating to wrestling around with the kids. I can't shovel the driveway; I can't mow that lawn. I'm really not supposed to drive, but I do.

"I used to be angry with a lot of people . . . not understanding why they would treat someone like that. Now, it's not a hate I have anymore. It's pity. I feel sorry for those people who got sucked into the whole thing. But I can see how they could get caught up in it."

Robitaille's attorney, John Laxton, remains angry. "What it boiled down to is that the doctor should have recognized the symptoms Mike had, but he didn't because of the rah-rah of the club. The mentality was, 'Get on the ice no matter what.' The doctor lost sight of the individual player in his zeal to help the team."

The problem, Laxton said, is that team doctors' loyalties tend to lie with those who hire them. Certainly, their jobs are highly coveted: They allow the physician to work with famous, motivated patients; they make him feel like an important part of the team's success, and they turn the doctor into a local celebrity, which, in turn, bolsters his regular practice.

"When the owner says, 'Hey, we've got to have this guy play,' the doctor doesn't want to get fired," said Frank Bassett, physician for Duke University's sports teams. "He doesn't want to lose this great job, so he thinks more of the owner's interest than the player's interest."

John Babinecz, a Paoli pediatrician who played four years in the NFL after starring at Villanova University, said the concept of team doctor "is contrary to everything I learned. Some physicians are tougher—they won't bow to the pressure of the front office. But let's face it, their job is not to keep people off the field."

And sometimes, they can save a job by keeping players on the field. That's what appeared to happen in 1971, when third-year linebacker Bill "Earthquake" Enyart was chopped down by a blind-side block.

At the time, the Oakland Raiders were giving tryouts to several doctors for the position of orthopedic consultant—even as Dr. Robert Rosenfeld held the job. Two physicians and the Raiders' trainer looked at Enyart's knee and recommended immediate surgery to repair a torn ligament. Rosenfeld, the last to examine Enyart, was treating the knee in the locker room when, according to Enyart, team owner Al Davis walked in.

"Davis was throwing a tantrum," Enyart recalled, "saying, 'There goes our bleepedy-bleep middle linebacking.' He was like a 4-year-old kid. Rosenfeld picked up on this and said, 'Wait Al, it may not be that bad.'"

Rosenfeld diagnosed Enyart's injury as stretched ligaments and put him in a straight-leg cast for six weeks. After two more months of rehabilitation, Enyart was cleared to play in the season's final game against Denver.

"The doctor kept promising Al Davis that if I didn't have surgery, he could get me back the same season," Enyart recalled. "And I played in the final game, so Rosenfeld kept his promise. . . . Whether or not I would permanently destroy my leg was not really an issue."

Enyart's knee kept swelling during the ensuing off-season, so Rosenfeld drained it several times and injected cortisone. When the 1972 season began, the knee was so swollen one day that Rosenfeld drew close to two ounces of bloody fluid from it as Davis looked on. Days later, Enyart was released.

"I still wanted to play, so I went home to a doctor in Oregon," Enyart recalled. "He took one look at my knee and said, 'Good God, you should have never played on this. You've got a complete tear of the ligament and cartilage. They let you heal like a caveman.' He said it had been so long and I had built up so much scar tissue that he couldn't really help."

Enyart was 25, and his career was over. He hired an attorney, who contacted the other doctors who had examined Enyart. One agreed to testify that Enyart's initial injury cut off the blood supply to the ligament, necessitating surgery within 24 hours. The doctor said he had given his diagnosis to Rosenfeld, who either ignored it or did not believe it.

Enyart sued Rosenfeld (who remains the team's orthopedic consultant), saying the doctor knew the extent of his knee damage and hid the information from him. His suit said that Rosenfeld was aware that, by not performing surgery, he was risking Enyart's health.

During the trial, Enyart's attorney produced a letter from Rosenfeld to Davis, indicating that Enyart's surgery was being delayed on the owner's suggestion.

In 1977, a California jury awarded Enyart $777,000. When the Raiders moved to file an appeal, Enyart settled the case for an amount that, as part of the agreement, both sides are keeping private.

Rosenfeld now denies feeling any pressure from Davis, or from the presence of other doctors competing for the job. He said his decision to delay surgery for ligament damage "is accepted practice now. That's what I did with Enyart and I know he fully recovered. ... He wasn't let go because of anything I did."

These days, Enyart is a real estate appaiser in Bend, Ore. His plan—and his acrimony—linger.

"The doctor knew my knee needed surgery and kept it from me," he said. "He told Al Davis what he wanted to hear. ... This is a classic case of the doctor's allegiance to the team."

In Enyart's case, he believed that the team doctor felt pressure from the owner. More often, however, the pressure comes from coaches, whose livelihoods depend on the athletes playing under them. The old axiom in sports is that owners can't fire all the players, so they fire the coach. If that coach's best players are on the sidelines, he becomes even more vulnerable.

"The coach is only as good as his horses," said Doug Swift, a six-year linebacker for the Miami Dolphins. "He always wants to have his front-line players being in their best possible condition and on the field. If he's being told by the team doctor that he can't have that, it's compromising his ability to get his job done." Swift, now an anesthesiologist at the University of Pennsylvania, was a first-hand witness to the subtle pressure some coaches would place on doctors.

"The coach will go to the doctor and say, 'Look, this guy, I want him to play. How's he doing? Is he going to be able to go?' " Swift recalled. "The doctor has to be able to sit there and say no."

Sometimes, the doctor does just that. Vincent DiStefano, Eagles team physician since 1971, remembers an episode in which he and head coach Mike McCormack had an angry confrontation on the sidelines in the middle of a game. McCormack had sent fullback Norm Bulaich back onto the field after the player had suffered an apparent concussion.

"I told (offensive coordinator) John Sandusky that he shouldn't go back in the game, but Mike was preoccupied," DiStefano recalled. "Bulaich went up to McCormack and told him it was all right for him to go back in. When I saw him in the game, I told McCormack he shouldn't be there, and then we started yelling at each other back and forth."

DiStefano said Bulaich suffered no further injuries after going back in that day, and the physician has had no similar confrontations since that episode more than a decade ago. The same cannot be said, however, for other NFL teams.

Stanford Lavine, the team doctor for the Washington Redskins from 1976 to 1985, said he felt pressure from the coaches on virtually every injury.

"They always wanted to know, 'Do you have to operate? How long will he be out? When is the soonest we can get him back?' " he recalled.

In one incident, Lavine had just finished examining a player's injured hip when he was approached by one of the Redskins' assistant coaches.

"He came up to me and said, 'Stan, you don't want to tell him what's really wrong, now do you?'" Lavine said. "I told him, 'Listen, I can coach a heck of a lot better than you can doctor. So stay out of it.' "

One of the biggest controversies over coach interference unfolded nine years ago and involved two celebrated names in hockey — Richard Martin and Scotty Bowman.

Martin, now 37, was the high-scoring left winger on the Buffalo Sabres' "French Connection" line of the 1970s. He scored 375 goals during his first nine seasons, played in seven NHL All-Star Games and was a fan favorite.

In 1980, Martin was tripped on a breakaway and crashed into Washington Capitals goalie Mike Palmateer. Martin's leg jammed into the ice, forcing his knee to bend unnaturally backward.

Sabres team doctor Peter Casagrande diagnosed Martin's injury as a hyperextended knee and advised Martin to rest until the symptoms had subsided. When the knee failed to improve, Casagrande—according to Martin's later testimony in court—told him not to rush back, saying, "You're the one that knows whether you can play or not."

A memo written by the doctor to club officials soon after the injury said, "I feel that (Martin) will be off game conditions for about two weeks." And Bowman, at one point, insisted that Casagrande had cleared Martin to play, the player later testified.

"The doctor says there's nothing wrong with you," the coach said, according to Martin's deposition. "Are you going to play? When are you going to play? How long are you going to keep this . . . whatever?"

Martin was out for most of 13 weeks. Casagrande performed several medical procedures and determined that Martin's injuries were limited to a sprained knee and a case of synovitis, meaning an inflammation of the joint lining stemming from early arthritis. Such a condition, Casagrande testified, was common in a player in his late 20s.

As time went on, Martin alleges, management became more abusive. Bowman, who had come to Buffalo from the Montreal Canadiens, berated Martin in front of teammates, Martin said, calling him a "chicken" and repeatedly questioning his manhood. Martin quoted Bowman as saying: "When I was in Montreal, we measured injuries in terms of minutes or hours, not in terms of days or weeks."

In his deposition, Bowman denied exerting pressure on Martin. "The doctors are in full control of the injured player," he said.

Martin played in eight games in January 1981 (scoring four goals) before the pain in his knee grew unbearable.

Eventually, Martin sought a second opinion. In February 1981, Toronto orthopedist Robert Jackson performed exploratory arthroscopic surgery and found several tears in Martin's knee cartilage, as well as floating cartilage fragments.

"I woke up after the operation," Martin recalled, "and was almost relieved to know there had been real damage. Finally, they would believe me. . . . Dr. Jackson told me that I should not have been playing on it. I was lucky I hadn't ripped my knee apart."

Soon after the surgery, the Sabres traded Martin to the Los Angeles Kings for two draft choices. Martin played two more games that season and the first three of 1981-82 before being told to retire by the Kings' physician, Vincent Carter. At the time, Carter said Martin "would become a hopeless cripple before the age of 40 if he continued playing."

Martin was 29, and his career was over. In 1982, he filed a $10 million lawsuit against the Sabres, Bowman and Casagrande, alleging that his career was shortened by improper medical treatment. The suit charged Casagrande with negligence, malpractice and concealment. It charged Bowman with fraud and with forcing Martin to play despite injury.

Casagrande, who has since retired, testified that he had kept club management informed of the injury as he diagnosed and treated it. Both Casagrande and his attorney, James McAskill, declined to be interviewed for this article.

In December, New York Superior Court Judge Henry G. Gossel dismissed the suit against the Sabres and Bowman, saying that the worker's compensation law provided the exclusive remedy for such injuries. Gossel kept Casagrande as a defendant, writing that the team doctor had not told the Sabres of the seriousness of Martin's injury until the team traded him. That trial is pending.

"If it's true that the doctor left the team in the dark—and I don't think it is true—who was he trying to protect?" asked Martin. "Was he afraid that if he told Scotty the truth that Scotty would call him a chicken, too? What good is a team doctor if he can't face pressure?"

Indeed, team doctors face pressure these days not just from coaches and owners, but from influences outside the club. Last year, Flyers team doctor John Gregg said he was the butt of constant criticism from Philadelphia fans after five operations were needed to repair Tim Kerr's badly damaged left shoulder.

Even when other orthopedic surgeons publicly defended Gregg's work and Kerr himself supported the doctor, the fans continued to lambaste Gregg on radio talk shows.

"I never experienced anything like that," Gregg said.

Similarly, Duke's Bassett came under public attack earlier this year after he held basketball star Danny Ferry out of one game because of back spasms. Even Bassett's wife—who has nothing to do with Duke's athletic program—has been the target of fan derision while sitting in the stands during home games.

"My wife and I get all kinds of flak from fans," Bassett said. "They say, 'Why did you do this? Why did you do that?' A lot of flak."

And, too, there are the agents of professional athletes, who frequently have their own ideas on the best course of medical treatment. Manning's agent (Grinker) and Wingate's (Andy Brandt) both played key roles in those players' decisions to seek outside physicians.

The agents see themselves as the lone advocate for a player's health—against a system that includes doctors working for teams, coaches striving for victories and the players themselves looking for fame.

Near the end of last season, California-based agent Leigh Steinberg sought to obtain a certified letter from the New England Patriots confirming that the team was clearing quarterback Tony Eason to play even though he wasn't healthy. The team balked at the proposal, but Steinberg—who represents many of the top quarterbacks in the NFL—said the inquiry itself could have been used against the team if Eason had suffered a crippling injury.

To the agents, the issue is safeguarding their clients' futures; to the team doctors, the issue is something else entirely.

"The agents are interfering," said Phillies team doctor Phillip Marone. "They're causing a conflict of interest between the doctor and the player, because they're telling the player, 'Don't go to Dr. X, go to Dr. Y.'"

But aren't agents presumably looking out for the players' interest?

"They're presumably looking out for their own pocket book," said Marone. "Come on, who are you kidding? The agent has one design in life: 'How much money can I make for you so that I get more money?' It's very obvious."

Once a player's skills have eroded and his agent is gone, the rest of his life may be one of regret—for playing with pain, for not questioning the team doctor, for not seeking a second opinion.

Wayne Moore, a former All-Pro defensive end with the Miami Dolphins, played with pain for eight years and will live with it for the rest of his life. He has been trying for nearly a decade to receive worker's compensation benefits from the NFL, saying that the team doctor cleared him to play while he had serious — and obvious — knee and back injuries.

The Dolphins, through spokesman Harvey Greene, declined to comment on the case.

Moore can no longer bend his right knee, he suffers from sever back spasms and he has arthritis in the fingers of both hands. Walking is becoming more and more difficult.

"Do you realize what it means to be this way?" he said. "I could never run with my kids. I could never do any of the physical things most fathers can do with their children. You feel bad. You feel like a cripple.

"My advice is, don't trust the doctor. Trust yourself. Never forget that you're just a body, a piece of meat. When you wear out, there'll be another body to take your place.

"That's the system. That's life."

The Pitfalls of Playing With Pain

(Third of three parts)

As Otis Armstrong slowly peeled himself off the turf at Mile High Stadium, his arms and legs still tingling from the impact of the collision, he noticed a frenzy of activity on the sideline.

The Denver Broncos' doctors and trainers were waving their arms and trying to scream above the din of the crowd, hoping to get Armstrong to leave the field.

The coaches were equally animated, beseeching the veteran running back to stay in the game and coax one more heroic effort from his tired, numb legs.

The coaches won.

"I can remember getting the ball on the next play, a critical third down," Armstrong recalled recently. "I had to get around a big defensive end to make the first down. I could barely feel my legs when I took that ball, and he got me before I could get to the marker.

"Now I'm coming off the field and everybody's yelling. The doctors are yelling at the coaches for not getting me out of there, and the coaches are yelling at me for not getting the first down.

"I just wanted to do my best. All I ever wanted was to do what was best for my team."

What was best for the Broncos, however, was not best for Otis Armstrong. Today, nine years after his retirement, he faces a dilemma: throbbing pain for the rest of his life, or a back operation that—if it fails—could lead to paralysis in all four limbs.

Worst of all, Armstrong knows there is one person to blame above all others. It isn't the team doctor or the trainers or the coach.

It is himself.

Like thousands of athletes in every major American sport, Armstrong thought it was a test of his courage to play with pain, a measure of his dedication to his teammates and to the game he loved. He never understood that the real challenge would come after he retired, when there were no cheers to soothe the suffering.

In a 1987 study conducted by the National Football League Players Association, 37 percent of the league's former players said they left because of a disabling injury; 62 percent said they still suffered from a game-related injury. The NFL Management Council keeps no such statistics.

Many of those in the NFLPA survey expressed resentment over the medical treatment they received and over the pressure coaches exerted on them to perform while injured. But many others also blamed themselves for not protecting their own interests—for cajoling team doctors into giving them one more shot for their aching knees, for popping handfuls of painkillers to get ready for a game, for forsaking a second opinion because it wasn't the loyal thing to do, for ostracizing teammates who were injured.

"The real tragedy is, players are the most trusting people in the world," said Bob Moore, a former tight end with four NFL teams who now is an assistant district attorney in San Francisco. "They rely on people with a blind faith that's almost childlike. They're taught their whole life to listen to authority, to do what they're told. If the doctor tells them something, they listen. They never question.

"And if that doctor says, 'OK, you can play,' you're not going to argue with him, that's for sure. So what you've got—especially if the doctor is not the most conscientious person in the world—is the worst possible doctor-patient relationship imaginable."

Under this imperfect system, Otis Armstrong was the perfect patient. He was willing to play without complaint or question. Even in the final months of his career, when he experienced momentary paralysis in his limbs after every hard tackle, he never placed his own safety above the fortunes of the team. When the team doctors forbade him to play after discovering the magnitude of his problem, Armstrong tried to persude them to let him back for one more game, one more quarter, one more play. He couldn't bear to quit.

"I thought I'd be playing forever," he said. "Even after they told me to retire, I remember saying, 'Ah, just give me some time and I'll be able to go again. It'll come back. It always comes back.' "

Years later, he finally realized that he had risked permanent paralysis and possibly death in the later stages of his career by playing with a condition called spinal stenosis—a narrowing of the spinal canal.

Suddenly, his loyalty to the Broncos evaporated. He sued the team over his medical care, but the case was thrown out of court. Then he was arrested for fraudulently acquiring an estimated 1,500 capsules of an addictive painkiller called Percodan, a synthetic heroin. To avoid a prison term, Armstrong agreed to get rehabilitation for his drug dependency.

"Right now, I don't know what I'm going to do with the rest of my life," said Armstrong, who is 38. "I'm so stiff and sore that I can't sit in one place for very long. I can walk OK for a few minutes, but then I start getting this sharp pain in my lower back and have to stop.

"It's a lonely feeling now, very lonely. I'll tell you what happens. You play for this team, and they take care of you so well: 'Anything you need, Otis. Anything at all.' Then one day it's all gone."

★ ★ ★

To be a professional athlete is a dream of millions but a reality for very few. Those who make it to the top can expect adulation, fame and money—sometimes lots and lots of money.

At the same time, however, there is always a fear that the privilege will somehow end prematurely, that some stronger, faster player will come along and take it all away.

When a muscle is pulled or an ankle broken, the physical pain is only a small part of the problem; the mental anguish of drawing a paycheck without helping the team also hurts.

"If you're not playing, you come into the locker room and it's awful," said John Babinecz, a former NFL linebacker who is now a Paoli pediatrician. "You shimmy off to the side or to the trainer's room, and you hope people don't see you there. You feel totally ostracized. You feel like you're in a different country.

"When I was hurt, I didn't want to watch the game, be in the stands, even watch on television. I would have done anything to be on the field, because I knew it was my job. I was a borderline player. I had to be in.

"There was so much pressure to produce that even if the physician is telling you not to play, you still feel you have to play."

These concerns span the full spectrum of players, from the best ever to play the game to those who never made it past their first training camps.

Ron Mix, a star offensive tackle from 1960 through 1970 with the San Diego Chargers, said he felt like "extra baggage" when he missed six weeks with a knee injury in his 10th pro year. Bill Enyart, a fullback who blocked for O.J. Simpson in the late 1960s and early 1970s in Buffalo, said he "wanted to crawl in a hole" on those rare occasions when he was hurt.

"Because you've walked this golden path, seen people fall by the wayside, you feel more and more invincible," said Enyart. "Then you're injured and thrown on the trash pile. That affects you. A sensitive guy goes into deep, dark depression. People don't really take injury as an explanation. They figure you weren't good enough."

The only way to feel part of the team again is to return. And the only way to return is to receive clearance from the team doctor. Sometimes, the physician is willing to compromise his standards to give the player what he wants—a chance to play. On other occasions, the player tries to take control of his own destiny by forcing himself back into action.

Dr. Joseph S. Torg, the director of sports medicine at the University of Pennsylvania, said the most dramatic example of this zeal to play that he had ever encountered happened 17 years ago, when he was the team physician at Temple.

During a football game in Storrs, Conn., a Temple player lay motionless on the ground at the bottom of a huge pileup.

The trainer, Ted Quedenfield, raced onto the field, checked the injured player and then frantically waved for Torg to join them.

When Torg reached the scene of the mishap, Quedenfield told him the player was paralyzed. Immediately a spine board was summoned, and the player was carefully rolled onto it and taken to an ambulance. The game was halted for close to 15 minutes.

As Torg waited for the ambulance to begin its race to the hospital, the player suddenly sprang up and announced his intention to re-enter the game. The impact of the collision had caused only a momentary paralysis. He felt fine again.

"We ended up trying to hang onto the kid to keep him from running out of the ambulance and back onto the field," Torg said.

Last winter, a similar—though less dramatic—incident occurred involving Flyers winger Tim Kerr, who has been plagued for the last several years with chronic shoulder problems.

Midway through the season, Kerr's left shoulder became inflamed, and he was advised to take time off by the team's medical staff and his personal physician. Pat Croce, the Flyers' strength and conditioning coach, explained to Kerr one morning that he could not play in a game the following night. Kerr agreed without challenge.

Later that day, Croce received a call at home from Kerr. This is how Croce recalled the exchange:

"Pat, I've got to play tomorrow," Kerr said.

"What do you have to play for?" Croce asked.

"I have to play. I've just got to play."

Finally, Croce told Kerr that there was no choice: For the sake of his shoulder—for the sake of his health—Kerr would not be allowed to play.

As a rule, though, the players don't want to hear that kind of command, even when it benefits their long-term health. The Buffalo Bills have a saying that sums up the attitude of players everywhere: "You don't make the club in the tub." In other words, you don't spend your days in the whirlpool—you play with pain.

And when the playing is done, you live with pain.

"You end up with a person who has made millions of dollars in a lot of cases but is never really going to enjoy it the way he should," said Leigh Steinberg, an agent who represents many of the top athletes in football.

"It's very similar to the concept of death. When you're in your 20s, it's impossible to believe that you'll ever die or grow old. Those things only happen to other people."

★ ★ ★

When his own playing days ended, former NFL tight end Bob Moore wanted to tell the world about the unheralded side of pro football. Although he had scant experience as a producer, Moore made a film in 1984 called "Disposable Heroes," documenting the life of pain that players face after their careers.

The film received wide acclaim, especially from players. Moore depicted in vivid detail the way former stars such as Jim Otto and Roger Stillwell now lead lives as semi-invalids because of the punishment they absorbed on the gridiron. Most of the former players in the film showed little regret over compromising their health for several years of glory.

What Moore did not reveal in the film was a personal incident that underscored how shortsighted athletes can be.

Late in his own career, Moore was in agony over a knee injury, but did not want to leave an important game. He knew the end was near for him, and wanted to preserve every moment he had left as an athlete. So he went to the team doctor during halftime and asked for a shot to kill the pain.

"He said he wouldn't do it," Moore recalled. "I got mad. I said, 'Look, I want a shot!' Then I grabbed him by the shoulders and told him he wouldn't be going out for the second half until he shot me up. I forced the guy to do what he didn't want to do.

"Now I consider myself a fairly intelligent person. If I was capable of doing something like that, you can imagine what other players are capable of doing. The truth is, in the middle of a football game—in the heat of battle—how many people are really thinking clearly?"

Stanford Lavine faced the same question in his first game as team doctor of the Washington Redskins in 1976. He was preparing to treat a massive defensive end who was writhing in pain from a hip injury when the player offered Lavine his own medical advice.

"He picked me right up off the ground and said, 'You're going to give me a shot for my hip-pointer," Lavine recalled. "I said, 'How can you be so sure?' And he said—remember, this is a big, big fellow —'Because I said so.' "

While most team doctors say the use of pain-killing shots has decreased in recent years, it clearly has not gone away. A case in point was raised by the Eagles' acquisition last year of offensive lineman Ron Solt from the Indianapolis Colts.

Shortly after Solt's arrival in Philadelphia, the Eagles discovered that he had received injections in both knees before each game the previous season to help him cope with tendinitis.

Eagles physician Vincent DiStefano refused to administer the shots, saying they could lead to a ruptured tendon. Without the shots, Solt was unable to play. Throughout the ensuing two-month controversy over his condition, Solt said he was willing to take whatever shots were necessary to allow him to perform. He even expressed disillusionment when the Eagles wouldn't compromise their standards.

Solt, Colts officials and team doctor K. Donald Shelbourne all have declined to discuss the case. DiStefano said it was simply a matter of placing the needs of the player over those of the team, which badly needed Solt's services.

"It came down to this," DiStefano said. "It was put to me that if this player comes in here, if we take him in a trade, and if he can't play, can he be made better so that he can play? And my answer was yes."

Did Solt ask for shots when he arrived in Philadelphia?

"I told him, I wouldn't do it," DiStefano replied. "He never got the chance to ask me. . . . If you inject a load-bearing joint, like the knee or the ankle or the toe joint in the ballplayer, you really should not have him go out and pound on it, because you can do damage."

For every case like Ron Solt's, there are dozens in which players received shots or medication to allow them to play. Former star linebacker Dick Butkus won a $600,000 settlement after charging in a lawsuit that the Chicago Bears' team doctor negligently overadministered cortisone, which caused him irreparable damage.

Ken Mendenhall of the Oakland Raiders won $35,000 in a lawsuit by proving that the club physician supplied him with mood-altering amphetamines to help him play through an injury. Ken Gray of the St. Louis Cardinals won a $45,000 court judgment several years ago after alleging that the team had given him drugs that made him perform "more violently" and diminished his "body integrity."

In each case, there was one telling point: The players accepted the shots or pills without complaint or challenge. The urgency to play superseded the risk to their own health.

★ ★ ★

When Mike Schmidt suffered a partial tear of the rotator cuff in his right shoulder last year, he began a highly publicized tour of orthopedic surgeons to get second, third and even fourth opinions after his initial examination by Phillies team doctor Phillip Marone. Ultimately, Schmidt accepted the prognosis by Dr. James Andrews of Birmingham, Ala., and had arthroscopic surgery to remove debris around the tear.

It was Schmidt's contractual right to get the extra opinions—especially with his career in jeopardy—but he later conceded that he did so with some misgivings.

"When I was a younger player, I would have never gotten a second opinion on anything," he said. "It takes a veteran player who's familiar with the system and is not fearful of ruffling feathers."

Most standard player contracts permit players to get second opinions for all significant injuries, yet—after winning that right in collective bargaining with management—most professional players don't exercise it.

"They think of themselves as members of a family," said Scott Righthand, an attorney representing former player Paul Hofer in a medical malpractice suit against the San Francisco 49ers. "Coaches preach togetherness all the time. And when you go outside the family for a second opinion, it's like slapping your father in the face."

"The player is afraid it'll get back to the coaches, the owners," said Tom DePaso, an attorney with the NFL Players Association and a former player. "He feels it shows a lack of faith and trust. And if a guy's job security is poor to begin with, this doesn't help."

So the athlete routinely accepts the team doctor's prognosis, even if he doesn't agree with it and even if it means playing with pain. To do otherwise is to contradict the concept of team ingrained in every player.

What many players don't realize until much later is that, with a few exceptions, they are members of the family only while they are actively contributing to the team. Once their playing careers are over, so too is their affiliation with the club.

It is like being injured again—the isolation, the rejection, the sense of not contributing to the team—only this time, the condition is permanent.

"When I was a younger player, I used to wonder why the old guys didn't come back (to visit)," said Charlie Krueger, a former star player with the San Francisco 49ers, who won a $1.5 million settlement last year over medical care. "Heck, they don't want to come back. When the new guys are making twice what you were making, they're young and you're not young anymore, who wants to see that?"

Otis Armstrong was one of the greatest runners in Denver Broncos history, but he is not part of the family anymore. In the days after his retirement, Armstrong said he struggled with his new role in the world—the former player, the former star, the former hero. Everything that he was meant to accomplish had already been accomplished, he felt.

Desperate to control the pain, he began visiting doctors and persuading them to prescribe Percodan. He never told them he already had hundreds of the pills; he said they never asked. Since overcoming his dependency on Percodan, Armstrong has been taking different medication—still strong, but not addictive.

No drug is going to give him permanent relief from his suffering, however, and he knows it. A complicated operation in which several of the disks in his back would be removed is the only cure, and that comes with a risk he is unwilling to take.

"There are no guarantees," he said. "There's no telling how I'll feel. If something goes wrong, I'm paralyzed for life. I'm not ready to have that surgery. I'm thinking about it, but I don't know if I'll ever be ready."

Whenever he begins to get up the courage to have the operation, Armstrong thinks of his former college roommate at Purdue, Darryl Stingley, who was rendered a quadriplegic after a tackle in 1977 while playing for the New England Patriots.

"I look at my old friend and I think, 'Nothing's worth that. Anything is better than that," Armstrong said. "Then I realize how close I came to being like that even without this operation. It scares me, really scares me. Sometimes you get so swept up in playing football, you forget everything else."

When he was a child and dreamed about playing football, the dream always ended with his final game. He never considered what would happen after that game.

Otis Armstrong doesn't dream much anymore.

"Kids approach me and say, 'I want to be a running back just like you, Otis' and I don't know how to answer them," he said. "I really don't. I mean, football is a great game, but what happens to you after it is not so great. Living like this is definitely not great.

"But what do you say to kids? It doesn't seem right to ruin their dreams."

Judge's Comments

The moral of this year's competition could be: Good sports reporting is good reporting, period.

Good reporting is characterized by detail and depth, accuracy and insight, observation and context. Clever writing is no substitute for hard digging, on the sports page or the front page. The winning entry, "Team Doctors: A Crisis in Ethics" by Angelo Cataldi and Glen Macnow of the *Philadelphia Inquirer*, is outstanding journalism.

With the real stories of real people, supported by experts' opinions and a wealth of background, Cataldi and Macnow explore a side of sport that seldom makes the papers until a Charlie Krueger wins a lawsuit or a Hank Gathers loses his life. Their series reminds us that sports is more than games. It is big business. It can be life and death.

There are other examples of excellent reporting among this year's best reporting entries. They illustrate both the breadth of this competition and the fact that you don't need a series to tell a solidly reported story. See, for example, Ron Borges' profile of Art Shell and Mike Tulumello's retelling of the rise and fall of Frank Kush. Both have the detailed observation and the depth of background that make good writing possible.

These and the other reporters whose work is represented in this collection offer rich entertainment for fans of sports and of good writing. They also offer models worth studying by students, young or old, of good reporting in any subject.

The Coach and His Champion

COLLEGE BASKETBALL

By *ALEXANDER WOLFF*

John Wooden will not be in Seattle this weekend. Instead, the greatest basketball coach ever—the man who so completely made the Final Four his private reserve that the fans and the press and the rest of the college game couldn't get in on the fun until he retired—will be at home, in Encino, Calif., in what is called the Valley.

He will not stay home because he is unwelcome in Seattle. Men like Bob Knight and Dean Smith have implored him to come, to grace with his presence the annual meeting of the National Association of Basketball Coaches, which is held at the Final Four. But their entreaties have been unavailing. "We need him at our convention," says current UCLA Coach Jim Harrick, who is the sixth man in 14 years to try to wear Wooden's whistle. "He is a shining light. My wife and I have offered to take him. I hounded him so much that he finally told me to lay off. The more you badger him, the more stubborn he gets. But I can see his point. The memories would be really difficult."

To most coaches, memories of 10 NCAA championships in 12 years, including seven in a row, would be sweet and easy. Indeed, this spring marks the 25th anniversary of Wooden's first title, the championship won by UCLA's tiny Hazzard-Goodrich-Erickson team, the one he likens to his first child. But beginning in 1947, when he was coaching at Indiana State, and continuing for 37 consecutive years, Wooden attended the coaches' convention and the Final Four in the company of his late wife, Nell. At 78 he's not about to start going alone, not now.

Nell was perennial, consensus All-Lobby. She knew the names that went with the faces, and she would whisper cues to her husband as well-wishers approached. He needed her with him, for she was as outgoing as he was reserved. A few coaches didn't cotton to Nell's presence, for they had left their own wives at home and knew that the usual boys-will-be-boys shenanigans would never pass unnoticed before Nell's Irish eyes. But her husband wasn't for an instant to be talked out of bringing her, just as today he isn't to be talked into going without her.

So Wooden will spend college basketball's premier weekend in much the same way he passes all his days now. The games on TV will be mere divertissements. He will take his early-morning walk, past the park, the eucalyptus trees and the preschool his great-granddaughter attends. Each evening he will speak to Nell in apostrophe before retiring. He may whisper the lines from Wordsworth that he finds so felicitous: "She lived unknown, and few could know/When Lucy ceased to be;/But she is in her grave, and, oh,/The difference to me!"

Sunday will be for church, for the long drive to Nell's grave in Glendale and for their children, their children's children, and their children's children's children. At night he will repair to the bedroom of the condominium he and Nell shared, in which virtually nothing has been altered since her death four years ago. Wooden sleeps fitfully these days, as if expecting a call. He talks often of death but does not fear it. "No fear at all, absolutely none," he says. "I'll confess that prior to losing Nellie I had some."

Upon finishing his morning constitutional—a doctor prescribed it in 1972 because of heart trouble—he often will sit down in his study, underneath the pictures of the 10 national championship teams that were hung, at Nell's suggestion, to form a pyramid, and a poem or aphorism will take shape. He remarks on how effortlessly this one flowed from him one morning:

The years have left their imprint on my hands and on my face;
Erect no longer is my walk, and slower is my pace.
But there is no fear within my heart because I'm growing old;
I only wish I had more time to better serve my Lord.
When I've gone to Him in prayer He's brought me inner peace.
And soon my cares and worries and other problems cease;
He's helped me in so many ways, He's never let me down;
Why should I fear the future, when soon I could be near His crown?
Though I know down here my time is short, there is endless time up there,
And He will forgive and keep me ever in His loving care.

And how did you imagine John Wooden spending his later years? The mind, the values, the spring in his step—they're all still in place. He could probably take over a misbegotten college varsity, demonstrate the reverse pivot, intone a few homilies and have the team whipped into top 20 shape in, oh, six weeks. He continues to stage summer basketball camps in which you won't necessarily meet famous players but you may actually learn the game. He answers his own mail, in a hand that you'll remember from grammar school as "cursive writing."

He books most of his own speaking engagements, although several outfits have solicited his services. Audiences rarely ask about Nell, but he tends to bring her up anyway. He usually refers to her as "my sweetheart of 60 years, my wife of 53, till I lost her." The cards he sends to family and the checks he makes out for the children's trusts, he signs in both their names. "That pleases Nellie," he says.

His life is lived to that end. "I won't ever leave here, because I see her everywhere," he says in his—their—living room. "I miss her as much now as I ever have. It never gets easier. There are friends who would like to see me find another woman for the companionship. I wouldn't do it. It would never work."

He takes the morning walk in part because she insisted he take it. He has continued to participate in the camps because his share of the profits goes into the trusts, and family was so important to her. He gives the speeches, usually on his Pyramid of Success—a homespun collection of life principles—because, if you riffle back through Norman Rockwell scenes of their life together, back to high school in Martinsville, Ind., you'll see it was Nell who persuaded taciturn Johnny Wooden to take a speech class to help him out of his shell. He struggled until the teacher, Mabel Hinds, who knew of his fondness for poetry, gave him a copy of Thomas Gray's "Elegy Written in a Country Churchyard," which made the speaking easier.

He still knows Gray's "Elegy" cold, and in Martinsville in January, at a banquet on the eve of ceremonies to dedicate the 12-year-old high school gym in his name, he recited it. With all manner of acclaim being slung at him, he intoned this stanza as if raising a shield to protect himself:

The boast of heraldry, the pomp of pow'r,
And all that beauty, all that wealth e're gave;
Awaits alike th' inevitable hour:
The paths of glory lead but to the grave.

"And they do," he added from the dais. "We're all going to go someday."

★ ★ ★

"As a coach, did you ever lose your temper?"

The postprandial question comes from the audience in Martinsville. Wooden's answer provides a lesson about self-control: "I always told my players to control their tempers, and I couldn't very well expect them to if I wasn't setting a good example myself. I lost my temper once in a while. But I never lost control. I never threw anything. I never threw a chair."

Not 20 miles from Bloomington, within the pale of Bob Knight, the banquet hall erupts with approval.

★ ★ ★

The sphinx of the Pyramid of Success rests his left forearm against his stomach, parallel to the ground. His left hand is a socket for his right elbow. His right forearm forms a hypotenuse leading to his chin, where the index finger sticks upright, hovering just over his mouth. When speaking, Wooden strikes this pose frequently and unconsciously. A photograph of him in the same pose—Nell's favorite—hangs in their bedroom.

It is an enigma, that finger to the mouth. Is it the stern Midwestern schoolteacher, meting out discipline, admonishing the class? Or is it the kindly grandfather, guiding the wayward and confused young, giving them assurances that everything will be all right?

Or is it both? Wooden's greatest achievement isn't the 10 in 12, or seven in a row, although such a feat will surely never be accomplished again. It is rather that he did all this during the roily years from 1964 to '75—an era in which 18- to 22-year-old males were at their most contrary—at UCLA, a big-city campus awash in the prevailing freedoms.

Your star player lies down in rush-hour traffic to protest the Vietnam War. (Stand up for what you believe, Bill Walton's coach always said, but be willing to accept the consequences.)

Four of your players ask to use your office after practice to conduct meditation sessions. (You let them.) One asks your permission to smoke marijuana, saying he'd heard it would relieve the pain in his knees. (I am not a doctor, you tell Walton. All I know is it's against the law.)

College players still take drugs, but none today go in to discuss it with the coach beforehand. What was it about Wooden that caused Walton to broach this subject? "Decisions are more apt to be accepted when you've listened to suggestions first," says Wooden. "I wanted them to see the reason behind what I asked of them, not to do things just because I said so."

Yet Wooden threw down the clipboard when he had to. Former UCLA center Steve Patterson remembers the day, in the fall of 1970, that he and forward Sidney Wicks asked to be excused from practice to show solidarity with a nationwide rally protesting the Vietnam War. "He asked us if this reflected our convictions, and we told him it did," says Patterson. "He told us he had his convictions, too, and if we missed practice it would be the end of our careers at UCLA.

"We blinked. I don't think he was necessarily unsympathetic to the statement we wanted to make. He may even have agreed with us. But I see the connection. I didn't at the time, but I do now. He continually challenged you about your attitude toward the team as a whole. He set the standards. He didn't let us set the standards, even though we wanted to."

Wooden's practice gym was a sort of one-room schoolhouse, transported from the Indiana plains. For two hours in the afternoon his pupils listened to material that seemed to have emerged from a time warp. They listened because they knew they would win if they learned their lessons. The fundamentals came complete with hoary precepts: Failure to prepare is preparing to fail. Be quick, but don't be in a hurry. Don't mistake activity for achievement. The purpose of discipline isn't to punish but to correct. Things turn out best for those who make the best of the way things turn out.

One sentiment is so dear to Wooden that he has mined the anthologies for two renderings of it. "The journey is better than the end" comes from Cervantes. And Robert Louis Stevenson said, "To travel hopefully is a better thing than to arrive." Says Wooden, "I appreciated that notion more later, after we started to win championships. The saying that it's tougher to stay on top than to get there—I don't believe it. It's very tough to get there. And along the way you learn, as Lincoln would say, not just what to do, but what not to do.

"People say we could never win those championships again, what with parity. But I'm not so sure it couldn't happen today. Winning breeds winning. If we had had freshman eligibility during the 1960s, we would have won another one (with Lew Alcindor, now Kareem Abdul-Jabbar, in 1965-66). When everyone has good players, teaching will be a telling difference."

Wooden taught basketball according to the simplest pedagogical principles. He used what he calls the whole-part method. Show the whole and then break it down, "just like parsing a sentence," he says, "or solving a math problem." He followed his four laws of learning: explanation, demonstration, correction and repetition. For 16 years there was talk of a new gym, and when UCLA finally opened Pauley Pavilion in 1965, Wooden made sure he didn't get just an arena, but a classroom with bleachers that roll back.

Wooden taught English at South Bend Central High before heading to Indiana State for two seasons and then to Westwood for the rest of his coaching life. He always preferred the practices to the games. The games were just exams, when the teacher's work was done. "There again," he says, "the journey's better than the end."

Piggie Lambert, Wooden's coach at Purdue, preached that the team making the most mistakes would win, for good things come to those who risk error by taking the initiative. Thus, initiative is part of Wooden's Pyramid. You would think, given his success, that someone might still coach his way today. But rare is the coach who doesn't have a tight rein, a hard derriere or both. How can a real teacher not indulge mistakes? "George Patton is not my idol," Wooden says. "I prefer Omar Bradley."

As he sees all the games the networks satellite-dish out, Wooden concludes that, besides turning the young men into dogs and ponies, television has transformed the coaches into showmen. Coaches today overcontrol. Instead, they should teach players the game and let them play it. Goodness gracious sakes alive—you may hear that truncated to Gracious sakes, but from Wooden you'll hear no stronger oath—coaches nowadays haven't even hit their 40's before they're writing books with titles like "A Coach's World" and "Born to Coach."

Wooden's first book is still in print. Published in 1966, it's called "*Practical Modern Basketball.*" Read it and you'll learn that basketball is a game of threes: forward, center, and guard: shoot, drive, pass: ball, you, man; conditioning, skill, teamwork. These last three elements made up Lambert's hoops trinity, and they are the three blocks at the heart of the Pyramid. The Wooden text also holds that the way to play the game—soundly, and with balance—isn't a bad way to live your life.

★ ★ ★

"You might have thought of that as a golden time, when you've climbed to the top of the mountain. But we were at the top of the mountain when we showed up." Greg Lee is talking about the Walton era, the three seasons Lee played at guard, between 1971 and '74. "Half the time we didn't even know who our opponent would be," he says. "Winning 88 straight games—that's not normal. It would have been better if we'd have struggled."

When Lee and his classmates were precocious sophomores, Wooden warned them that, as seniors, they would be intolerable. Headstrong young men like Walton, guard Tommy Curtis and Lee—"I'd like to be able to say I didn't contribute to the problems," Wooden says, "but I did"—didn't prove him wrong. But Wooden bent too much, and his normally steady hand seemed to waver. He relaxed some of the inviolable principles on which he had always insisted. He excused Walton from practice on Mondays and Tuesdays because of the center's aching knees. Detecting inconsistency, the team took advantage.

That March, as if to vindicate 25 years' worth of strictures suddenly allowed to go flaccid, UCLA squandered a seven-point lead in the second overtime of the NCAA semifinals and lost to North Carolina State. "Bill was such a megastar he probably didn't need to practice," says Lee. "But maybe the team needed him to practice."

Lee, now coach at a high school near San Diego, has learned that lesson in discipline in retrospect. But Wooden, even if he denies it today, relearned it then and there. The next season, with the Bruins again playing on his exacting terms, they became champions once more.

★ ★ ★

Since his retirement, the catty strains of Wooden revisionism have made their way through the coaching fraternity. Unlikely as it may seem, between 1948 and 1963 Wooden did not win an NCAA crown at UCLA, and during this period the critics accused him of being a jockey of referees and opposing players. They said that he overheated the old "B.O. Barn," the Bruins' second-floor gym, because he knew his teams could stand it. They said that he had two sets of standards, one for stars and another for everybody else. But the most persistent whisper has always been that the cornerstone of the Pyramid was no middle-American verity, not conditioning or skill or teamwork, but a Los Angeles contractor and UCLA booster named Sam Gilbert.

Gilbert was everything Wooden wasn't. Worldly and wealthy, he offered players advice and, in violation of NCAA rules, gave them gifts and paid for their girlfriends' abortions. Black players, in particular, received healthy doses of his street wisdom and regular invitations to the lavish spreads at his house on Sunday mornings. "I remember we were on a road trip in Chicago, and five guys all got on the bus together wearing matching coats with fur-lined collars," says Lee. "It was pretty conspicuous. It's not like Coach was an ostrich about Sam, but he wouldn't confront the problem."

Wooden insists that no one enrolled at UCLA because of Gilbert. But once a player became a Bruin, few were denied his largess. With the inertia born of a successful program, and with Wooden's lack of interest in matters outside the gym or the classroom, Gilbert went unchallenged. After becoming the UCLA coach in the late '70s, Larry Brown, who resented Gilbert's sway with his players, tried to run him off. Gilbert responded by threatening not only to cut off Brown's testicles but also to do it "without him even knowing it." In 1987 a Florida grand jury, unaware of Gilbert's death four days earlier, indicted him in a drug-money-laundering scheme.

In the simplistic analogy, Gilbert is the hoodlum on the fringe of the school yard, and Wooden is the teacher who can only tell his pupils to Just Say No. "I warned them, but I couldn't pick their friends," says Wooden. Today Wooden owns up to breaking NCAA rules himself. He invited players to have meals with him and Nell during in-season school vacations so they would not be alone in dormitories on campus. He helped pay the rent of a player with a child and a sick wife. He bailed out of jail another player who had been picked up for delinquent parking violations. These transgressions all conformed to Wooden's higher rules.

"I honestly feel Sam meant well," says Wooden. "He felt whatever he did was right, even if it was against the rules." As different as he and Gilbert were, Wooden felt much the same way.

★ ★ ★

"I never had a smarter player than Mike Warren," Wooden frequently says. He also says, "I never had a better athlete than Keith Erickson." This is a salutary lesson about race, from a man who grew up in Indiana, then a hotbed of the Ku Klux Klan. Warren, who later starred in "Hill Street Blues," is black; Erickson, white. In a sport infected with racial code phrases like "heady ballplayer" and "great athlete," Wooden's comments are March on Washington stuff. But he says he isn't the slightest bit aware of their stereotype-busting implications. Wisdom subdues bigotry. With the experience to judge, one need not prejudge.

★ ★ ★

By her husband's count, Nell was twice at death's door before she finally succumbed. A heart attack, which she suffered while undergoing a hip-replacement operation in 1982, put her in a coma. Friends and family took turns visiting St. Vincent's Hospital in downtown Los Angeles, not to see Nell in her quiet as much as to succor her husband. He spent 10- and 12-hour days at her bedside, and he might not have found time to eat were it not for their solicitude.

"The doctors told me to talk to her," says Wooden. "They said that I might not see any signs, but in her subconscious she might be hearing me." Three months after Nell entered the coma, as her body lay suctioned and plugged with intravenous tubing, he took her hand and squeezed it, and he felt a squeeze back. There are no nets to cut down when something like that happens.

But shortly thereafter Nell had to go back into the hospital to have her gallbladder removed, and that, the doctors said, was a no-hoper. No way she could weather the trauma. Yet she survived the surgery, recovering enough to live life rather than just muddle through it. She even made one last Final Four—Seattle, in fact, in 1984. She was in a wheelchair but was still alert and vivacious, still matching the names with the faces. "It was," the coach says, "the last enjoyable thing she did."

That is why this weekend in Seattle would have been so difficult. Early on Christmas morning in 1984, Nell had to be rushed to the hospital. By then a number of ailments, including cancer and emphysema, had gotten ornery. At 73 she just wasn't going to pull off any more miracles. Nell fought on through the rest of the winter, playing out the season. She died on the first day of spring.

Before every tip-off back at Martinsville High, Wooden had looked up from his guard position and caught her eye in the stands, where she played the cornet in the band. She would give him the OK sign and he would wave back. They kept up that ritual even as Johnny Wooden (Hall of Fame, inducted as a player in 1960) became John R. Wooden (Hall of Fame, inducted as a coach in 1972). He's the only person with the old one-two combo. Few knew that he clutched a cross in his hand. Fewer knew that she clutched an identical one in hers. She took it with her to the grave.

The reclusiveness that ruled Wooden's first year as a widower alarmed doctors, family and friends alike. Former players and assistant coaches conspired to telephone regularly until Wooden's granddaughter, Caryn, gave birth to a girl, Cori, and he brightened somewhat. "I try to be thankful for the time Nellie and I had together," says Wooden. "But sometimes you wonder what you could have done. There's a certain amount of second-guessing that goes on."

He never went off to scout opponents, never brought the practices home and didn't make more than a dozen recruiting trips in his entire career. What could so faithful and doting a husband possibly regret? "We did things because I wanted to, not because she did," he says. "We never went to Ireland. Nellie always wanted to go to Ireland. We had planned to, too. But something would always come up. And Nellie loved to dance. I was not a dancer, you know."

He averts his eyes, betraying his small-town bashfulness. That's what Nell, at 13, had to crack; that's what she and her friend Mary Schnaiter would talk about when they repaired to the quarries outside town. Of course, Johnny was already smitten. "She was as cute as can be," says Mary. "Little, with a turned-up nose. She could do just about anything she wanted."

And my, the life John and Nell spent together. You can almost hear Alistair Cooke in the voice-over: Johnny, born in Hall, Ind., in 1910, one of four sons of a simple and devout couple, spent much of his youth in a farm-house with a three-holer outhouse out back. His father forged the iron goal he learned to shoot at. John and Nell waited out his four years at Purdue, only to have their savings—$909 and a nickel—wiped out in a bank failure on the eve of their wedding.

So rock-solid a couple was grossly misplaced amid the shifting-sand values of Los Angeles. When John and Nell left Indiana State for UCLA, they found the support of two familiar Midwestern pillars. Wales Smith, the minister at the church they joined in Santa Monica, had been in Wooden's class at Martinsville High. Ralph Irwin, the doctor they chose, had performed an emergency appendectomy on Wooden in Iowa City. With a pastor and a doctor they could trust, John and Nell needed little more. "Oh, you're from back East!" people would say. Crossly, Nell would correct them.

She would speak up at times when John wouldn't. She upbraided the fans who she thought were too greedy. She threw withering looks at the caviling men along press row. She badgered J.D. Morgan, UCLA's shrewd and parsimonious athletic director, about her husband's insulting salary and the anemic retirement package awaiting them. "I know John Wooden never lies," one coach said during the early '70s, "but he can't be making twenty-nine-five." At the time he was. And he never made more than $32,500.

He had no shoe contracts or courtesy cars, either. In the early days, before all the titles, before Pauley was built, Wooden's Bruins practiced amid the gymnasts and wrestlers and shared a locker room with the other men's sports. The dust from all the gym classes would build up by practice time, and Wooden and his managers had to mop the floor themselves. The undisciplined circumstances under which he was asked to teach ate away at him, but he and Nell never really considered going elsewhere, even as offers from NBA teams and several schools in the Big Ten came his way. Their son, Jim, had fallen for surfing; their daughter, Nan, for Hollywood, where she and her girlfriends staked out the stars, autograph books clutched to their breasts. Soon enough Wooden made peace with the broken promises and his chaotic classroom. "I whipped it," he says, "by recognizing it."

Some people think Wooden was too deferential to Morgan. Certainly, the same couldn't be said of Nell. "She really thought they were taking advantage of him," says Nan. "And Daddy never wanted to complain, because he never wanted for anything. But Daddy didn't have to get mad. He could stay very serene, because his other half was getting it out. Nobody was his champion the way Mother was."

Championing a champion took its toll. During his early days as a coach, Wooden would stop smoking the day practice began and forswear cigarettes for the balance of the season. In 1955, he quit entirely. But it wasn't so easy for Nell. From the time she first acquired a taste for cigarettes, Nell had relied on smoking to help her cope with the stress. Her husband desperately wanted her to give up the habit that would hasten her departure from him, but she played games with him: stashing butts in her purse, retiring to her daughter's house to get a fix.

As the dynasty pushed into the '70s, success was spoiling what should have been glorious times and edging Wooden toward retirement. "Sometimes I'm very slow making up my mind," he says. "But once I make it up, I'm very slow to change it."

On the floor of the San Diego Sports Arena in 1975, after Wooden had won his last NCAA title, a booster sought him out and said, "Great victory, John. It makes up for your letting us down last year." The attitude implicit in that statement disgusted him. There would be no second thoughts, no regrets, about retiring. He didn't want to step down. He had to. "Daddy's job wasn't fun for us" says Nan. "It really wasn't."

★ ★ ★

Here is a lesson about learning. Back in the late '60s, when he was in the midst of winning those seven straight titles and had little reason to question himself about anything, Wooden attended a press conference at which the Los Angeles Lakers announced that they had traded for Wilt Chamberlain. A reporter asked Wilt about his reputation for being hard to handle. Would the Laker coach have problems handling him? "I am not a thing," Chamberlain said. "You handle things. You work with people."

Upon returning home that day, Wooden opened a copy of "Practical Modern Basketball." He turned to the section titled "Handling Your Players," crossed out "Handling" and wrote in "Working With." He phoned his publisher and asked that the change be made in all subsequent printings.

"John was a better coach at 55 than he was at 50," says Pete Newell, the former coach at Cal and San Francisco, who has known Wooden for more than 40 years. "He was a better coach at 60 than at 55. He's a true example of a man who learned from day one to day last."

★ ★ ★

In the outer lobby of the old Martinsville High gym hangs a picture of the Artesians' 1927 state championship team. "Gone," says Wooden, pointing to the player in the top left-hand corner. "Gone, gone, gone, gone," he continues, moving his finger from teammate to teammate. "Almost gone," he says, his finger finally coming to rest on his likeness.

When speaking engagements take him east, he'll route himself through Indianapolis, rent a car, drive the highway south and zip into the various graveyards around Martinsville, where his and Nell's forebears are buried. At each one he'll say a prayer. The neighboring gravestones are graced with names like Way and Byroad and Schoolcraft, names that sound as if they came from a novel about Puritans.

His preoccupation with death lifts only when Cori, 3, and her cousin, John, who's pushing 3, come by to visit. Cori is the philosophical one, and little John is the instigator. It was John who got Papa, as they call their great-grandfather, to turn off all the lights and play a flashlight game that the kids call Ghostbusters. Nell must have been cackling from behind the credenza.

Meanwhile, over the hill in Westwood, a variation of the same game goes on. "The problem we're having is John Wooden," a Bruin named Kenny Fields said a few years ago. "He won too much. Now our fans can't accept anything less."

Wooden has scrupulously avoided commenting on the performance of any of his many successors. Indeed, Harrick says he has to crowbar advice out of him. Watch Wooden watching the Bruins, from his second-row seat across from the UCLA bench, occasionally with Cori and John scrambling around him: He claps rhythmically to the pep band during timeouts, but otherwise he betrays little reaction to the basketball before him.

Wooden won't say this explicitly, but the man UCLA should have hired back in 1975, the man the old coach praises whenever he has a chance, is Louisville's Denny Crum. That single move might have forestalled all the Bruins' recent travails. But Morgan refused to consider him as Wooden's replacement simply because Crum, a former UCLA player and assistant coach, had been divorced. Such were the impossible standards of John's and Nell's legacy.

★ ★ ★

So we come to the lesson of the peaks and the valleys. If you should catch one of those Final Four historical shows on late-night cable, be sure to study Wooden's Bruins in victory. They're happy campers, storming the floor and cutting down the nets, but always they hold something back. "Of course, I will have reminded them in a timeout," says Wooden, "for every artificial peak you create there is a valley. I don't like valleys. Games can be lost in them."

He had seen Phil Woolpert win back-to-back national championships at San Francisco in 1955 and '56 and then struggle in the crucible of trying to keep winning. Then he saw Ed Jucker also win two in a row, at Cincinnati in '61 and '62, only to leave coaching because of similar pressure. That's when he resolved never to exult unduly in victory or to languish in defeat. "One's life," he says, "should be the same."

But with Nell's death his very faith wavered. Never mind that a favorite plaque of theirs hangs in his study and reads GOD NEVER CLOSES ONE DOOR WITHOUT OPENING ANOTHER. "He did not want to live," says Gary Cunningham, his old assistant. "A lot of us were worried, and disappointed, too. What he had instilled in our lives he wasn't practicing in his own." All that winning, and look what one loss did.

A few weeks ago Cori and Papa looked up as an airplane passed overhead. "See that airplane, Papa?" said Cori. "I'm going to take that airplane and fly all the way to heaven and get Mama and bring her back, so Papa won't be lonely anymore."

Gracious sakes, Cori, no. Stay right here with Papa. For later, there, he'll have Mama. For now, here, he has you and John, two previous generations of Woodens, and—should he ever change that mind that's so hard to change once it's made up—a convention full of rudderless coaches of basketball, who desperately need to learn how to teach the game.

Before this extraordinary life gets played out, before the buzzer sounds, won't someone please call timeout to remind him? He has taught so many of us such wonderful lessons. He has one more lesson, his own, to study up on.

Frank Kush

COLLEGE FOOTBALL

By *MIKE TULUMELLO*

Editor's note: He was more than a football coach. He was a warrior, a master, a celebrity. His supporters were more than fans. They were his followers, his believers, his faithful. Frank Joseph Kush brought big-time football to Arizona State University, and the people loved it. Ten years ago this week, the legend began to crumble. Soon, it was gone. For the record, Kush was accused of striking a football player during a game. "I never punched the kid," he still insists. The story, however, goes far beyond that simple act. After dozens of interviews, including a lengthy one with Kush, and after sifting through hundreds of documents, the full story of the demise of a legend can be told.

The last chance for Coach Frank Kush to save his job came in the final days of his legendary career at Arizona State University.

Fred Miller, the athletic director and theoretically Kush's boss, drove out to a night football practice and asked Kush for the umpteenth time if he thought he might have punched an unremarkable punter named Kevin Rutledge during a game the previous season.

If Kush had said yes, he might still be the coach at ASU. He'd likely be closing in on 250 wins. There would be talk about whether he might someday pass Bear Bryant as the winningest big-time college coach in history. The stadium would bear his name.

Kush said no.

In the past, Kush's word was good enough for Miller, who wasn't so much his boss as his fishing buddy and cheerleader. Kush had built a multi-million dollar football program, that had in turn funded a sparkling athletic complex.

Miller, however, now had decided his friend was lying. He had already gathered enough evidence to recommend that Kush be suspended. But in his heart of hearts, he had hoped Kush would change his story. So he gave the coach one last chance.

But Kush continued his denial. He even told Miller he was nowhere near Rutledge during the game.

Kush's fate was now sealed. The man whose stature had grown to mythical proportions, thanks to winning football teams, his own earthy charm and a boosterish media, could not be saved.

Kush had become a legend for demanding the strictest discipline in others. Now his career gradually would wither—amidst explosive charges not only of professional misconduct but of a personal skeleton—because he did not heed his own teachings.

★ ★ ★

Frank Kush grew to be tough early in life. He was among 15 children of a Polish-born coal miner in Pennsylvania. He lived over Mine No. 35 in the town of Windber. His father, a stern man who didn't spare the rod to enforce discipline, died at 50 of black-lung disease.

The biggest family paycheck Frank ever spotted, after the company took out for rent and food, was $2.62 for two weeks work. His parents wanted a better life for their children, so they stressed education.

It helped that Frank was an undersized yet tenacious football player, otherwise they never could have sent him to college. He was good enough to start at Michigan State on teams that lost one game in three years and won a national title. Kush was named All-America at offensive guard.

After a stint in the Army, Kush got married and landed an assistant coaching job at Arizona State College in Tempe. When head coach Dan Devine left to take over at Missouri after the 1957 season, the 28-year-old Kush took his place. The salary was $10,000 a year. Kush had found paradise.

Kush's teams were, like him, small, quick and tough. They used technique rather than muscle. And they were good. Kush produced winning teams, and his following grew so much that Sun Devil Stadium expanded from 30,000 to 70,000 during his era.

By 1975, Kush had become a god in Arizona. From 1970 through '75, his teams went 62-9 and produced five bowl winners. The Sun Devils had a bonafide top 10 team. Maybe even top five. They gave the Valley, an area that was desperately grasping for major-league status, its identity in sports.

It simply wasn't true that Valley fans had no pro team. In their hearts, they had the Sun Devils.

"We banged the drum hard at creating the whole mystique of the Sun Devils," Miller says today. "We were very successful."

An occasional student or professor might grumble that the players weren't steered to the classrooms or libraries. Miller later would acknowledge that no administrator or faculty member *ever* pressured him to emphasize the players' academic pursuits.

The student newspaper, *State Press,* would run occasional stories critical of Kush: about his business venture with a controversial partner on a project across the street from the football stadium; about his trips to the dog tracks with recruits.

None of this bothered the "professional" media, which loved Kush as much as any beery booster. The negative news was ignored.

During this time, a subgroup of the Sun Angel Foundation quietly established the Legna fund (angel spelled backward). Thousands of dollars a year poured into a retirement fund for Kush. The only way he wouldn't get money from the booster group would be if he quit as Sun Devil coach.

Kush's financial future was set. He was the big man on campus.

Expensive dinners were staged to benefit Kush, and to a lesser extent Miller. John Wayne showed up at one. Another netted Kush $45,000 and Miller $18,000. This affair subsequently turned up as a violation of NCAA rules.

This pie was expanded when Kush's team went 12-0 in 1975 and finished second in the national polls. He was named national coach of the year. He reportedly turned down a multi-million dollar offer to coach the National Football League's Philadelphia Eagles.

Kush had become the most popular sports fixture ever in the Valley. Nothing, it seemed, could stop him now.

"In college athletics, you sell the coach," Miller later would say ruefully. "The trouble is, some coaches believe it."

★ ★ ★

Camp Tontozona, the Sun Devils' mountain practice field 100 miles north of campus, opened with little fanfare in 1979. The usual ingredients were there. The Sun Devils had a highly rated quarterback in Mark Malone and enough other talented athletes to field a respectable team.

But media coverage of the camp was different. There seemed to be more than the usual number of cameras around. And they were focused squarely on Kush, whose tactics of swatting helmets and grabbing face masks were well known.

The previous college season had ended in infamy, when Woody Hayes lost his job as Ohio State coach after punching a Clemson player on national TV. But compared to Kush, Hayes was a pussycat.

On August 20, the *Phoenix Gazette* ran a photo of Kush yanking on a player's face mask. The photo then was sent out nationally by wire.

The photo prompted John Schwada, the low-visibility ASU president, to take a remarkable step. He summoned Kush for a meeting and reminded him that discipline had its limits.

Kush replied that his methods had been successful and that he would coach the way he saw fit.

"If I can't, tell me to resign," Kush later recounted.

Miller and his assistant, John Wadas, recall watching Kush walk out of the meeting with Schwada. The message was clear: Kush had built a multi-million-dollar athletic department, and he was bigger than Schwada, Miller or anybody else.

He was right, of course.

A mythology had grown up, thanks to Kush's boosters in the press, about those who left camp. The timid players who hitchhiked back to Payson and then to Phoenix drifted into anonymity. Those who turned around and headed back to endure camp became men.

That's why the news on September 4 of Rutledge's complaint to the Arizona Board of Regents seemed almost comical. A marginal player was claiming he was harassed out of a scholarship by Kush. If Rutledge couldn't take it, so what?

Miller pronounced the suit "could very well destroy the structure of amateur sports as we know it today."

But three days later, the charges grew uncomfortably specific. Buried in the local papers was Rutledge's claim that he had been punched by Kush after a 27-yard punt on October 28, 1978 at the University of Washington.

This was a black-and-white claim. Either Kush did or he didn't. Still, the issue shouldn't have been a big deal. If Kush had said he punched the player, or may have done so, he could have apologized and be done with the issue. He could have joked that the punt was a lousy one anyway; the entire state would have laughed.

Instead, Kush chose to say, "That statement is absolutely totally untrue."

After a quick look into the matter, Miller added, "This is categorically untrue."

These statements made Gene Felker uneasy. Felker was director of the Sun Angel Foundation, the booster group full of the biggest cigars in town. From his seat at the game about 70 yards away, Felker had seen Kush shake Rutledge's face mask and take a swing at the punter.

Felker told Miller what he saw; he thought the athletic director had put himself in a box. Miller listened but said little.

Later in September, coaches began taking statements from players. One lineman copied what he had seen in the movies: "I, Bryan Caldwell, in sound mind and body, never saw Coach Kush punch Kevin Rutledge in the face."

Caldwell called a booster named Rick Lynch, who in court later quoted Caldwell as saying, "I just signed my name to a lie."

Lynch operated a drag strip, where he employed many players during the summer. He and Kush had had increasing differences over the years, but Lynch said Kush still thought enough of him in 1978 to ask him to start up a fund to help non-scholarship players. Payments from this fund later were cited as violations by the NCAA.

Kush believed ASU needed a stronger walk-on program now

that it was joining the Pacific-10 Conference, a move Kush had opposed.

Lynch said Kush told him, ' "You be the bagman,' " according to the Long Island newspaper *Newsday*.

Lynch had grown closer to the players than Kush over the years. He believed he might be the only person able to stand up for them. He began calling them and urged them to tell the truth about Rutledge, a player he did not know. When Kush found out, he drove to Lynch's office and urged him to stay away from the players.

Kush also was lining up an alibi. During a coaches' meeting, he turned to Bob Owens, his defensive coordinator and said, "You were standing next to me on the sidelines," Owens testified in a civil lawsuit filed by Kevin Rutledge.

Owens was worried. He generally did not stand near Kush, and during the 41-7 loss to Washington—the worst of Kush's career—he tried to stay as far away as possible.

Owens became even more concerned in early October when Kush gathered with Owens and the offensive coaches.

To save their jobs, Kush told them they had to keep their stories straight and stick together "even if it meant lying or perjuring ourselves," Owens said in a sworn statement.

Kush told him to relay his message to the defensive coaches. They were disbelieving. So Owens summoned another assistant, Bob Karmelowicz, to tell the other coaches what he had heard.

Karmelowicz agreed that Kush said they needn't worry about perjuring themselves "if our stories are the same."

Thus began Hell Month for Kush.

On Saturday, October 6, Felker met Kush for a morning drive around Tempe. Felker told Kush that despite his statements that he was nowhere near the punter, Felker had seen an incident where the two had made contact. Kush said this wasn't so.

The next day, Lynch called Felker. They met in a parking lot at 44th Street and Camelback Road in Phoenix. Lynch played a tape of a player's description of the alleged punch.

On Monday night, Lynch arranged for a reporter from the *State Press* to meet lineman Gary Bouck at a Scottsdale restaurant. On the condition of anonymity, Bouck described the alleged punch. Lynch had tried the same tactic with other local papers without success. But the student paper ran the story the next day.

In past years, student editors would hear howls of indignation from administrators when they ran negative stories about the athletic department. This time, they heard nothing.

On Tuesday, Lynch met Miller at a hotel and played the tape. Miller said that wasn't good enough.

Lynch wasn't sure whether to trust Miller. But he heard through a minister that Miller was a devout, family-oriented man. He decided to take a chance.

On Wednesday, Lynch arranged for Miller to meet Steve Chambers, another player who said he had seen the punch, at a local grade school.

Then Miller and Wadas drove to a boarded-up gas station in Tempe to meet Caldwell and Bouck. Lynch and one other player also were present.

"There's no reason you ought to trust me, because I've come out on the record as supporting Frank Kush," Miller told the players. "But this is a question of ethics I want you to tell me in your own words what you saw."

Speaking one at a time, the pair laid out the story. Then Miller said, "What these young boys have told me is more important than friendship."

Lynch recalled later: "Once I saw the look on Miller's face, I knew what he was going to do. His face was quivering. He looked like he was going to cry."

Miller was angry. He'd decided he'd been had by Kush.

Miller asked Felker over to his house, where the Sun Angel chief repeated what he had told Miller a month ago. Then Miller drove to Schwada's house just south of campus. There, in the president's kitchen, Miller recommended that Kush must go.

The plan was to suspend Kush after the Washington game. Miller didn't want to disrupt the team before the biggest home game of the season. As always, the game came first.

Miller would come to regret this decision more than any he ever made at ASU.

On this same Wednesday evening, Kush and his lawyer, Harry Cavanagh, invited Bouck into Kush's office. Kush told Bouck that players were calling him a "rat fink" for telling the *State Press* that he had seen the punch. Kush repeated his claim that he was at the opposite end of the field.

Bouck decided he'd be a fool to call Kush a liar to his face. So he told Kush he couldn't have been the paper's source because he had seen nothing. "I just wanted to tell him exactly what he wanted to hear," he later recalled.

Word of Kush's demise began to leak out about the time of the gas station meeting. The *Phoenix Gazette* began to pick up the scent.

Then the story was confirmed, by of all people, Schwada. The ASU president had attended an informal luncheon Thursday with *Republic* and *Gazette* executives. According to sources within the company, Schwada spilled the story while persuading the company's management to sit on it.

That set in motion a chain of events that helped Kush and damaged Miller.

The *Gazette's* sports editor, Joe Gilmartin, found out what was happening, but he was in Pittsburgh covering the World Series and thus in poor position to fight for the story. Gilmartin, hoping to confirm the story, called Kush on Friday and told him he was on his way out.

By this time, Miller had driven to practice to ask Kush one last time if the punching might have happened. And he had just found out about the cover-up allegations.

On Friday night, Kush drove to Miller's Tempe home and confronted the man who suddenly was acting like the boss.

"You don't believe me, do you?" Kush asked.

Miller didn't, and the two had what he calls "a damned donnybook" on Miller's patio.

"I've been set up! I've been had!" Miller charged. When Kush left that evening, he knew the score.

The next day, the lawyers started getting involved. Attorneys for Kush were briefed on the alleged punching and cover-up accusations by those for Miller and the university. Miller called Schwada one last time for his final approval.

One lawyer present remembers the voice over the speaker phone: "Fred, you have no choice."

Kush cleverly jumped ahead of the game. He staged his own news conference on Saturday at the Sands Hotel in Phoenix. "I am told the reason I am being fired is that Dr. Miller did not believe it when I denied punching Kevin Rutledge . . ."

He may as well have announced the outbreak of World War III. Or that he would now start coaching archrival Arizona. For Sun Devil fans, the news was simply beyond belief.

Kush returned to his home in Tempe, where he dined on his usual pre-game meal of cheeseburgers and salad. Miller sent an underling to tell him not to come to the game, but Kush showed up anyway.

He was dressed not in his usual maroon and gold attire, but in gray slacks and a blue sweater, attire that his boosters would copy for the rest of the season.

Miller met him in the locker room at the south end zone about an hour before the game and pulled him into a small room nearby.

"What the hell are you doing here?" Miller demanded. Kush began a teary dialogue, interrupted when Bob Owens, whom Miller had appointed as interim coach, poked his head in the door. Owens said the crowd was in an ugly mood, Kush had better take the field.

Miller relented.

The scene at the Washington game seemed more suited for a British soccer match. The crowd went into a frenzy when the players carried Kush *onto* the field. Raw emotion carried the Sun Devils to a 12-7 win.

The fans near Miller's press box seat kept him occupied, banging on windows, screaming and making obscene gestures. One of his attorneys, Paul Eckstein, would later note that the controversy over the impeachment of Gov. Evan Mecham—in which Eckstein was a prosecutor—seemed rather subdued by comparison.

"If those fans could have gotten their hands on Fred Miller, they would have killed him," Eckstein says.

Miller may have killed himself professionally after the game.

He staged a news conference in which he came off as well as Alexander Haig after the shooting of Ronald Reagan. Following his attorney's advice, he refused to answer questions. The strategy was sound legally, but a public-relations disaster.

"I don't know if Fred ever recovered from that," Eckstein says.

The attorney failed to take into account the power of a sports superstar like Kush.

The political powers reacted as emotionally as any pro-Kush fan sitting in the end zone. Burton Barr, an influential state legislator, said "Miller and Schwada are the ones who ought to go." Other legislators warned ASU's budget could suffer.

Harry Rosenzweig, the president of the Sun Angels and Barry Goldwater's closest friend, canceled his group's plan for a golf course and said ASU officials "should consult the powers that be" before making major decisions in the future. Felker, meanwhile, was publicly identified as a witness to the punching. He was on his way out as the Sun Angels' director.

A remarkable series of televised news conferences took place the week after Kush departed, with the sports media grilling Miller and lobbing softball questions to Kush. ("Could your accusers have misconstrued something you said?")

Kush held the edge until Wednesday, October 17, when Miller released a damning report that included eyewitness versions of the punch, and chilling accounts of Kush telling his assistants to lie for him.

Miller had always thought it would be enough to be correct, that right would win out. "I was wrong about that," he later conceded.

By now, Miller had become a marked man. There were death threats. One of his neighbors painted his car with the slogans, "Fire Fred, Keep Kush."

There were occasional acts of kindness. At the next home game, a visiting athletic director, seeing the "Screw Miller" sign hanging around the stadium, cried and kissed Miller on the cheek.

But then reality would set in. At the same game, a sportswriter muttered an obscenity at Miller, who started to attack the writer. Wadas, a former wrestler, tackled Miller.

The flames were fanned by the pro-Kush slant of many sportswriters and broadcasters.

"I think the press was the biggest evil of all," Wadas said. "The writers had built him up and then they had to justify why they built him up. The media was out of control."

Miller and Wadas decried the coverage, but deep down they knew they were partly to blame. They had helped create the Kush myth and the publicity machine for Sun Devil football.

"Maybe we did too good of a job," Miller later said.

Wadas was more succinct: "We created a monster."

In the weeks after Kush departed, charges and counter-charges grew ever more serious. ASU now was the destination for investigators from the NCAA and even from federal, state and local police.

In the three weeks after the public eruptions, charges surfaced that athletic department funds may have been criminally mismanaged. Kush also was accused of misusing funds. Police investigated but the mud didn't stick in either case.

Later, the FBI probed long-whispered rumors of gambling ties involving Kush and some friends. The investigation delayed Kush's chances of getting a professional job. The FBI closed its case without filing charges.

One piece of dirty laundry was authentic. John Rehfield, the athletic department's academic coordinator, revealed he had arranged a scheme whereby eight football players received credit for an extension course in California they never attended.

The Sun Devils had to forfeit five of their six wins in 1979. Even the circus triumph over Washington now was a loss.

The whole controversy became a feeding frenzy for lawyers. Kush sued the university, charging his rights had been violated. Kush and Lynch sued each other.

Kush, meanwhile, fretted that he was a victim of society. "Discipline is going out of style," he said.

How ironic. At the time, Miller's attorneys were starting to prepare a list of charges on Kush's suspension.

Six allegations were being prepared. Most concerned the familiar tales of punching and coverup, Kush's supposed knowledge of the bogus-credit scheme and a "pattern of physical assault and harassment." There was a final charge. It alleged "serious personal misconduct."

The charge would play an important behind-the-scenes role in the upcoming legal contests.

★ ★ ★

Neil Cumsky was in a hurry. The Phoenix lawyer was racing across Los Angeles in a rented car early one Sunday morning in December. He was driving down a winding road, desperately trying to find the house of Bruce Allen, son of George Allen, the famous football coach. Cumsky needed to get to the younger Allen before he received a house call from Kush, attorney Harry Cavanagh and a court reporter.

Allen had given a sworn statement to Cumsky's law firm that he had accidentally witnessed sexual activity involving Kush while walking into the football film room at the University Activity Center. The incident had taken place in late 1978, Allen had said, while he had been a graduate assistant.

The incident comprised the "serious personal misconduct" charge. And it was the hidden nuclear bomb in the arsenal of Miller's lawyers.

Cumsky and Eckstein had some misgivings about using the material. They felt it was a fair weapon; the incident had taken place in a public building in an area where a high school coach was walking around. Yet it was so personal that its use could backfire. They might never use it. Still, it was important to them that it be kept as *potential* ammunition.

Allen was feeling heat to recant the testimony. Miller and the Sun Devils were in Hawaii for a football game. Cumsky would be Allen's sole source of support.

Allen was only 22 years old. He had a promising career in athletics ahead of him. He didn't want the material to go public, yet he vowed he would tell the truth in any legal matter.

Cumsky was only 29 himself. But it was his job to shepherd Allen through the confrontation with the heavyweights, Kush and Cavanagh. "They never taught me about this at Yale Law School," he was thinking.

Cumsky, who had caught an early plane out of Phoenix, arrived minutes ahead of Kush and Cavanagh. He was seated with his back to the front door when the pair walked in. Cumsky recalls turning around and greeting them: "Good morning, gentlemen." Cumsky thought the blood seemed to drain from the faces of Kush and Cavanagh.

But Kush plodded ahead. He put his arm around Allen and asked to see him alone. The two walked outside.

Allen recalls Kush asking, "Isn't this terrible?" Allen agreed it was.

"Don't you wish this hadn't come up?" Again, Allen agreed.

Kush asked if he would like to make another statement. Allen said he told the truth in the first statement; he didn't think another was needed.

When Kush left Allen's house, Cumsky sensed he was more flustered about this matter than the Rutledge folderol. "This was a critical event," Cumsky said later. As Kush walked out the door, Cumsky sensed that in this rare moment, the coach had lost with the game on the line.

★ ★ ★

Stepping outside his usual legislative duties, Barr arranged a settlement for Kush. The offer was for $200,000 if Kush dropped his suit against the state. With ASU's hearing on Kush's suspension less than 48 hours away, Kush stepped into a private room and called his wife, Fran.

Then he tearfully talked about his 25 years at ASU and signed the papers. He also received an estimated $180,000 that had accrued in the Legna fund. The fund somehow was allowed to continue even afterward: Kush later got $80,000 to finally end the arrangement.

Miller had desperately wanted the hearing so that the full story would be told. His interests were ignored. In the end, he was hung out to dry.

Miller had run the athletic department like a corporate high-roller, dunning money from the wealthy boosters to build the school's spectacular sports facilities. He had little power with faculty or students.

A few weeks later, Schwada—whose office had been visited by representatives of the boosters—fired Miller. He had done the dirty work. But now he had outlived usefulness.

"They didn't care about the truth coming out," Miller said later.

Ten years later, Schwada still refuses all requests to be interviewed about Kush.

★ ★ ★

After the regents routinely dismissed Rutledge's complaint, the punter pressed a suit in court.

Depositions taken in the Rutledge-Kush case contained dirty secrets known to ASU insiders. Kush was accused of hitting players with boards, ship's ropes, tree limbs and other objects.

Players in Kush's doghouse sometimes underwent the "hamburger drill" in which the offending player had to collide with teammate after teammate. Kush replied that he was only trying to motivate players by appealing to their pride.

Owens said Kush ran off as many as 10 players per year. "You can't just tell a player he's off the team" because it would be detrimental to future recruiting, Owens said. He said the coaches' justification for running the program in this manner was that it was "an entertainment enterprise" and not an educational one.

Rutledge's civil lawsuit went to trial in early 1981. His lawyer, Robert Hing, argued to move it out of Maricopa County. He produced a poll that showed Kush had nearly 100 percent name recognition and a 3-1 favorable perception. Rutledge's unpopularity, meanwhile, rivaled that of John Harvey Adamson, a notorious murderer.

Hing's motion failed, as did his attempts to include in the trial testimony about abuse of other players, rules violations, the cover-up at ASU and the sex matter.

Meanwhile, Kush's lawyer, Warren Platt, masterfully portrayed Rutledge as a "quitter." He produced witnesses who saw Kush grab Rutledge's face mask but did not see a punch. He argued over whether Rutledge's chin strap was buckled and what time during the game the punch supposedly occurred.

He also was allowed to bring in a host of big names from the coaching establishment to defend Kush's methods. Herb Brooks, who had guided the U.S. Olympic hockey team to its miraculous 1980 gold medal, was among them. He joked that he didn't punch players, he hit them with a hockey stick.

Kush, who previously had said he was on the opposite side of the field as Rutledge and later that he never punched Rutledge, testified he couldn't "ever recall" hitting or confronting Rutledge.

By a 5-3 vote, he jury rejected Rutledge's claim that Kush had punched him. He also lost all other aspects of his case. Appeals dragged on for years. Kush emerged the victor.

Today, Rutledge and his father, Gordon, seem to think their struggle was worthwhile, that ASU is now on a more ethical track in athletics. But at the time the punter was bitter. "If you tell the truth, you get burned. You lie and you make out like a winner."

But a more important jury, the NCAA, found ASU guilty of 30 rules violations, including the phony-credits scandal, payments to players and a booster offering a cotton farm to a recruit. Kush was cited in five violations, Lynch in three.

Kush went on to a professional coaching career in Canada, the National Football League and the upstart United States Football League. The results were mixed. The man whose face could practically have been chiseled for eternity onto Tempe Butte became known as a merely average coach.

Kush is now a public relations man at Turf Paradise, a horse-racing track in Phoenix.

Bear Bryant's record is safe. And the stadium does not bear the name Kush.

Boy Wonder

TENNIS

By *THOMAS BONK*

There hasn't been a real American Tennis Hero since 1985, the last time an American man ranked No. 1 on the computer, or maybe 1984, the last time an American male took a Grand Slam title and the last time America made it to the finals in the prestigious international Davis Cup competition. No one has quite fit the bill. Not Ivan Lendl, who only lives in America. Not John McEnroe, who used to be the best. And not Andre Agassi, who looked like he could be the best . . . last year.

Then in June, Michael Chang, a teen-ager from Placentia, stunned everyone (including himself) with a victory at the French Open, and the search for an American Tennis Hero suddenly took the form of a question: Is this any job for a shy, quiet, 134-pound, 5-foot-8 Chinese-American 17-year-old with cropped black hair, a "born-again" victory speech, a dad for a coach and a serve your mother could return?

Until his success at the French, Michael Chang had been nothing more than a standard-bearer for the most overworked word in U.S. men's tennis: potential. Like a string of prodigies from Tracy Austin to Aaron Krickstein, he had frequently been the youngest high achiever at every level. He had been the youngest player to win a match at the U.S. Open in 1987 (when he was 15); the youngest to win the U.S. Junior National Championships (when he was 15½); the youngest to play on Centre Court at Wimbledon in 60 years (in 1988); the youngest to play on a U.S. Davis Cup team in 61 years (against Paraguay, last January).

And then came Paris, where Chang delivered on that much-vaunted potential. On the red clay at Stade Roland Garros, he became the youngest man ever to win a Grand Slam singles title. His was the first triumph by a U.S. men's player in Paris in 34 years.

Now he must prove that he's not just a flash in the pan, a one-event Boy Wonder. So far it hasn't been easy. He played respectably on the grass courts of Wimbledon, where a big serve is an advantage, making it to the round of 16. But in two recent outings on hard courts, the surface Chang grew up on, he lost early against players at the bottom of the computer rankings. Starting tomorrow in Flushing Meadow, N.Y., he has another chance to live up to his potential. All he has to do is win the U.S. Open.

★ ★ ★

Deep down inside, beneath a sort-of-cool, sort-of-not exterior, Michael Chang feels utterly ordinary. He lives, after all, in his parents' tract house in Placentia. He likes his mom and dad, who are not just his parents but also partners in his tennis career. His high school counselor says he got good grades; he likes to fish; he gets an allowance; he's eager to get his driver's license. But Michael Chang is also extraordinary, even without the Grand Slam title. He attended high school all of two days a week his sophomore year and dropped out at 15. His allowance, reported to be $100 a month, comes out of a million-dollar-plus annual income. Last year, his first as a professional tennis player, he played in 15 tournaments, traveling the world, albeit with his mother as chaperone. And then there's all the attention.

On this day, the neighborhood calm along the trim streets bordering Placentia's Alta Vista golf course has been replaced by the buzz of a media event. A string of reporters and technicians makes its way to the Changs' home. A television magazine crew camps out in the dining room, cables crawl along the carpet, and hot lights shine in every direction. Outside, a black stretch limousine waits to take Chang to the NBC studios in Burbank and a guest appearance on "The Tonight Show."

After finishing his television interview, but before he gets into the limo, Chang poses for more pictures for a magazine article. In the midst of all this, he finds time to talk with one more reporter asking yet another series of questions about why he's so good, about why he won in Paris. This is not Chang's favorite leisure activity—he'd rather be bass fishing—but he endures it pretty well. Fame has arrived at Michael Chang's door, and he seems to have been expecting it. "It doesn't totally bother me or anything," he says. "In a way, it's been coming on little by little, so I'm getting used to it. It's not like it's taking me apart or anything. It's definitely part of being a professional tennis player."

He answers questions in as few words as possible. How has his life changed since he won the French, rocketed from No. 23 to No. 5 in the world rankings and added $290,752 to this year's income?

"Well," he says, with no trace of sarcasm, "I'm richer."

But when the questions turn toward what he is really, really like, Chang gets uncomfortable. His already laconic style grinds to a halt.

"You know, that's kind of hard to say—how you really are," Chang offers. "Ask somebody else."

At 17, he finds it difficult to define himself in words. But he is adept enough at self-expression on the tennis court. Pressed to describe his strengths there, he says, "my mind," and taps his head, then pats his thighs and adds, "my legs."

His well-developed thighs give him speed and power, vital in a sport where players must chase down shot after shot if they expect to win. And he is fast, with a quickness that's been compared to Bjorn Borg's. But men's tennis today is increasingly dominated by power players, Boris Beckers who can smash unreturnable serves at 120 mph. Unless Chang grows taller, his serve will always be a weakness. But his speed and technically excellent strokes still allow him to build a game on finesse.

A key to that finesse is the mental side of Michael Chang. In the end, it's the game that differentiates the masters from the technicians. Generally, it takes years to develop the dual ability to concentrate despite distractions and to continue playing hard after falling behind.

No less an authority than John McEnroe thinks Chang has a head start on the others. "Listen, this guy mentally is unbelievable for that age," he says. "Chang is very, very strong mentally."

Arthur Ashe, another elder statesman, agrees: "He is easily the smartest young player I have ever seen. He has an intuitive sense that I can only compare to a chess prodigy at age 9. You see him do things on the court that you would expect to see from someone who's been on the tour for years."

"People do not see the mental part of tennis," Chang explains. "You may wonder why (a player) handles situations better. You see a guy make an unforced error, you just think 'Oh, gosh, he just missed the shot.' But it's something else.

"In the juniors, I always had tight situations. I was always competing with guys who were bigger, stronger, older than I was. Just to be put in that situation—you can't run away from it. You have to deal with it. If you don't deal with it, you're going to lose."

The championship potential of Chang's mind and his legs became very clear at the French Open. Many regard the two-week French as the most grueling of the four major annual tennis tournaments, the so-called Grand Slam events: the Australian Open, the French Open, Wimbledon and the U.S. Open.

The French tournament is played on clay courts dusted with a quarter-inch of crushed red brick. The clay surface slows down the ball as it bounces, and players have time to get to each shot and return it. A big serve is not as vital as being able to grind out a match. And it isn't easy to hit "winners"—unreturnable shots that simply beat an opponent cold. Points are longer than on grass or hard-surface courts; matches of five hours are commonplace. The French Open rewards endurance and mental toughness as well as good strategy and precision shotmaking.

This year, Chang found himself in the half of the draw with Ivan Lendl of Czechoslovakia, the No. 1 player in the world. They met in the semifinals, and the outcome seemed to be a given. Even his father, Joe Chang, who acts as his coach, didn't bother to stay for the Lendl match. "There was no way Michael could win," the elder Chang said.

Lendl won the first two sets and needed just one more to take the match. But Chang began to wear him down. Running to return shot after shot, he tied the match at two sets apiece. Then Chang lost a key tool: Muscle cramps in his legs made it difficult even to sit down during changeovers, much less chase the ball effectively. So in the fifth set, he had to beat Lendl with his head.

Eating bananas and drinking water during breaks to help cure the leg cramps, Chang played defensively, lobbing the ball over Lendl's head to buy rest time for himself as Lendl ran to return it. He looked for openings to blast winners past Lendl, who seemed unable to change his own game plan and take advantage of Chang's obvious distress. And the strategy worked.

Lendl eventually faced a match point on his serve to stay in the competition. His first serve was long. Before he could serve again, Chang moved up inside the baseline, just steps behind the service line. The crowd of more than 16,000 cheered wildly at Chang's audacity. It was a ploy he'd used before, a move that telegraphed the insult: "I know you're going to blow the shot." Lendl pleaded for quiet, got only a little, then, flustered, sent his second serve skidding across the top of the net and long to give the match to Chang.

From there, Chang slugged two-fisted backhands and looping topspin forehands in the final where he once again came from behind and wore down his opponent, beating Stefan Edberg of Sweden, ranked No. 3 in the world, to claim his first Grand Slam title.

What had happened to his opponents? And how had he managed to dissolve Lendl's legendary composure? "I don't know," Chang says. "Having to play a 17-year-old, being two sets up, I get cramps —maybe he was thinking too much. It's like a hesitation, to compare it to bass fishing. You have a hesitation in the line, and the bass might feel some kind of resistance and let go."

Maybe that's it.

There is one thing Chang does know for sure about the victory in the crucial match against Lendl: "I said a prayer and my cramps went away."

★ ★ ★

The day after he met the press at his home in Placentia and appeared on "The Tonight Show," he and his family appeared at the Chinese Christian Church of Thousand Oaks. On this Saturday evening, there was not a seat left in the sanctuary. The Changs had jumped at the opportunity to tell others of their Christianity during the special two-hour service honoring Michael. As Chang, his father, and his mother, Betty, took turns speaking, a man from the church stood beside them, translating Joe's and Michael's English into Chinese and Betty's Chinese into English.

The congregation cheered loudly when Michael got up from his seat in the front row of the church and strode to the pulpit. He spoke softly, careful, at first, not to look anyone in the eye.

"If there are any of you who don't know me, my name is Michael Chang," he said. "I'm 17 years old, and I'm a professional tennis player."

With building rhythms, he walked his audience through a list of his recent accomplishments, asking them to consider the force behind each victory.

Was it just coincidence, he asked, that on a day when he was suffering from severe cramps he had beaten the No. 1 player in the world? Was it just coincidence that he had come from behind to defeat Ronald Agenor later in the tournament? And was it coincidental that he'd come from behind yet again to defeat Stefan Edberg?

"Come on, let's face reality. Those weren't coincidences," he said to loud applause. "That wasn't me playing out there. Jesus Christ is alive and well."

Baptized 17 months ago—about a year after he joined the pro tennis tour—Chang told the churchgoers he had been inspired to read the Bible by a sermon he heard.

"I decided to see what the Bible said about friendship and love," he said, and when he discovered insights there, he kept reading. "Now, I'm 17," he added, "and I understand."

Michael and his parents attend the Chinese Christian Church when he isn't traveling, despite the 160-mile round-trip from Placentia to Thousand Oaks. It is the family church—Chang's grandfather was a founding member.

Chang pursues his faith with fervor, sometimes to mixed results. At the French Open, moments after his greatest tennis triumph, Chang accepted his trophy in the box of Philippe Chatrier, president of the International Tennis Federation, and thanked God for his victory. Scattered boos were heard.

Chang simply plowed on, undaunted. Professions of faith in the winner's corner may "annoy" people, he says, "but to me, it's the truth," a steadying force amid the pressures of his life. He attends occasional Bible study classes on the road, prays before meals, frequently pulls a Bible from his workout bag and reads between matches.

His religion, he says, has helped him make sense of the events he sees in the world around him. It's also given him a framework for answering more personal questions—sorting out his purpose in life. "You sort of wonder about the things that happen in the world, like in China. . . . And then you sort of wonder what would happen if this world were perfect. No evil. Everything good. You're sort of curious."

One thing he is particularly curious about is his own success. "You think there are reasons for it," he says softly, "then you just wonder. It's just like a person gets cancer and says 'Why me?' Well, you don't know why."

But, he continues, "God has an idea for me, I think—to spread his word through tennis. I realized God gave me talent at this young age. It is what enables me to make contact with the world.

"Evangelist with a racket, that's pretty much it."

★ ★ ★

Michael Chang began playing tennis when he was 6 years old, first engaged and then engulfed in a game that was his father's passion. Ever since, his dad has been the primary influence on his game and his career—the major architect of an 11-year effort to develop and then market the product that is Michael Chang. I am matching Michael's needs with the needs and hungers of the public, Joe Chang says.

Chang, a research chemist who develops products for Unocal, fled China and its revolution in 1948, going first to Taiwan, then emigrating to the United States in 1966. He met and married Betty Tung in 1966 when he was a graduate student in New Jersey and she was going to college in New York. Betty was born in India, the child of a Chinese diplomat, and came to the United States when she was 11. The couple's first son, Carl, was born in Hoboken, N.J., in 1969; Michael was born in 1972.

In 1974, the family moved to St. Paul, Minn., so Joe could take a job with 3M, but Joe will always remember that year as the beginning of his tennis addiction. "I got hooked," he says. "I read all the books and the magazines and played all the time. I spent so much time on the tennis courts, my wife finally asked me, 'Why not take the kids out?' And that changed our whole lives."

Michael began playing in 1978 and by 1979, the whole family was so involved in the sport that Joe decided to move the family to La Costa, near San Diego, so the boys would play year-round. "That was when we really wanted to develop their tennis," he says. "They were so good already. We played Tuesday through Friday, took Mondays off, and played in tournaments on the weekends." The Changs skipped the traditional route into youth tennis—tennis camps and coaches—playing, instead, among themselves, round-robin games in hour-and-a-half sessions on weekdays. They took on non-family competition on the weekends. That set Michael apart from his peers, whom he'd meet on the court but otherwise have few opportunities to get to know.

Michael won his first tournament, at the tennis complex in San Diego's Balboa Park, at age 7, and though both of the boys steadily worked their way up through the rankings, it was clear early on that the younger son would be the family prodigy. Over the years, Joe brought in and dismissed a series of coaches—Phil Dent, Roy Emerson, Dennis Ralston, Ian Russell, Pancho Segura—never relinquishing his role as Michael's primary trainer. He keeps detailed graphs and flow charts monitoring Michael's progress and sees himself in the role of information gatherer, gleaning knowledge from the experts and passing it on to his son.

In 1985, Joe refinanced the Changs' house to cover the costs of travel and training. Betty arranged her household duties to free the weekends for her sons' tennis matches. While Michael kept performing, kept advancing, he clearly felt the pressure of his family's intense focus on his development. "If I said forget it (about tennis)," he told *World Tennis* magazine in an interview cited by critics of his father's role in his career, "my dad would be incredibly mad. Just looking at the way my parents and my brother have helped me, you want to give something back by working hard, showing that you care and that your parents didn't waste $100,000 for you to screw around. This is a family thing."

When Reebok offered 16-year-old Michael a multi-million dollar contract to turn pro in February, 1988, he quit high school, got a GED certificate and hit the circuit.

Betty Chang, a smiling, gregarious woman, says hers is an egalitarian family in which everyone has a say at round-table family councils. It is there that decisions are made by consensus, she says, not imposed by her or her husband. The decision to let Michael turn pro, says Joe, was an easy one.

"It was a once-in-a-lifetime opportunity," he says. "He was mature enough. And even if he *wasn't* mature enough, the money and the opportunity they were giving us were too good."

Today, Michael's endorsements alone exceed $1 million annually, which means at the age of 17, Chang is a millionaire without even picking up a racket. In addition to Reebok clothes and shoes, he endorses Prince tennis rackets, Yale locks and such products as ceiling fans, security systems and noodles. His earnings put him fifth on the Grand Prix prize money list this year with $387,412, his career winnings $556,646, and many expect him to finish the year as the youngest male player to earn $1 million in prize money.

But critics wonder about the costs of Michael's binding family ties. Tennis legend Segura, 68, the pro at La Costa Hotel and Spa, coached Michael when the Changs lived nearby. He praises Chang's mental toughness, but worries that the teen-ager isn't allowed to use it.

"A boy should be able to make decisions for himself, like he does on the tennis court," Segura says. "God forbid anything should happen to those parents. We have to respect our parents, we love them, but we got to be men."

Unlike his brother, a junior at Berkeley, Michael won't be attending college—at least for a while. That decision, too, has the blessing of his parents. "Kids these days don't go to college to learn something, they go just to get a degree so they can make a living," Joe reasons. "But getting a degree and getting an education are two different things. If Michael really wants to develop the knowledge he thinks he needs, then he can go to college in five years. By then he'll know what he wants to do after tennis. In 10 years, he will be financially set. He can go to college anytime later."

On the road, Michael is insulated from the demands of ordinary life by his mother, whom he describes as a friend. She's a dominant force: Betty Chang even took over the kitchen of a London hotel to prepare Michael's meals.

Michael insists that he didn't miss much by dropping out of school, that he simply matured early and made his career choices before other people did. But he does lag in some of the experiences common to other teen-agers: Driving. Dating. Hanging out. When Johnny Carson asked him to describe the logistics of his last date—"Did she drive? How did you get where you were going?"—a chagrined Michael Chang told the amused audience: "My parents came with us."

★ ★ ★

In the youth movement of sports, the pressure to succeed is tremendous and athletes sometimes find that early success is fleeting. The term used to describe such a condition is burnout, but psychologist Jim Loehr, director of sports science for the United States Tennis Association, thinks Michael Chang will not flame out early. "When you take a young player and catapult him into stardom, in tennis particularly," says Loehr, "(he goes) from childhood directly into adulthood. There are many adolescents who are not ready for that.

"Michael Chang is truly the exception. From a psychological perspective, I see him as really a great role model for young kids, perhaps one of the best all-time."

Lots of people hope Loehr is right.

When Chang won in Paris, Reebok ran full-page ads in the *Los Angeles Times*, the *New York Times, USA Today* and the *Boston Globe* celebrating his victory (and that of Arantxa Sanchez Vicario, another 17-year-old company representative). The ad said: "Some kids go to Paris to study history, others go to make it." Reebok's Chester Wheeler, director of sports marketing, is thinking of an encore: "Our next idea," he says, "is that he win the U.S. Open."

Michael, says Joe Chang, has a slightly less lofty goal: to do better at the Open than he did last year, when he lost in the round of 16. To that end, says his coach, Chang will play the three hard-court tour competitions that precede the tournament, then go to New York a week early. "He takes a one-week rest, then, based on how he does in the three tournaments, we go through certain drills—the strokes, the serve, the strategy. Typically, he drills two hours in the morning, takes a three-mile run, then he plays a match in the afternoon. We want to build a pattern, a routine that is similar to the tournament schedule.

"I don't think he can go in thinking he will win," says the most talkative Chang. "It's a long two weeks, and everything has to be just right to win a Grand Slam. Most of all, he will need a lot of luck."

Michael himself, on media day back in Placentia, grappled with the question of luck, fortune, fate. "You think about the world. You think 'Why is there life on this world? There's got to be a reason for it. Otherwise, you just live and die . . . as if your life were nothing."

"You wonder why all these things happen. You just wonder about things."

He tries not to rush himself or to think much about how soon he'll achieve his goal of being the best tennis player in the world: "I really don't think of it that way because I don't want to put pressure on myself." Facing the pressure to be the American Tennis Hero, to live up to what even he might call a miracle in Paris, Chang ventures his fall-back position, the part of his preparation that considers defeat as well as victory: "I think there will be times when maybe I won't be doing so well and I'm sure people will be saying, 'Now where is your Jesus Christ?'

"For me, I feel as if being a Christian I have a job to do on this earth and that's my first priority—to get that job done. You can't win all the time. You can only do as much as you are made to do."

Airborne

by free-lance photographer Diane Weiss. West German Boris Becker, the 1989 Wimbledon and U.S. Open tennis champion, makes a diving stretch for a shot during an indoor professional match in Philadelphia. Copyright ©1989, Diane Weiss.

Yakety-Yak

by Andrea Mihalik of the Philadelphia Daily News. It was an off-camera moment for CBS Sports announcers Verne Lundquist and Terry Bradshaw, or so they thought. When the CBS camera stopped, Mihalik seized the moment and caught both men in unrehearsed conversation with other parties. Copyright ©1989, Philadelphia Daily News.

Is Perfection Good Enough?

HIGH SCHOOL BASEBALL

By *SCOTT REID*

Early Wednesday evening Jon Peters raced his mother's car over the hills of North Brenham. As he drove he didn't notice R.E.M. on the radio.

Follow me. Don't follow me.

Behind him, reporters in three cars and a van carrying a team of photographers from *Sports Illustrated* chased the Brenham High School pitcher across the Santa Fe railroad tracks that run along the third-base line of Fireman's Park Stadium, up West Main Street as it runs into Highway 90, past the Dixie Motel, past the Bluebonnet Electric Company, then left at the sign for the Phillips 66 station that says "We Now Have Gas."

They went down a rough, narrow gravel road, finally stopping at the Peters' secluded brick house that overlooks a rolling 22-acre ranch; 73 miles northwest of Houston, where the hills of Central Texas fade into the plains of the southeast. Where for the past two years, Peters, perhaps the most famous high school pitcher ever, has stepped away from the shadow of the media.

Wednesday the shadow stepped with him.

Before sundown, Peters, who has never lost a high school game, was scheduled to complete two photo sessions and then give two interviews. By the time he takes the mound tonight at Fireman's Field in his attempt to break the national high school record for consecutive victories—50—a second group of *Sports Illustrated* photographers will have arrived in Brenham, along with a crew from NBC's "Today Show." If Peters beats A&M Consolidated he'll be interviewed live Monday morning by Bryant Gumbel.

"This is even bigger than Blue Bell ice cream," Brenham mayor

Dorothy Morgan said, referring to the town's other claim to fame.

By now, however, the media attention is routine for Brenham and Peters. Five television stations were on hand a year ago when Peters shut out Oak Ridge, 5-0, for his 34th consecutive victory. Then Brenham and the nation thought Peters had broken the national record for consecutive victories set by West Covina (Calif.) Edgewood's Mike Pill, who won 33 consecutive between 1975 and 1977. *Sports Illustrated* planned to put him on its cover, but Peters was bumped by Pete Rose, who was suspended for 30 days for shoving an umpire. This week Brenham coach Earl Hathaway teased Peters that Rose will knock him off the cover again.

After the *Sports Illustrated* article appeared, Peters' record was disputed by Clyde Parrish, a South Carolina high school coach who said Tim Moore won 50 consecutive games while pitching for McColl (S.C.) High School from 1977-80. The National High School Federation verified Moore's mark.

So, after Peters pitched a two-hit 3-1 victory over Katy Taylor Friday, the media returned to the town of 10,066. Among the chaos, Peters has tried to keep his normal routine. He still plays pool every Thursday night at friend Kevin Picone's house, still runs his daily two to five miles around Fireman's Park and still takes solitary walks in the fields of bluebonnets and buttercups behind his house.

"It's peaceful up here," Peters said. "I can relax out here, think things through here. Sometimes I'll come out here with something bothering me and after walking around for a while it doesn't seem like it was that big of a problem."

On the ranch he can walk past the mound his father, Val, built for him when he was in grade school, climb over the wooden fence and put the media and the pressure of the record behind him. But he can't walk away from everything. Some shadows never fade.

There are days when Jon Peters reflects on a season full of headlines and still feels empty; feels that the record bid was more fun the first time around, the victories a little sweeter, the cheers a little louder, the walks through the bluebonnets a little easier.

"It felt better last year," Peters said. "I enjoyed it more because I had Jeff to share it with."

★ ★ ★

"Baseball is the big thing in this town; we're a baseball town," said Morgan, who also teaches government and economics at Brenham High. "There's such a community spirit for baseball. Our children grow up together on the baseball fields here."

Jon Peters and Jeff Toll were no different.

They bought baseball cards at Perry Brothers fabric store or anywhere else they could find them, played Pee Wee and Little League and hung out at Fireman's Park every chance they could. Peters was such a regular at the Montreal Expos annual tryout camp that Expos' scout Red Murph made him an assistant while he was still in grade school.

By the time he was 11 Peters was already a star.

"Pressure goes along with playing baseball in Brenham, Texas, because the expectations are so high that go along with it," said former Brenham coach Lee Driggers, who coaches at Hardin-Simmons University. Driggers, in 1986 and 1987, coached two of Brenham's five state high school championship teams. Since 1967 the town has produced 11 professional players, including Cecil Cooper, who starred for the Milwaukee Brewers. Forty-seven Cubs have received college scholarships.

"The first time I saw him I knew he was special," Driggers said of Peters, then a seventh grader who had already pitched two victories in the Little League Junior World Series. After going 13-0 with a 1.97 ERA his freshman season in high school, Peters led Brenham to the Little League Senior World Series, where he was the losing pitcher in a 3-1 loss to Taiwan in the semifinals. He hasn't lost since.

As a sophomore, he caught the attention of the major-league scouts with a 15-0 record and a 1.09 ERA. In 104 innings, he struck out 209 while giving up just 31 walks. "If he was throwing like that today he'd be in the major-league draft," Driggers said.

Less than a day after winning a Class 4A state semifinal game, Peters pitched three innings of relief against Fort Worth Brewer, striking out the first eight and then getting the ninth to pop out to clinch Brenham's second consecutive state championship.

That summer, the 6-foot-2, 190-pound righthander was supposed to be the youngest player in the Junior Olympics but was sidelined by shoulder surgery. Despite a 14-0 mark and 0.96 ERA last year and a 8-0 record and 0.70 ERA this spring, his fastball, his primary pitch, has only recently approached the 89 miles per hour he consistently threw in 1987. There aren't as many comparisons to Nolan Ryan as there were two years ago. These days the name David Clyde also comes up. As an 18-year-old, Clyde made his major-league debut with the Rangers in 1973. Five years later he was out of the majors, without ever having a winning season.

Next year Peters will play for Texas A&M instead of the minor leagues. A pro career might come later than he once thought, Peters said, but it will come.

★ ★ ★

Jeff Toll was first diagnosed with leukemia when he and Peters were in grade school. However, by the time he entered high school, doctors said he had the disease licked. Toll talked about playing baseball in high school after his strength returned. In the meantime Driggers made him the team manager.

But in January 1988 the leukemia returned. While Peters made his record bid last spring, Toll was bedridden at Houston's Texas Children's Hospital. Peters never doubted which one of the two was stronger. "Seeing everything he was going through and how he kept fighting made what I was doing seem so much easier," Peters said. "He really inspired me to get the record."

As soon as Peters won his 34th game, apparently breaking the record, he waded through well-wishers to call Toll on a pay phone outside the stadium. Bystanders couldn't tell which of the pair was more excited. "I just told him I was proud of him," Toll said at the time.

"Jeff was always bragging about Jon," Morgan said. "He was his No. 1 fan and his closest friend."

Just before this baseball season, Peters lost his friend.

"Jeff's death tore up the school and I think it tore up Jon," Morgan said. "But Jon was strong for everybody. He never showed his emotions. He never does. The other day I told him he was a fine young man. Because that's what he is now, after all this, a man."

To this day the winningest pitcher in high school baseball history walks in the shadow of a friend who never played an inning.

"Jeff would love this," Peters said of the media hoopla. "He'd eat this up. It would be more fun if he was here. Yes sir. It would be a lot better if I could share it with him. He suffered so much, but was always so positive. I miss that. And I wish I could talk to him, just have him around.

"Sometimes I think I've adjusted to his death, but I still really miss him a lot."

Watching the sun set Wednesday night, Peters' eyes finally betrayed his emotions.

Tennessee Revives Bad Memories

COLLEGE BASKETBALL

By *TERI THOMPSON*

The University of Tennessee, which dumped its basketball coach, Don DeVoe, after a first-round loss in the NCAA tournament, found a nice replacement last week.

Unfortunately, the school discovered the new guy has a handicap that has nothing to do with his golf game: He's black.

In one of the more chilling stories to come along since the days of separate drinking fountains, Tennessee athletic director Doug Dickey said over the weekend that his new coach, Wade Houston, wouldn't be extended a university-paid membership to the Cherokee Country Club in Knoxville because "obviously Cherokee Country Club does not have black members, and (joining) is not an option (for Houston). It's not an issue with us. We just have memberships we retain at the athletic department and it's our decision to do what we want to do with it."

What Dickey was saying was that Cherokee Country Club is an all-white club—as all but one country club in Knoxville are—and that despite the fact that both of Houston's predecessors, plus Dickey himself and football coach Johnny Majors, have memberships, Houston will be kept out.

Because he is black.

Not because he can't play golf. Not because he doesn't choose to participate in the phony social structure that accompanies most country clubs. But because of the color of his skin.

Cherokee's official position is that there is no exclusionary policy based on race, creed or religion, but that the club has the right to refuse any application it chooses.

If you believe that smokescreen, then you also believe Watergate was a harmless break-in. And that Doug Moe doesn't swear.

This is nothing but bigotry at its finest, racism at its height. It is also a shocking example of the plantation mentality that pervades college athletics.

Houston is good enough to coach the basketball team. He's good enough to recruit the basketball players Tennessee wants on the court. But he's not good enough to swap nassaus with the mucky-mucks on the golf course. Or to sip gin-and-tonics with the swells after the tennis game. One of the justifications, if you could call it that, the country club is using to keep Houston out is that there is an unwritten rule that a newcomer to the community must go through a waiting period, and that Houston couldn't be accepted immediately because of that, anyway.

"It's not in the bylaws, but any person that comes in the community should be here about a year," says Cherokee president Hank Bertelkamp, who, as it happens, was once a captain of the Tennessee basketball team and served on the committee that helped select Houston as coach. "A lot of people wouldn't know him."

Bertelkamp, who must qualify as the second-biggest hypocrite in Knoxville, behind Dickey, went on to say the waiting period would have applied to a new white coach, too.

Funny, though, DeVoe did not remember a waiting period when he arrived from Wyoming. In fact, he was hired in the spring, and his kids were swimming in the club's pool by summer.

"I don't recall any waiting period," said DeVoe. "I think they transferred it from Coach Mears to me," he said of his predecessor, Ray Mears. "I guess there could have been one, but I remember we were using the club quite early in my tenure at UT."

Bertelkamp even went so far as to say he's "been a proponent of Houston. I'm in his court. He's a wonderful, wonderful guy."

Sure, as long as he stays off Bertelkamp's golf course.

Clearly, there is no justification for this kind of treatment. If we were shocked by Al Campanis' ignorant insensitivity and horrified by Jimmy the Greek's, we should be intolerant of Doug Dickey's.

The president of the university, Lamar Alexander, rightfully withdrew all the school's Cherokee memberships yesterday, including Dickey's, but I'm not sure the matter should end there.

How can Tennessee keep an athletic director who says his basketball coach "is better off than I am" because he can keep the money the university would have paid for the dues, and adds that Houston can "play golf at Willow Creek and eat at Club LeConte."

Willow Creek, for your information, is a public course, and as far as we know, even in the South blacks are allowed to play on public courses. Club LeConte is a private club that does not discriminate.

Thanks, Doug, for that bit of illumination.

But Dickey is not the only culprit here; the people who belong to the country club itself are at the real heart of darkness.

"Everybody wants to monitor the membership and have the kind of club they can be proud of," said Houston. "It's their decision. It's their club."

I'm sure the members of the Cherokee Country Club are quite proud of their decision and their club today.

Their greens are safe. Too bad about their handicap.

A Sore Subject

COLLEGE FOOTBALL

By *MARK KRAM*

Bob Waters is strapped to a wheelchair and hooked to a respirator, the plastic tube of which curls beneath his office desk to a rectangular speaker. His breathing is labored. Unable to walk or shake hands, either to feed or bathe himself, he weighs his dismissal as the head football coach at Western Carolina University with sadness and disappointment. University chancellor Myron Coulter had promised Waters that he could remain the coach for as long as his health allowed, but as wife Sheri Waters pointed out, "Bob lived longer than the chancellor expected him to."

The illness that has afflicted Bob Waters is amyotrophic lateral sclerosis (Lou Gehrig's disease), and it is incurable. In the four years that have passed since the disease was diagnosed, a period in which the ex-San Francisco 49ers quarterback has been paralyzed in his legs and arms, Waters set a shimmering example of how even grave encumbrances need not deprive one of hope or value. He had adjusted to his breathing apparatus and other confinements and had presided over practices with both courage and pride. "I love this school," he said. "I never would have tried to hurt it."

The removal of Waters last month as the head football coach at Western Carolina has set off a controversy in Cullowhee that has torn some friendships and divided others. When Coulter acknowledged that he relieved Waters because the football team had been in decline, and that the school needed a coach who patrolled the sideline with "vigor," some criticized him for abandoning his commitment to Waters and taking a narrow view of the place athletics should have at a school the size of Western Carolina.

Still only 51—but thin and ashen—Waters coached the Catamounts for 20 mostly successful seasons. The team went 2-9 in 1988, but he believes he possesses the vitality and personnel to turn the Western Carolina program around. Rejected in his attempt to convince Coulter that he still had command of the program, which had evolved from the NAIA to the NCAA's Division I-AA, Waters considered the events that transpired this spring and spoke of how the "larger picture" seemed to elude the chancellor. Which is to say: Winning is a high priority, but Western Carolina is not North Carolina.

"I decided when I was diagnosed that, if I could continue coaching, that it would send a signal to other disabled people that there is still a place for them," Waters said. "I still believe that, and it worries me that those people will now think that I have quit, that I have neither the strength nor desire to continue the battle."

The former coach lowered his eyes and added: "We were doing bigger things here than just winning and losing football games."

★ ★ ★

Western Carolina University occupies a parcel of land in the sprawling grandeur of the Great Smoky Mountains. When Coulter announced that Waters had been reassigned to position of assistant athletic director—a job Waters hasn't decided whether to accept—the tranquility that commonly prevails on campus erupted into heated demonstration. Between 30 and 40 students paraded to the administration building bearing a petition with 500 signatures in support of Waters and staged a "sit-in." When Coulter addressed the crowd, and tried to explain his position, one of the students shouted:

"Stop sidestepping the issue!"

The "issue" had been as clear as it was volatile to Coulter. Seated in an armchair in his spacious office, his dignified hands cradling a cup of decaffeinated coffee, Coulter acknowledged that it was a "painful decision" but an inevitable one. While he conceded that the Southern Conference is not the Atlantic Coast Conference, and that the athletic department at Western Carolina is not the revenue source it is at other schools, Coulter added that "excellence" in sports still is an expectation. "I have that same expectation for the English department," Coulter said. Asked if he would reassign an English professor because of a handicap, Coulter said:

"That depends."

The chancellor paused and sipped his coffee. "For example," he continued, "if the handicap interfered somehow with his performance, there would obviously have to be a change. In the case of the football team, there has been a decline in the program, and I sense that some of our athletes were not responding. A coach has to project an aura of strength and vigor on the sidelines."

That Coulter seemed to confine his concerns to such a limited scope is disconcerting to Waters and his supporters. While it is true that Waters required special care on the sideline—his wheelchair had to be placed on an elevated platform and protected on either side from errant passes or careening running backs—it also is true that his intellect remains as vital as ever. "People see the wheelchair," Sheri Waters said, "and somehow think that his faculties have abandoned him." Waters had been told to expect that, and one of his priorities has been to accept interviews, if only to prove that his disease has altered neither his perceptions nor will. "However," Waters said, "there is the belief that it has (altered both)."

No one on the Western Carolina football staff subscribed to that belief. Offensive coordinator Don Dalton, a former quarterback at Western Carolina, said Waters is as "sharp as a tack," and spoke of how he and the other assistants enjoyed driving the coach to and from practice and helping with his various other needs. While Waters sat in his office and interviewed candidates for the head coaching position in the final week of spring practice, Dalton sat in an adjoining office and told of how he applied for the athletic directorship at the school but withdrew his name when he was told that he would have to remove Waters. "This is a special man," Dalton said. Upset at how the chancellor has treated Waters, especially in light of the allegiance the former coach has demonstrated to the school, Dalton shook his head.

"Toughness comes from in here," Dalton said, tapping his chest. "Coach is a strong, caring person and should have been allowed to decide when *he* wanted to resign. We, as a staff, had adjusted to his limitations and were eager for the season to start."

Linebacker coach Tommy Scott agreed. "We did well recruiting and we had worked hard in spring practice," said Scott, an assistant to Waters for five seasons. "I can see the other side. We were 2-9, but with a break here or there we could have been 6-5 and people would have been happier. Coach is an amazing person."

Neither of the assistants is pleased with the abruptness with which Waters was relieved; Waters is equally perturbed. Coulter had told him again in December that he could remain as the coach if he chose, and so it was a shock when, at the height of spring practice in February, Coulter dropped by the athletic office and told Waters that he was planning a change. Coulter offered Waters four alternatives: either he could take a reassignment to assistant athletic director (at a reduced salary); take retirement; take disability; or resign. Coulter gave Waters a week to think it over and two more weeks when Waters asked for an extension. When Waters drafted a proposal of his plans for the season ahead, and asked Coulter for just one more season, Coulter said no.

"I gave him that proposal," Waters said, "and he spat on it."

Coulter denied doing that. "I read it," he said. "I definitely read it, and it seemed to me that his plans were precisely what I would expect from other coaches in other sports. I would not say that (the proposal) was an extraordinary one."

Word that Waters had been relieved spread across campus and into neighboring hamlets that surround Cullowhee. In some circles, chiefly within the athletic booster organization, "The Big Cat Club," the announcement was received as a step toward rebuilding the football program and winning. In other circles—staff, players and students—it was received as a blow. Some former Western Carolina players approached Waters with the idea of protesting the removal with a boycott of the 1989 season. Waters was unsupportive. "I did not—and do not—want that to happen," Waters said. The idea was dropped.

The current Western Carolina players are in large part supportive of Waters. Senior quarterback and co-captain Todd Cottrell, dressing at his locker before the final day of spring practice, said he and his teammates are saddened to see Waters leave. Told that the chancellor believed the team had stopped responding to Waters—that Coulter thought a football coach should project vigor—Cottrell disagreed. "Coach is inspirational," Cottrell said. While conceding that Waters did not "run up and down the sidelines" and shout at the team in a deafening baritone, Cottrell remembered how Waters would work as hard or harder than some other coaches he has seen.

"No one who ever comes into contact with the coach will ever be the same," Cottrell said. "I know he has helped change how I look at the world."

Senior offensive tackle John Martin concurred. "Coach is a class act," Martin said. Contending that Waters should have been given the single extra season he had requested, that "it did not seem like a lot to ask for," Martin stood outside the Western Carolina locker room and reflected on the impact Waters has had on his life. Though it was true that the team had not performed well, and true that some people thought Waters should be relieved, Martin thought college athletics (especially at Western Carolina) "stood for something bigger." While an assistant wheeled Waters out for practice—his final practice—Martin said:

"Seeing him, his courage, is sort of like a parable to me," Martin said. "There are some coaches who shout and scream, but it can seem so pointless. Coach Waters, just by his presence, has provided us with lessons that some of us are probably not even aware that we have learned. I know I will always remember him. I also know that no one on this team ever had complained of being tired or hurt."

Martin walked off to join his teammates, but turned and added: "I will miss him."

★ ★ ★

Western Carolina named a new football coach yesterday. Coulter interviewed four candidates for the job and chose former University of Georgia assistant Dale Strahm. In looking back on his removal of Waters, and the anger it stirred, Coulter said that while he agreed that Waters set "a global example" to the handicapped, the chancellor also had a responsibility to the people who follow Western Carolina football. Approaching the issue philosophically, Coulter added that "each of us will reach that day when we can no longer do the job and will have to step aside.

"And," Coulter said, "each of us will have someone to push us."

Coulter said he still considered Waters "a friend" and hoped that he would take the assistant athletic directorship. The chancellor even has told Waters that he would not cut his $73,044 salary. Athletic director Bob Setzer, a former assistant football coach who had a part in removing Waters, acknowledged that "the wounds are deep," but added that he also hoped Waters would accept the job as his assistant. "I need his help," Setzer said. Waters is the former athletic director at Western Carolina and has, according to Setzer, valuable knowledge concerning budgets and fund raising.

"What has happened, happened," Setzer said. "I know Bob is disappointed, but we have to look ahead."

Waters still is not certain if he will accept the new position. "Although I suppose I will," he said. Stationed on the sideline during his final practice as his team did wind sprints, Waters spoke to his team in private at the end of the workout and reiterated, according to Miller, his intentions to continue to "battle this disease." When he finished, he sent his team home and returned to his darkened office, where his desk is decorated with a commemorative football that the 49ers presented to him. There he spoke of how therapeutic it had been for him to coach football and how he would now have to rechannel his energies in some other place. Some other place where people will see that he still is Bob Waters and that he has not withdrawn.

"No sir," he said, "I still have something to give."

Iditarod Rescue Is Sweeter Than Victory

DOGSLEDDING

By *LEW FREEDMAN*

From the Anchorage Daily News

Help. Mike Madden knew he needed help. Everything was going fuzzy. All his muscles were going weak. Push on, his mind told him. Stay awake. Help was in Iditarod. Keep going.

The cold night was clear and filled with stars. The trail was empty, the whole area was empty. Just deep snow, flat land, and stunted, tiny spruce. Madden urged his dog team forward. And then he couldn't anymore. He slumped over the handlebars of his sled. Blinking the blurriness from his thoughts, he clutched his snow hook and drove it into the snow. Then he rolled off the sled and fell alongside the trail.

Musher Jamie Nelson found him there 20 minutes later.

Nearly 150 miles ahead in Grayling, the race for the lead of the 17th annual Iditarod Trail Sled Dog Race was unfolding. But back on the desolate trail between the ghost towns of Ophir and Iditarod, on the night of March 10, a different drama unfolded: the race to rescue North Pole rookie musher Mike Madden from death.

For nearly 18 hours, veteran Jerry Austin and rookies Nelson, Mitch Brazin, Kathy Halverson and Lynwood Fiedler forgot the race and acted as a Red Cross team. They gave up their chances at top-20 money and rookie-of-the-year honors, to feed, warm and care for Madden until a military helicopter could airlift him from the wilderness to a hospital in Anchorage. At Humana Hospital, doctors found Madden riddled with salmonella.

A week later, when they mushed under the finish banner flapping in a whipping wind on Front Street in Nome, 1,100 miles and over 13 days from Anchorage, the group learned this: Mike Madden was well, Mike Madden was here. Mike Madden would like to buy them a drink.

★ ★ ★

Madden, a sturdy 6-footer, felt wearier than he should have in his first Iditarod as afternoon turned to evening that day. His right knee was throbbing from the three-stitch cut he suffered when he wounded himself with an ax in McGrath. They were tiny warning signals, but Madden didn't know he had eaten poison.

Madden, 27, a carpenter who put his life on hold for eight months to train for the Iditarod, was traveling with Nelson, another first-time racer from Togo, Minn., and the 1988 winner of the John Beargrease Sled Dog Marathon in her home state. Madden's real problems began when they stopped to rest at about 6:30 that night. He didn't have the energy to feed his dogs.

"She was wearing just a vest and a wool shirt and commenting on how beautiful it was out," said Madden. "I had on parkas, goose down, pile. I was just chattering my teeth and my head was real rummy."

Madden told Nelson he couldn't think real well. It is 90 miles between Ophir and Iditarod, one of the longest stretches between checkpoints in the race, and perhaps the most barren. They were about 30 miles from Iditarod. Nelson suggested building a fire, but Madden felt worse.

"I said, 'I've got to go to a checkpoint,' " said Madden. "She said, 'I'll follow you.' "

Madden mushed out of camp, but within moments fell asleep on the sled. He had covered only a short distance when Nelson came upon him lying on the ground. She acted swiftly, bundling Madden into layers of clothing and a sleeping bag.

"It was something anybody would do," said Nelson. "But I'd never dealt with that. I realized there was something wrong, but I didn't realize how bad it was."

The cavalry arrived soon; Brazin of St. Michael, Halverson of Trapper Creek, Fiedler of Canyon Creek, Mont., and Austin. All but Austin were new to the race across Alaska. Austin was in his 10th Iditarod. Ordinarily, Austin, of St. Michael, would not have been anywhere near here; he would be mushing with the leaders. Not this year, though. His dogs' diets were out of whack and he was mushing just to finish.

Nelson, Brazin, who is a close friend of Austin's, and Halverson, were with Madden when Austin and Fiedler stopped. There was no reason for a gang of mushers to be parked.

"Kathy Halverson said, 'We have a little problem here,' " Austin said.

Mushers understand the rigors of the outdoors. They face severe cold, high winds, blizzards, all the time. They know the fierceness of the country, and what it can do to a human body under stress from long days on the trail. They reacted instinctively. They built a fire, cocooned Madden in thick layers of warm clothing and sleeping bags, boiled water and forced him to drink liquids.

"We didn't know what was wrong," said Brazin, 28, who is a commercial fisherman. "We just had to use a bit of common sense."

Hot and cold. Hot and cold. Madden sweated and shivered. He lay on his bed of snow, wrapped like a mummy, barely conscious.

"I was completely delirious," said Madden.

Brazin said Madden "was off the wall" yelling things like, "God, take me inside," and "What about the three gallons of coffee?"

Austin, who is respected for his wisdom and coolness on the trail, took charge. He examined Madden, searching for a clue to the illness. Was it blood poisoning from the cut? Hypothermia from exhaustion and cold? The flu? He couldn't tell.

The mushers' hands were too cold to really tell if Madden had a fever and their thermometers were broken. The thermometers measuring the air temperature worked, though, and they showed minus-15 degrees, cold that can be rough on a body even when everything's functioning well.

The mushers huddled and discussed options. Madden clearly needed expert medical assistance. But what was the most efficient way to get him out of this remote place, possibly the worst spot on the trail?

Packing Madden into a sled bag and hauling him over bumpy terrain into Iditarod might do more harm than good, they thought. Fiedler seemed to have the freshest team and Austin knew the trail, so they were picked to ride into Iditarod. The others would camp with Madden until a helicopter arrived.

Fiedler and Austin dumped equipment to lighten their sleds and mushed on aware that for once speed meant more than moving up in the race standings. After seeing Madden shake and listening to his incoherent answers there was genuine concern that Madden could become the first musher ever to die during the Iditarod.

"It really kind of put the fear of God in us," said Fiedler, 35, a life insurance salesman. "It makes you realize how quickly things can happen. It was definitely serious. It wasn't a matter of someone just feeling weak."

As he mushed away with Austin, Fiedler recalled the history behind the Iditarod. The race was begun in 1973 to commemorate the 1925 diphtheria serum run. Dog teams relayed the life-saving serum to epidemic-devastated Nome.

"I couldn't help but think, that's what this race is supposed to be all about," said Fiedler, "people with dog teams helping other people."

★ ★ ★

Madden's memories of the long night are limited. He remembers Halverson asking, " 'Hey, how are you?' Just checking on me, just to see if I was there. It's all real vague," he said.

There were times the whole world spun and there were moments of lucidity. He remembers thinking, "God, I wish that helicopter would get here."

But he said he never thought he would die.

"I was hurting too much to think that," he said. Nelson, Brazin and Halverson alternated shifts.

"We had been up for such a long time, all of us, that we had to catch some Zs," said Brazin. "Every 10 minutes we'd ask him how he was."

Bernie Willis of Anchorage, another rookie, stopped and helped for a while. But a few mushers passed without asking if anything was wrong, and the rescuers were angry about that.

"The people who didn't stop, or even ask . . . a guy's lying there in three feet of sleeping bags," said Brazin. "We were all sitting around a camp fire shivering to death."

Meanwhile, on the trail, Austin and Fiedler were pushing their dogs. Fiedler had to put one in the sled. It took several hours to mush into Iditarod and they arrived in the middle of the night.

"It was a good excuse for us to move fast, which was more than we have been doing," Austin joked later.

It took time to reach someone on the radio. Then the helicopter went to Grayling to pick up Iditarod volunteer Dr. Dan Stevenson, an Air Force doctor from Fairbanks. Austin climbed on as a trail guide, leaving his dogs in Fiedler's care. The chopper left Iditarod in the dark, searching the trail for the camp. Austin said the helicopter operators told him they hoped he knew what he was doing because they had about 10 minutes worth of spare fuel. Austin got them there.

Stevenson's thermometer worked. Madden was running a temperature of 103.4. Stevenson had trouble getting Madden to understand questions.

"Where are you?" Stevenson asked Madden.

"Twenty-first," said Madden, mentioning his place in the race when he got sick.

"No, where are you?"

"You mean I lost 21st?"

Madden ultimately gave the right answer: on the Iditarod Trail.

The mushers helped lift Madden into the helicopter and watched it fly away. Nelson noticed Austin still there and said, "Oh, no, they forgot you."

Austin wasn't overlooked. He volunteered to mush over the same terrain he had just covered, this time driving Madden's dogs the 30 miles into Iditarod.

In the helicopter, Madden broke into tears. Not tears of relief at being rescued, but tears of frustration at being out of the race.

"I had such a nice team," he said.

Stevenson told the mushers they had done well as amateur physicians and told them it was a good thing they had. Another two hours without help, he said, and Madden might have died.

"When the doctor came and said that another two hours and they might have taken him out in a body bag, that kind of hit home," said Brazin. "We were pretty quiet there for a while."

★ ★ ★

At the hospital, Madden was diagnosed as being hyperthermic, overheated rather than underheated, and suffering from salmonella. No one knows how he got it, but guesses focus on getting contaminated dog food on his hands.

Madden spent one day in Humana and then flew to Nome. Still slightly weak, but upright, he wanted to be there when his rescuers mushed in along the Bering Sea coast. They started coming in Friday night and when Austin crossed the finish-line there was Madden bearing a gin and tonic.

The mushers sacrificed about 18 hours of race time to help Madden and that surely cost one of them rookie-of-the-year honors and perhaps several of them prize money. Austin finished 22nd, less than three hours late for the $3,000 20th-place money and Brazin was nine minutes behind top rookie Richard Self.

If they lost money, they found a special bond.

"The competition was kind of stifled," said Brazin. "It didn't even seem like a race after that."

Madden was grateful the mushers cared more about sportsmanship than dollars.

"I feel real fortunate to have people on the trail like that," he said. "Whether I would have died, I don't know. If I was by myself, maybe yeah."

Instead, he was able to raise a glass to toast them all at the finish line.

The Chase

by Christopher Smith of the Brantford (Ontario) Expositor. Diminutive Canadian soccer players pursue the bouncing ball during action in an early morning game of mini-soccer. These youngsters play on a small field that helps keep the ball in play and enhances action. Copyright ©1989, The Expositor, Brantford.

Sweet Victory

by free-lance photographer Elizabeth Karnazes for United Press International. After Hector (Macho) Camacho had earned a split decision over World Boxing Association lightweight champion Ray (Boom Boom) Mancini in a March bout in Reno, he celebrated by taking a dive into the arms of his adoring fans at ringside. Copyright ©1989, Elizabeth Karnazes.

Last Week's Miracle, This Week's Tragedy

BASEBALL

By *MARK BRADLEY*

"Sports," said the forlorn golfer Mike Reid, "is like life with the volume turned up." A guy could think a hundred years and never come up with a better description than that. If, as Thoreau wrote, the mass of men lead lives of quiet desperation, athletes lead theirs loudly. Sometimes you wish there was a mute button.

Sometimes the news regarding our little games is so grim you wish everybody and everything would just hush. You'd just as soon not know that Ricky Berry killed himself, that Donnie Moore shot himself and his wife, that Stacey Toran got drunk and got dead, that Tim Richmond died in mystery. You'd rather not see a life-affirming story unravel six days after the happy fact; indeed, you wish you *hadn't* seen the clip of Dave Dravecky collapsing on the mound. Those who have won't ever forget it, no matter how hard they try.

Of sports, Mike Reid said: "The friendships are tighter, the laughter is louder and some nights seem a little longer." Likewise, the sorrow cuts deeper. Sports are supposed to be *fun.* When they turn out otherwise, when the good yields to bad, the hurt seems exponential.

This sort of hurt isn't the kind that comes with mere losing; this is about lives wasted, about dreams denied. It's about questions that have no answers. Why does an earnest and decent man like Mike Reid, so near the victory of his life, lose the PGA on the final three holes? Why did Ricky Berry, 24 and healthy and financially independent, pick up a gun and end his life? Why is Dave Dravecky a miracle last week and a tragedy this?

In the afterglow of Dravecky's triumphant return from cancer, Giants manager Roger Craig said: "I've been in the game a long time, but I've never seen anything like this." Tuesday night in Montreal, Craig used almost exactly the same words, only this time his heart weighed two tons. Said the Expos' Hubie Brooks: "I hope I never see anything like it again."

The sight of Dravecky crumpled on the mound was enough to shake even the truest believer. Here was a man who'd heard the most terrifying diagnosis of all—malignant tumor—and had not only lived but had rehabilitated an arm that looked, to use Kevin Mitchell's phrase "like Jaws took a bite out of it." Ten months after surgery, Dravecky beat the Cincinnati Reds in as joyous a game as baseball has ever known. He started again Tuesday, leaving on a stretcher.

Dravecky was throwing a pitch when his humerus snapped. Understand: The humerus is the biggest bone in the upper body, a bone that almost nobody ever breaks. When people break their arm, they invariably break either the radius or the ulna, bones below the elbow. The humerus connects the elbow to the shoulder. In Dravecky's case, the humerus was the bone frozen during his cancer surgery. Likely the surgical removal of the deltoid muscle contributed to the bone breaking, but why now? Why not the first time he tried to throw a ball again? Why not while pitching on rehab assignment in Tucson? Why not in the Cincinnati game? Why now?

Said Bryn Smith, pitching against Dravecky this night: "It looked like his arm could've kept going along with the ball." Hubie Brooks likened the sound to a firecracker. Giants and Expos alike rushed to Dravecky's side, who kept saying: "It's broke." Everyone could see it; nobody believed it. After all the man had been through, how could this *happen?*

"It was like an act of God," Craig said. "But just for him to be out there in the first place was an act of God."

As he was being carried from the field, Dravecky asked another Giant to call his wife Jan, who'd wept unashamedly throughout Dravecky's comeback game. While Dravecky waited to be examined in the training room, he and teammate Bob Knepper, Christians both, said a little prayer. And then, in a moment poignant beyond words, Expos catcher Mike Fitzgerald walked in wearing his gear and, bending low, kissed Dravecky on the cheek.

Said the Expos' Damaso Garcia: "You see this man's courage and it's a dream to see him come back. He has motivated everybody in baseball. I went out there (to the mound) and he was just holding his arm. I was in pain, just being there with him."

Now Dravecky is done for the season, maybe for his career. Far more chilling, one doctor says: "If there are tumor cells around, they could be stimulated by the fracture." You think about that and you shake your head. You wish you could stop thinking about Dave Dravecky, but you can't. This time the volume of sports was as loud as a firecracker, and you wish you'd been wearing earplugs. Some sounds are too sad for human ears.

The Bayonne Bleeder's Bloodiest Brawl

BOXING

By *JOSEPH TINTLE*

No longer can Chuck Wepner come and go as he wishes. Gone are the days of driving fast cars, wearing expensive jewelry, and dating scores of women.

He wakes up when he's told to wake up. He eats when he's told to eat. He goes to bed when he's told to go to bed.

It is the first time in 50 years that anyone has ever told Chuck Wepner what to do.

For the past year-and-a-half, the former world heavyweight contender, who fought Muhammad Ali for the title in 1975 and inspired the film character Rocky Balboa, has been serving a 10-year sentence at Northern State Prison. It is a lonely, sad place that stands near Exit 14 of the New Jersey Turnpike in Newark, where Wepner has been paying the price for possession and conspiracy to distribute cocaine.

Recently, however, he was admitted to Northern State's Intensive Supervision Program, which allows him to live and work outside the prison's walls as long as he adheres to an 8 p.m. curfew and performs community service.

"It's a lot better than sitting in prison," said Wepner, who stands 6-foot-5 and weighs 245 pounds—20 more than his fighting weight. If all goes well, he said, he'll be a free man in 17 months.

As he tries to rebuild his life, Wepner has returned to work as a salesman for his former employer, Majestic Wine & Spirits, in Union, N.J. "But always," he says, "I think about my days in the fight game."

One of Wepner's most painful days in boxing took place a little more than three miles from his home in Bayonne. At the Jersey City

Armory 20 years ago next June, he fought Sonny Liston in one of boxing's bloodiest brawls.

The year was 1970, and Wepner realized that only a win over a top-10 contender could thrust him into the world heavyweight scene. So he signed to fight sixth-ranked Sonny Liston, a frightening hulk whose sinister glare often intimidated opponents before any punches were thrown.

This would not only be an important fight for Wepner, but for Liston as well. The former world heavyweight champion, age 38 (or so he claimed; some estimates ran as high as 46), could not afford another loss. A defeat would end an 18-year boxing career that had peaked eight years earlier with a first-round KO of Floyd Patterson for the heavyweight championship of the world.

After that victory, and a second one-round humiliation of Patterson, the Liston myth took hold, with sportswriters regarding him as one of the ring's heaviest hitters ever. But the infatuation lasted only until he lost title fights to Cassius Clay in 1964 and 1965.

Although no longer a serious contender after his losses to Clay, Liston fought 16 more fights from 1966 through 1970. He won 14 straight before Leotis Martin stopped him in December 1969 in a bout for the vacant NABF title. The loss placed Liston at the crossroads of his career.

At the same time, Wepner was facing his own crossroads. Al Braverman, Wepner's manager, had always arranged his fights. But not this one. Canadian promoter Loren Cassina set it up.

In April 1970, Cassina received a message that Liston wanted to speak with him. They met in a coffee shop at the Bonanza Hotel in Las Vegas. Liston said he wanted another fight, and Cassina suggested Wepner, a stand-up, no-nonsense boxer. Liston agreed and contracts were drawn up. Wepner knew a victory over Liston would assure him of a shot with top-contender Jerry Quarry and a big payday.

(As it would turn out, the bout with Wepner was the last of Liston's career. He died of an apparent drug overdose in December 1970.)

At the Liston-Wepner press conference in Jersey City in June, the fighters were a study in contrast. Liston was bull-shouldered and boorish, with all the personality of an embalmer. Wepner, who stood four inches taller than the 6'1" Liston, was pleasant and glib and acted as if Liston didn't scare him at all.

"All this talk about Liston the cop beater, Liston the jailbird, Liston the tough guy doesn't mean anything to me," he said. "I'm from Missouri. Sonny's going to have to show me how tough he is."

Then a writer asked the former champion what he'd do to Wepner. Liston's forehead wrinkled as he flashed his infamous stare. "The outcome," he said, "is gonna be bleak. I'm gonna open Wepner's face."

Which is what happened a week later when the opening bell

clanged on June 29.

Wepner fought a stupid fight from the outset. Against Braverman's wishes, he traded punches with Liston. But that was Wepner, always forsaking defense. A few of his punches grazed the slow-moving Liston. Midway through round two, Liston began jabbing at Wepner's face, twisting his glove to the right or to the left upon impact. During one exchange, Liston broke Wepner's nose. But Wepner landed a few rights that staggered Liston. After that, Liston dominated.

Before round three, Braverman exhorted his fighter to box defensively. "The big ape's got an 84-inch reach to your 78-inch reach," he said. "Does that tell ya something?"

"Yeah," Wepner said with a smile, "it means I'm in for a long night."

Braverman, whose sense of humor vanishes in the ring, slapped Wepner across the face and pulled his hair. "No, dummy," he said, "it means ya gotta back off once in a while or else he's gonna eatcha up."

But Wepner never took a step back. In his mind, to step back indicated weakness. He had never done it before and he sure as hell wasn't going to change now. So Liston easily pressed his advantage. He thundered uppercuts against Wepner's chin, and during rounds three, four, and five, his jab opened gashes above Wepner's eyes.

"Jab after jab after jab," Wepner recalled. "They kept coming like the monthly bills." In the fifth, Wepner slipped to the canvas after absorbing a right to the midsection. It was ruled a knockdown.

By round six, rivulets of blood were blinding Wepner. For the rest of the fight, all he could see was Liston's outline against the hot glare of the overhead lights. And all he could feel was the pounding of a left jab tearing his face apart, just as Liston had predicted.

The ringside physician, Dr. Reginald Ferrar, tried to examine Wepner after the third round and the sixth, but Abe Greene, the New Jersey boxing commissioner, restrained him. Earlier that day, Wepner had told Greene about his concern that the fight might be stopped prematurely because of his excessive bleeding. "They don't call me the 'Bayonne Bleeder' for nothing," Wepner said.

The commissioner understood. "This was Chuck's biggest fight of his career up until then," Greene said several years after the bout, "and he didn't want a soft-hearted referee or doctor to stop it early. So I got together with referee Barney Felix and Dr. Ferrar and emphasized that bleeding didn't mean a thing to Chuck. I reminded them to note this fact. I had an understanding with them that if the fight became a bad-looking sight, we'd stop it. But only after I gave Barney the signal to do so."

The fight dragged on. In round seven, a left-right combination broke Wepner's cheekbone and he tottered across the ring. How he bore the pain is beyond comprehension. Even Liston was puzzled. "Fall down, man," he pleaded during a clinch in a rare moment of compassion.

Liston then dug a left and a right to Wepner's body. In the eighth, he fired a jab to reopen the gashes over Wepner's eyes, and streams of blood squirted halfway across the ring. Wepner's left eyebrow, soaked with blood, dangled lifelessly as he headed back to his corner. Cries of "butchery" and "murder" rang out, but the fight continued.

"All I can remember about that round," Wepner said, "is that every time I got bashed, I kept seeing the words, BOOM, THWACK, and CRUNCH appearing wherever Liston's fists struck. Just like in the old "Batman" TV show."

By round nine, blood was still pooling in Wepner's eyes. Braverman had tried to patch him up between rounds, but it was impossible to treat six cuts at once. And now Wepner had no idea where Liston was. He punched only at the air while Liston zeroed in with his incessant jab and followed with hooks.

At the bell ending the ninth, Braverman led his battered boxer to their corner. Before the fight, Braverman's shirt had been navy blue. Now it was scarlet, completely soaked with sticky, pasty blood. "Liston might've driven all the blood out of you," Braverman said, "but he sure hasn't driven out your heart."

Meanwhile, Felix stared at Wepner. What he saw was a clump of caked blood blocking Wepner's nasal passage, making it difficult for him to breathe. Slowly, Wepner sucked in puffs of air through lips that had been split by Liston's jabs. Strains of pain showed in a face that was a bleeding, chopped up pulp, made uneven by bumps, bruises, and cuts.

Felix then looked to Greene, hoping to get the signal to stop the fight. He got it.

But as he was about to wave his hands, Braverman exploded. "Don't you dare stop it!" he said. "What the hell's the matter with you? One more round, that's all, one more round. Chuck's gotta go the distance." Wepner sat quietly, unable to see through swollen eyes.

"How many fingers am I holding up?" Felix said to him.

"How many guesses do I get?" Wepner responded.

That was it. Felix waved his hands. The bout had ended, Liston winning by 10th-round TKO.

In the words of the *New York Times'* Dave Anderson, the fight was "a bloody sacrifice that evoked more sympathy for the loser than prestige for the winner."

Wepner would require 75 stitches to patch up a two-inch slice under his left eye, a three-inch gash over the left eye where there was once an eyebrow, a nick in the corner of the eye near the nose, a 2½-inch gash over the right eye, a two-inch cut extending from the forehead to the eyebrow, and a slight tear under the eye.

In his dressing room, Wepner sat bloodied, battered, and bruised.

"Jeezus," said his father Charley, a former fighter. "Will you look at him. It looks like someone went to the butcher shop, pulled out the reddest hunk of meat, cut it open, and let the blood fly out."

Meanwhile, Wepner calmly fielded reporters' questions. Even the silliest ones.

"Was this your toughest fight?" someone said.

"No," he said, adjusting an ice pack on his face. "I think I escaped relatively unscathed thanks to my scientific boxing techniques."

The reporter pressed on. "Did you block any of his punches?"

"All of them—with my face."

"Hey," Braverman said, "if you guys don't ask some intelligent questions, I'm gonna clear the room."

"Weren't you afraid of Liston's power coming into the fight?"

"Nah, I'm from Missouri. You gotta show me. Unfortunately, Sonny did."

As the reporters dispersed, well-wishers came in to console Wepner. One of them was Sonny Liston. He gripped Wepner's still-bandaged hand and said, "Man, I ain't never done this before. But I gotta tell ya that you're the gamest guy I ever fought."

As Liston was walking away, a reporter asked him if Chuck Wepner was the bravest man he'd ever known.

"No," Liston answered, "his manager is."

Lamarr Mondane: Uncovering the Legend

BASKETBALL

By *JEFF RUDE*

You talk about playground legends, you got to bring up a guy named Lamarr Mondane. I've seen him just rain jump shots on people—4, 5, 6 shots in a row. . . .

Danny Ainge had heard the advertisements on radio, had seen the 30-second spots on television, and was taken by the name and style. *Lamarr Mondane.* Gunner.

Using a felt-tipped pen, Ainge wrote the name on his Boston Celtics practice jersey last spring. "That's the guy I wanted to be," he said. Then he went out and acted the part.

"I'd yell 'Layup' or 'Money' when I'd shoot a 15-footer in practice," Ainge said. "All the guys on the team would call me Lamarr Mondane. When I'd shoot a crazy shot, to everyone else I was Lamarr. Lamarr was the wild side of Danny."

Ainge, nearing the National Basketball Association record for Mondane-ish three-point baskets, carried on like that for a few weeks. Then came what he called a "shock." Danny Crawford, the NBA referee from Chicago, had read about Ainge's routine and broke him the news about his alter ego:

Lamarr Mondane is no fictitious character, no Madison Avenue creation used to shill for Yuppie basketball shoes in a TV commercial. He is genuine, a long-range shooter from Chicago's West Side, from Marshall High, from Malcolm X Junior College, from Northeastern Illinois University, from Chicago's best playground games, and now from various city leagues in which, at 36, he still rains jumpers.

"I hadn't even thought that he might be a real person," said Ainge, hardly alone in his ignorance.

Wanting to witness, Ainge requested a meeting. Soon after, at a Bulls-Celtics game in Chicago, Ainge met Mondane. It was at halftime, during the Celtics' shootaround, that they were introduced. They shook hands, they chatted. Moments later, during the second half, Ainge would launch a three-pointer and hear teammate Robert Parish exclaim at him as they ran down the Chicago Stadium court: *"La-marr Mon-dane!"*

For the real Mondane, a downtown security officer by day, the evening was far-out as well. He watched the game from the stands with longtime friend Bernie Washington, the Chicago advertising executive who fathered the popular "Money" commercial. Afterward, Mondane visited the Celtics' locker room, where Ainge showed him off to other players. "Nice guy, that Lamarr Mondane," Ainge would say later. "He must have thanked me 15 or 20 times for the tickets I got him."

But *real* nice guys finish fantasies sometimes. When this season started, Ainge, feeling he had lost claim to his newfangled identity, surrendered the Mondane act and went back to being himself.

. . . People just started to call him "Money." 'Cause when he shot, it was money in the bank. . . .

★ ★ ★

Dangling from the chain around Lamarr Mondane's neck is a pendant that spells "Money." People started calling him that in high school, back when his 5-foot-9 frame carried about 155 pounds, 20 fewer than today. The name took hold in the '70s when, without a three-point semicircle to inflate his 30-point average, he led the country's junior colleges in scoring.

"When the game was on the line, everybody called him 'Money,' " said Doug DeVincent, for whom Mondane averaged 21.4 points from 1976-78 at Northeastern, an NAIA school on the North Side.

Skip Dillard, who later fashioned the same nickname, used to go watch Mondane play. Mark Aguirre, Bob Love, Rickey Green, Sonny Parker, Mickey Johnson and the like competed against him on asphalt and wood. Isiah Thomas looked up to him on Saturday mornings at Columbus Park. If the subculture of inner-city ball was your thing, you knew of Lamarr Mondane.

"He was always the top pick in our games," said Thomas, the Detroit Pistons guard. "He would pass it, but you'd pass it back because his J was better. I don't remember calling him 'Money', but people did call out 'Layup' when he pulled up from the top of the key."

A basket from the top of the key is worth three points in high school and college these days, but only two when Mondane was in school. The significance of the rule change isn't lost on the men he played for and with. "He would have averaged 40, easy," said John Sampson, a Northeastern teammate.

"If we would have had a three-point line then . . . Lamarr would have been at half-court taking shots," said DeVincent. He didn't specify whether that would have been good or bad. "A great shooter" is what he did say, Mondane's two-season shooting percentages of 40.0 and 40.8 notwithstanding.

Mondane has taken his shot all over town. West Side, South Side, North Side, the suburbs. Inside, out. Margate Park, Hamlin Park, the Broadway Armory. The Niles Center last winter. On Saturdays, the Lawson YMCA. Just the other week, even highbrow Winnetka. But you won't find him on pavement as much anymore. "The knees and joints can't take it," he says.

Mondane's lifestyle and personality belie his on-court extravagance. He's apt to drink orange juice after games. He lives in a two-bedroom apartment on the North Side with his mother and sister. He says no to alcohol, tobacco and drugs. And he will tell you he has "never" considered himself a playground legend.

But then came the stories.

• Foster Park, Evanston, early '80s. Mondane shows up three minutes into the game, his team, the Washington Stars, ahead by about eight. "I remember going in in the second quarter, hitting seven three-pointers in a row, missing one, then hitting five more threes," he says. "Then I sat down the rest of the game. I didn't want to press my luck."

• Cabrini-Green, final of the city's "toughest" outdoor summer tournament, mid-80s, 1,500 people watching. "We were down 17 at the half, and then Lamarr went crazy," said Bernie Washington, the ad executive, the coach of the Stars. "He would cross half-court, start shaking like he was going to make a move to the basket, and then pull up. His first shot, three. His second shot, three. His third shot, three. He just paralyzed the other team." And won.

A prevailing theory in the asphalt jungles is that hundreds of playground regulars are better than some NBA players. The breaks just didn't come, for whatever reasons. Grades, timing, reputation. One of Chicago's hottest shots, legend has it, didn't enhance his chances when he pulled a gun on Bob Love during a summer league game years ago.

In Mondane's case, his 5-9 height was a shortcoming. His defense and grades were too, some say. Even so, Mondane remembers someone who "claimed to be a scout" inviting him to the Cleveland Cavaliers' camp years ago. But nothing materialized. And Ed Badger recalls having arranged for Mondane "sight unseen," to try out for the Bulls in 1978 when he was the team's coach. But that opportunity was dismissed when Badger was.

. . . He'd come down and shoot a 15-footer, everybody on the side be hollering, "Layup." . . .

★ ★ ★

On Saturdays at the Lawson Y, they tend to stare at Lamarr Mondane. "Once I get rolling," he says, "people on the sidelines will be cracking up, saying 'Money,' yelling out 'Layup' like in the commercial."

The commercial has given rebirth to his legend, introduced him to a mass audience. And like Ainge, people outside his circle have thought Lamarr Mondane mythical. Even Harvey Hartenstein, Mondane's varsity coach at Marshall, was fooled. "Is that him? I just assumed that it wasn't the same kid."

The eighth-graders John Sampson coaches at St. Matthias Catholic School were skeptical when Sampson told them Mondane was his friend. Until Mondane showed up one day. "When I walked into the gym, their eyes got bigger than silver dollars," he said. "They were touching me to make sure I was real."

Said Sampson: "I noticed a lot of kids were saying 'Money' when they shot."

This Mondane mania is growing. "I've been in gyms when people shoot jump shots and call themselves Lamarr Mondane," he says. "And they didn't know me."

When South Shore's McGlother Irvin rained in three straight three-pointers during a Public League quarterfinal against Marshall this year, fans shouted, "Money . . . That's it, Lamarr." Just the other day, in a white-collar two-on-two game outdoors at downtown Presidential Towers, one participant yelled "Mondane brings rain" as he shot.

Mondane also brings stares and questions. In a tournament this winter in Niles, an opponent asked him after a game, "Do you ever get called Lamarr? You look just like the guy in the commercial."

"I should," Mondane said. "Because I am."

The man excitedly ran across the gym, returned with his children and gushed: "This is him! This is him!"

. . . Slam dunks are tough, but when a 35-footer come raining out of the sky, it'll wire you up. . . .

★ ★ ★

The book on Mondane is that he's as proficient making 25-footers as 2-footers. "The reason he used to shoot long jump shots is because he couldn't make layups," said Crawford, the NBA ref, who grew up with Mondane and preceded him in the Northeastern record book. "He had unmolested layups a few times and missed. But he'd shake and bake and hit from 35 feet."

"I heard in his younger days he would shoot as soon as he crossed half-court," said DeVincent, his Northeastern coach. "For me, he would shoot from 30. He could shoot from 40. But he didn't do that all the time because he would have been sitting next to me."

Mondane sobers such talk, saying his range is 20 to 25. Whatever, just as striking is how high he jumps when shooting. Sampson, for one, says Mondane could touch the top of the box on the backboard.

. . . Make you holler, "Money . . . Money."

★ ★ ★

The commercial was filmed on a New York playground from dawn till dusk one cold March day last year. That's a lot of shooting

—for cameraman and legend.

"I got tired at the end," Mondane said. Of shooting? "Oh, no. Not tired of shooting."

Mondane estimated the wind-chill factor at 5 to 10 degrees. The wind was blowing the ball all over. Not a shooter's day, so he adjusted. "He just had to move in from 40 feet to 30 feet," said Washington, the ad exec.

The "Money" commercial was Washington's brainchild. He wrote the scripts. He conceived a Legends marketing campaign and sold it to Reebok International. Two spots have been added, one called "Showtime," based loosely on Chicago's Billy Harris, and "Wizard," written with Chicago's Ralph "The Rocket" Walker in mind. But unlike Mondane, neither Harris nor Walker appears or is mentioned.

"Money's" money from the project is unclear. Mondane said he has received about $4,000, that he gets residual checks every 13 weeks. But John Morgan, Reebok's basketball marketing chief, countered: "It was a one-time buyout with him."

What's more, Reebok soon will sell basketball shoes called Money, Showtime and Wizard—and Mondane will not be cut in on the profits, Morgan said.

"Fictional—that's the way we kind of like to keep it," Morgan said. "There's a player called 'Money' in every big city."

Perhaps. But there is only one Lamarr Mondane. As Danny Ainge well knows.

Rooted in Tradition: The Raiders' Art Shell

PRO FOOTBALL

By *RON BORGES*

From the Boston Globe

Howie Long can still recall the first time he laid eyes on Art Shell, but, in case he ever forgets, he only has to rub his hand across his cheek for a reminder.

"I was a rookie with the Raiders," Long recalled. "We only had one day of pit drill (where defensive linemen battle offensive linemen with a back running behind them. It is hand-to-hand combat of the most primordial variety).

"I was working against the second unit. All of a sudden Earl (Leggett, the Raiders defensive line coach at the time) told me to get in there. I looked up and, man, there was this guy who weighed about 400 pounds staring at me.

"Art came off the ball and hit me like I'd never been hit before. He drove both his fists into my chest and knocked the wind out of me. He slammed his helmet into my face and drove my face mask back into my head until it split my cheek. I didn't do too well."

When Art Shell, who now serves as Long's boss since becoming the first black coach in the Silver and Black's history (as well as the first in the past 64 years of the NFL), is asked about this he smiles a bit, takes a moment to shuffle through the pages of his life, then remembers.

"Earl came to me and said he had this young kid he thought was pretty good," Shell said. "He wanted me to test him. He told me to give him my best shot. I did. Howie stood the test."

It is just like Shell to come to that conclusion. He does not mention the air flying out of Howie Long's lungs or the look on his face as his mask caved in around him. He doesn't even hint about the split cheek.

"He stood the test," is what Shell recalls, making scant mention of his own performance. Long, now an All-Pro defensive end, is not surprised to hear this.

"Art isn't the kind of guy who's boisterous," Long said. "I stood the test all right . . . if you call staggering back to the ball standing. Art had the hardest head butt ever. Of course, he'd never tell you about it."

He'd rather use it instead. Then, if you chose to, he'd let you tell someone about it.

Perhaps that attitude, as much as anything, explains how Shell has managed to right what appeared to be a sinking Raider ship this season, one that had fallen to 1-3 and was taking on water faster than the Three Stooges' dory under the leadership of former coach Mike Shanahan.

Shanahan is a brilliant football mind. To a man, the Raiders concede that. But he is an Xs-and-Os kind of guy, a strategist, a manipulator of his troops, and like many such tacticians he is not, shall we say, a people person.

"He wanted us to wear our uniform jerseys to Stacey's funeral," one Raider claimed. (Stacey Toran, a safety, died in an auto accident this season.) "He said some guys didn't have suits and some guys did and this way we'd look like a team. The veterans had to go talk him out of it. Geesh!"

The Raiders have always been a team, but only in the loosest and truest senses of the word. They are a team on Sundays or whenever you happen to want to play them. And they are a team whenever the outside world tries to intrude on them.

Otherwise, they do what they want, go where they want, wear what they want, say what they want. They are a team in the sense of an Art Shell, one that seldom intrudes except when it counts. Shanahan, the first head coach to be hired from outside the Raider family, could never quite grasp that.

"Mike is a brilliant guy," Long said. "His problem was a philosophical thing. When Art came in he took the lid off the teapot. It was boiling and some steam needed to be let off. The boys needed to run free."

So Shell let them, but that alone has not caused the Raiders' reversal from a 1-3 start to 5-6 status with a outside shot at the playoffs. No, there was a bigger problem with the Shanahan regime than ill-advised rules like no sunflower seeds in the locker room, assigned seats at meetings and, heaven forbid, no sitting on your helmet during practice, although their existence was bad enough.

Shanahan never could fathom that helmet sitting, for example, was a Raider sideline tradition that carried with it mythic connotations. The technique of how to balance your bum on a football placed for comfort on top of your helmet was passed down from generation to generation. It was as tricky as the Raiders got and it was a TRADITION not to be trod on lightly.

"Art got us back to the things that really matter," said cornerback Mike Haynes. "Sitting on your helmet has nothing to do with winning games.

"Art changed the environment. He understands what it means to play Raider football. Mike really didn't."

That was the real problem, of course, because the Raiders have never made much of Xs and Os. They are into bruises and abrasions, always playing football the way the game was intended to be played.

Always have. And, with the exception of 20 games under Shanahan in which they lost 12, always will.

"The only way I know to win is power, toughness and explosion," Shell said. "A great team has to have those qualities. We had to get that back.

"Mike believes in finesse football and the short passing game. We believe in power football and throwing deep. We're going to attack on offense."

Shanahan tried to make the Raiders a scheme team rather than a mean team. He seemed to feel coaches won more games than players, and in some towns maybe that's true. But the Raiders are different, a point managing general partner Al Davis drove home by telling Shanahan to drive home to Denver a month into the season after deciding to put a Raider back in charge.

There was historic import in all this because Shell also happened to be the first black head coach in the NFL's modern era, but to Davis and Shell what was important was not that he was black, but that he was silver and black.

"My job is to create a winning atmosphere," Shell said. "The Raiders attitude is about relaxation. I don't want them walking out on the field like they're standing at attention.

"I know I have to win. If I can't, I set myself up to be the first black head coach fired. But that pressure has to be on the coaches, not the players.

"The losing was very tough for me. I know what this organization is about. I grew up in a winning tradition with this organization. I'm proud of being the first black coach, but after we won our second game no one mentioned black. That's progress."

So was winning. And hitting.

"We're playing beat 'em up football again," said assistant coach Terry Robiskie, who once ran behind Shell's blocks. "We're not trying to trick anybody now. It's the bloody nose effect."

By bloodying people's noses . . . and occasionally caving in their face masks . . . Shell's Raiders won three straight and four of their first six. While he would be the first to admit this team is not yet a brother to the Raiders of old, at least now he can see it's kin.

So when he speaks to the players in these early days of his tenure as guardians of the Silver and Black it is not on the evils of sunflower seeds or helmet sitting. Rather, it is to drum home the story of TRADITION.

"I tell them about the players we had," Shell said. "Sometimes I get to telling stories and I get carried away, but I've asked the veterans if I'm going overboard and they said they enjoy learning about the TRADITION.

"I tell them about Jack Tatum's hits and Snake (Ken Stabler) sticking his head in the huddle with a minute to go, saying, 'Boys, let's win it and go home happy.' Once I told them about Dan Birdwell. He was an old veteran linebacker when I got here and one day he sat me down and said, 'Arthur, you gotta play this game like the guy across from you just hit your Mom with a 2x4 and you're there watching.' That's the Raider TRADITION.

"When I start, I tell 'em 'we're going back into the Twilight Zone,' but it's really more like sitting around the campfire telling stories."

Just like back home in Charleston, S.C., where Art Shell first learned about family and TRADITION.

★ ★ ★

Shell grew up quiet and happy in the Daniel Jenkins Projects in a house sandwiched between a sulphur mill and a fertilizer plant. At night the air was odoriferous, to be polite about it.

As the eldest of five, he shouldered much responsibility and did it quietly, spending many hours listening to his sickly mother, Gertrude, tell him stories.

"She liked to talk and I liked to listen," he says. "I had a good childhood."

But childhood came to an end at 15 when his mother died at 35, victim of a heart attack while her eldest son was playing in the front yard.

Art Shell remembers many private moments from those days, but what he chooses to recall publicly is his father calling the family together after the funeral and promising one thing.

"He said he'd keep us together," Shell said. "He told us family was the most important thing."

And so it has remained with the Shell family and the Raider family, even when his playing career was coming to a close. Although his skills had diminished from the days when he was an eight-time All-Pro and perhaps the finest tackle ever to dent someone's face mask, family always came first.

"My last year (1983) I wanted to retire the second day of training camp," Shell recalled. "I'd done it all in so many big games. I was happy with my career. I didn't want to just hang on.

"I couldn't do the things I wanted any more, so after the morning practice I went to Tom (Flores, then Raider coach) and told him it was time for somebody else to step in. He asked me to stay in case Bruce Davis wasn't ready.

"You don't want to embarrass yourself. You don't want to embarrass the organization. You don't want to embarrass your family. But I couldn't leave the organization hanging. I stayed."

He would do the same five years later when, by now a veteran Raider assistant, Shell was faced with the opposite situation.

Shanahan was in the midst of his first season as coach, a losing year of transition in which he was trying to rework the Raiders in the image of the Denver Broncos. Al Davis (known to most simply as The Boss) didn't like it. Art Shell didn't particularly like it, either, especially the losing part.

So he spoke up.

"I thought we didn't have the players on the field to win," Shell recalled. "I just made a statement to Nick Nicolau (a new Raider assistant Shanahan brought with him from Denver) about why a certain individual wasn't in the game. He took exception to it."

Actually, he did a bit more. He reddened Shell's cheeks by responding, "Why don't you just leave? Mike doesn't want you here."

Shell was stunned. He was angry. He was insulted. But, most of all, he was in control of himself. As always.

"Who the hell is Nick Nicolau to make that kind of statement?" Shell says now. "Sure, I was shocked. I thought we were working TOGETHER. I thought I knew him better. But I'm glad I didn't do anything because it would have reflected badly on the organization. I think I responded in the correct fashion.

"When I got home, I have to admit, I kicked myself in the butt a few times for not choking him, but I knew only one guy ran this organization. For a guy like Nicolau to tell me to leave, well, forget it. Only one guy could do that—Al Davis.

"Around here, you've got to understand who the boss is. If you understand that, it makes things easier. You'd have thought they'd have known."

They, of course, were the outsiders. They were the people who are gone now. They were Shanahan and Nicolau and the others Shanahan brought from Denver. They didn't know Al Davis was The Boss. They didn't know about The Family and how Shell and Willie Brown (whom Shanahan fired and Davis rehired as his aide) and Joe Scannella and Tom Walsh (two assistants Shanahan also tried to fire only to have Davis tell them to keep working) were part of The Family. If you are really smart, you don't mess with The Family.

They didn't know that, so they're gone. And Art Shell is here, quietly running the show.

★ ★ ★

Not even being an All-State football and basketball player was enough back in the early 1960s to help a quiet boy named Art Shell find a outlet for his athletic talents.

The big Southern schools had not yet accepted the idea that you could win more games using black athletes than by ignoring them. And neither had most other big-time colleges outside the Big 10. So Shell decided to let the Big 10 know about a big guy from Charleston.

"I wrote Woody Hayes a letter at Ohio State," Shell said, chuckling at the recollection. "I did it in my senior typing class. I kept it in an envelope, but I never mailed it. Who knows what might have happened if I had?"

Nobody does, but anyone who knows Shell knows it would have been out of character to have sent it because such a letter would involve blowing one's own horn. Regardless of how softly the notes came out, that is something he simply cannot do.

Instead, he does the work, as he did at the University of Maryland-Eastern Shore, and hopes others blow his horn.

It is why, 30 years later, he never thought to mention that Jesse Jackson called to chat after Shell was named head coach on October 3, yet he willingly spoke of Art Jr. telling him how proud he was to call himself Art Shell's son and how it had overwhelmed him to hear those words for he felt the same about his own father, who had died of a stroke 10 months too soon to see his offspring make history.

On the morning of January 24, Shell learned he had made the Pro Football Hall of Fame, joining his best friend and old Raider blocking mate, Gene Upshaw, in Canton, O. In football terms, at least, he was immortal.

But less than 30 minutes later, immortality dissolved when his sister, Eartha, called and told him their father had suffered a stroke. He would die less than a hour before Shell's plane landed in Charleston.

When Shell arrived at the hospital, he walked into his father's room and sat with him, two men alone, the child now a man trying to explain himself to a father now gone.

During the weekend of his Hall of Fame induction last summer, Shell huddled often with his family and the talk was often about his father and mother. It left a man of 300 pounds in tears because what was more important than family?

"This has been a difficult year," Shell says today. "Some things have been great. The Hall of Fame. Becoming a head coach in the NFL. Some have been difficult. I miss my dad, but I know he's proud of me."

Anyone wearing silver and black would tell the old man he has good reason to be.

Anybody's Ball

by Tracy Baker of United Press International. Boston Celtics Robert Parish (left) and Dennis Johnson (right) reach for a loose ball, but Detroit's Adrian Dantley appears to have the advantage during a National Basketball Association game played in Detroit. Copyright ©1989, Tracy Baker/UPI.

The Big Splash

by Billy Weeks of the Chattanooga Times. Mud volleyball may not appeal to everyone, but it does have some supporters on the University of Tennessee-Chattanooga campus. This student made a real splash after a winning point during an intramural competition. Copyright ©1989, Billy Weeks.

Knowing Billy Was a Privilege

BASEBALL

By *BRUCE JENKINS*

From the San Francisco Chronicle

It takes 10 years to become eligible to vote for the baseball Hall of Fame, and my first ballot arrived the other day. With the privilege finally at my disposal, I was ready to cast my support for Joe Morgan, Jim Palmer, Bill Mazeroski, maybe a couple of others.

Yesterday morning, I felt like tearing up the original and submitting just one name: Billy Martin. It was a fleeting notion, based more on emotion than good sense, but as I remembered my many encounters with Billy over the years, it seemed terribly appropriate.

A lot of sportswriters are finding it difficult to praise Martin now that he's gone, because it would represent the height of hypocrisy. Whether it was his drinking, his dealings with the press, his handling of pitchers, or a series of private comments that bordered on racism, there was always plenty of ammunition for the anti-Billy crowd.

Maybe I've got a screw loose, but I always found myself defending Billy Martin. He reminded me greatly of Al Davis, Bobby Knight and Frank Sinatra, with whom my father, Gordon Jenkins, had extensive dealings in the music business. They were complete and utter louts on the surface, among the very nastiest human beings on the planet, but as I got a little bit closer, I discovered a wonderful sort of mad genius in all of them, from their staggering acts of humanitarianism to their priceless sense of humor. I always felt if we lost any of them, the world would never quite recover.

Now we've lost Billy. If you didn't have any use for the man, you can bail out now. Surely there's a list of Billy's Top 10 Fights that you can have some fun with. But I'm remembering him just as I knew him—one of the fondest acquaintances and greatest talents I've ever known in sports. If you're talking about the combination of personality and true contribution to the game, he's in the company of Ruth, Cobb, Stengel, McGraw—the real heavyweights.

★ ★ ★

It was nice to hear Bobby Brown, the American League president, make mention of Martin's playing ability. They were teammates on the great Yankee clubs of the early '50s, and Brown was always amazed by Billy's ability in the clutch. Over five World Series, he hit .333 in 99 at-bats, with five homers and 19 RBIs. He made that unforgettable, lunging catch in Game 7 of the 1952 Series, racing in from second base to catch Jackie Robinson's pop-up and save a 4-2 victory. He flat-out won the 1953 Series, ending it with a ninth-inning single to center off Clem Labine in Game 6.

And there was a line in Martin's playing record that will always stand out. It was the 1947 season in Phoenix, then a member of the Arizona-Texas League. Billy hit .392 in 130 games that year, with 230 hits and 48 doubles, and somehow, with the handicap of just nine home runs, he drove in 174 runs. That's some serious ball.

As a manager, he just might have been the greatest ever. Mack, McCarthy, Stengel, Huggins and McGraw won with superior talent, more often than not. Billy won with dirt, with cheap imitations. "If you notice, he never had one particular style," Earl Weaver once said, "Look at the teams he had in Minnesota, Detroit, Texas, New York and Oakland. They all played with different styles. Whatever it took. Billy always looks at his talent first, then manages accordingly."

Of the 10 seasons I spent on the baseball beat, the two with Martin (1981-82 A's) were by far the best. Billy had a pathetic infield and a nonexistent bullpen in that '81 strike year, yet he took Oakland into the playoffs, and it was no fluke. Many have claimed that Martin "burned out" that starting rotation of Mike Norris, Steve McCatty, Rick Langford, Matt Keough, and Brian Kingman, but those critics didn't spend enough time at the ballpark. They didn't watch Martin day-to-day, how he lifted those men to the height of baseball glory. To this day, none of them rip Billy, and neither do the writers who covered his teams elsewhere. They saw a true genius at work, and when you have that privilege, you don't sit around wielding your nerd wand. You appreciate every single minute of it.

Billy simply outthought everybody else. There was that classic night in Seattle, when manager Maury Wills tried to have the batter's box moved up a couple of inches. Langford was pitching that night, and Wills figured, what the heck, let's bribe the groundskeepers into a little creative drawing. Let's get to that Langford sinker before it drops out of sight.

The problem was, Martin saw the whole thing. He stood there in the dugout, arms folded, watching Wills' scheme unfold. Who else would have done this? Who else would have noticed? Billy noticed. And he waited until the perfect time—the pregame exchange of lineup cards—to bust Wills in a massive way.

★ ★ ★

The height of Martin's glory with the A's came in the so-called "mini-playoffs" in the fall of '81. I can still see Billy in the hotel bar at Kansas City, downing a few beers *before* one of the games, regaling the national press with tales of the A's superiority. Then they went out and won. I could never find fault with Billy's behavior that day. He was in his element. It was absolutely fine.

Martin's unraveling in the 1982 season was painful to watch, but for me, one story always sticks out. On the A's last road trip, Billy spent an afternoon with Mickey Mantle before the final game of a series with the Rangers in Arlington. They probably had a drink or two. Billy showed up late, just minutes before the game, and discovered that Jackie Moore (then a coach) had pulled the A's off the field during batting practice. The players had lost all discipline in Martin's absence, acting like a bunch of kids with a substitute teacher, and the scene got pretty ugly.

With tight newspaper budgets in effect, the *Oakland Tribune* was the only paper covering that series. Kit Stier, the respected beat writer and a stand-up guy, had a strong suspicion of the Mantle connection, but wrote only what he'd seen at the ballpark.

I showed up for the season-ending series in Kansas City, and when I visited Martin in his office before the opener, he'd just finished reading the *Tribune* story. He took one look at Stier and unleashed one of the most vicious verbal tirades I've ever heard, absolutely savaging him in front of the team. He banned Stier from all future team buses, team flights, everything, and the language he used was unspeakably hideous. This lasted a full two minutes, leaving everyone in shock.

★ ★ ★

A bit later, I found myself alone with Billy in the visiting dugout. Well, it's just the two of us, I thought, and Billy's stark-raving mad. Maybe he'll give me a nice little story. The thing was, though, Billy liked Kit. "Go get him, will you?" he asked me. "Tell him I'd like to apologize."

That was Billy Martin. When you got right down to it, if he respected you, he'd do anything for you. He did it for Kit Stier, for me, for his friends, umpires, people in need. He was the greatest terrible man on earth, and now even George Steinbrenner can't bring him back. I find that just depressing as hell.

The Mouth That Roars

COLLEGE BASKETBALL

By *DAVE DYE*

Right there . . . freeze it!

You can't be serious. Four days with Dick Vitale?

And live to write about it?

Sounds like an M & M'er . . . a marathon with the maniac.

You'll have to give some VT, baby . . . more Vacation Time.

Here's the itinerary: Catch up with the Mouth of College Basketball on a Sunday afternoon in West Lafayette, Ind., for Michigan-Purdue (ABC), drive to Bloomington immediately afterward for Monday's Indiana-Iowa game (ESPN), then fly to Syracuse, N.Y., on Tuesday, and finish it off Wednesday night with the Orangemen facing Villanova (ESPN).

Three games in four days with the self-proclaimed "one-eyed wacko."

There must be some type of special insurance for this.

Pack the bags and put some cotton in the ears. We're gonna be rockin' 'n' rollin' on the road with the Dickie V. show.

★ ★ ★

Sunday, January 29, West Lafayette, Ind.: It's about 6 p.m., a few minutes after the Wolverines had put away Purdue, 99-88. NC (no contest).

Vitale hustles so he'll get to Indianapolis for a radio show, but the moment he takes off his headset, he's swarmed for autographs. It happens everywhere he goes nowadays.

Though frequently ripped by television critics, Vitale seems to be the people's choice.

"I couldn't stand him before," says Todd Barrett, a 26-year-old basketball junkie from East Lansing. "He got on my nerves. But he knows the game so well, I've gotten to the point I can put up with some of his stupid stuff."

The "stupid stuff" is part of Vitale's shtick. When a game becomes a rout, he's been known to say something as corny as, "See ya later, alligator . . . in a while, crocodile."

He's the king of abbreviations—"Get a TO, Mr. Knight. Get a TO, baby. Get a timeout, Mr. Knight. Doesn't want the timeout. He can be stubborn. But he's going to the Hall of Fame, and I'm going to Zeroland."

And he's a mad man for dunking descriptions—"Dipsy-do dunkaroo . . . Slam bam jam."

The routine is working. He's a celebrity at every gym he walks into. His notoriety has swelled even more since "Vitale," his autobiography, hit the book stands. It's currently in the top five of best-selling sports books.

"I'm flattered by all that stuff," says Vitale, 49. "It blows my mind. It's still new to me, but I can't understand why some guys don't like the attention. I love it. It's a beautiful feeling to see people get that excited.

"It's fantasy land to think you could have a book. I know this will come to an end, maybe soon. It's been 10 years now, and that's just the way it is. I'll have to be ready to move on. But I'm going to have a lot of fun and enjoy while it's here."

With such popularity has come increasing demands on his time. In every city, Vitale gets swamped with interview requests from radio, TV and newspapers. He checks into a hotel and picks up a stack of messages. Everyone wants his opinion.

Vitale *is* college basketball.

"Bigger than the game," says ESPN partner Tim Brando.

An appealing candor has turned Vitale into the perfect authority for college basketball writers and talk-show hosts.

"I haven't cut back to this point, but I think I'm going to have to," he says. "Saying no really bothers me. I never thought I'd have to, but now I do.

"It's gotten out of hand. What's happened is I'm very easy with my phone number, I'm very easy with my availability, and I like doing it."

The trade-off for this new fame, he's finding out, is some stabs in the back. Vitale struggles to handle such attacks, even from people he knows are simply jealous of his success.

"One thing you worry about in this business, as you climb the ladder, people, your peers, are always taking shots at you," Vitale says. "I know I have sensitivity to this. I hear things sometimes, and you walk away and it hurts.

"You shake your head and say, 'Why?' You know why? Because, obviously, I must be succeeding.

"I heard a guy recently bury (criticize) a coach. I'll be honest; he buried (Ohio State basketball Coach) Gary Williams. I'm not going to mention the guy's name. He buried him about recruiting, about this and that.

"When I walked out, I told our producers, 'You know what? Gary Williams has arrived in the Big Ten. He has arrived.'

"When they're not taking shots at you and popping at you when you get up to our level, it means you're not doing something right."

It's almost 6:30 p.m., and Vitale has a personal driver, Jay, waiting to take him to Bloomington with a stop first in Indianapolis. At 8 o'clock, he must host "Dick Vitale's Sunday Night College Basketball Show," an hour-long program on syndicated radio.

Much of the talk in the car centers on Michigan. How can the Wolverines look so great one day and so pitiful the next?

"Michigan's problem is they've got too many guys who are used to being the first option (in the offense) in high school and still haven't adjusted to being the third or fourth option," Vitale says, using guard Sean Higgins as the prime example.

Sometimes Vitale's opinions (he's never had one he didn't express) get him in trouble. Earlier this season, he called for Kentucky Coach Eddie Sutton's resignation amid the NCAA's investigation into alleged violations.

"If you say great things about a school, they flat out love you," Vitale says. "They loved me at Kentucky last year. I spoke at Kentucky's banquet a couple of years ago. This year I'm scared to go to Kentucky.

"I went there, I had a police guard sitting behind the bench. Their fans were very upset that I would question the situation. You learn in this business they can quickly turn on you.

"Other programs appreciate honesty. Like a Michigan. Ann Arbor treats me great, their fans. The kids are phenomenal.

"I've been kinda critical about their schedule. But I think they respect it because they know what I'm saying is the truth. They know it's the truth when I say for a 10-day period Michigan underachieved. I'm not saying that they've underachieved all year because you can't say that. They played well against Ohio State; they played well (today).

"I think there are just some fans that become so wrapped up and obsessed with their teams, that no matter what you say, if you don't say it positively, you're a bad guy."

Jay pulls into a hotel near the Indianapolis airport around 7:30. Vitale runs into the restaurant without closing his door, tells a companion to order soup and a pasta salad for him, then heads for the telephone to call his wife, Lorraine, at their home in Bradenton, Fla.

Vitale gets just 10 minutes to eat, then returns to the pay phone near the lobby. One of the employees finds him a chair.

"People think I'm in some studio," Vitale says.

He gets a call from a fan upset that he criticized Illinois' Larry Smith for taking a poor shot in a game last week.

"Who me?" Vitale says. "You must be thinking of (Al)

McGuire."

The caller insists that Smith didn't take a bad shot.

"Bad shot," Vitale says firmly. "Next case."

"But it . . ."

"Bad shot. Next question."

The caller is scared off by Vitale's interruptions and hangs up.

"I'm sorry, I was just messing around with you," Vitale says on the air.

Before moving on to Baltimore, Vitale calls in his Top 20 for the Associated Press poll. He chooses Illinois No. 1 since the No. 2 and No. 3 teams (Georgetown and Louisville) also lost in the last week.

Vitale heads straight for the hotel lounge after arriving in Bloomington at 10:30.

"I don't drink alcohol," he says. "But I like going to clubs. I love the discos."

Tomorrow promises to be a busy day. "I don't even want to think about it," Vitale says, heading for his room before midnight.

★ ★ ★

Monday, January 30, Bloomington, Ind.: Ten years ago, Vitale broadcast ESPN's first college basketball game—Wisconsin-DePaul from Chicago. He showed up 20 minutes before tip-off.

"I didn't know what time to get there," he recalls. "My producer was *so* mad. They'd been trying to find me for a couple of hours."

Now there's a production meeting in the morning to establish a game plan for the telecast. Vitale, Brando and the behind-the-scenes crew meet in producer Fred Gaudelli's room.

Vitale, a former University of Detroit and Pistons coach, takes over. He puts on a mini-basketball clinic, suggesting that they emphasize the screens set by Indiana's Brian Sloan.

Vitale uses a chair and a couple of bodies to demonstrate the difference between a front and rear screen and what is and isn't legal.

"The thing I miss most about coaching is doing the clinics," Vitale says. "I really enjoyed that, all the Xs and Os. Now my speeches are motivational."

The book signing at Indiana's student bookstore starts at noon, and Vitale receives a hero's greeting as he walks in.

Let the comedy show begin.

An attractive woman asks him to sign a book, and Vitale's flirtatious side is quickly revealed.

"You're pretty. I'm going back to college. You don't have a boyfriend? Look at all these animals (pointing to a group of male students nearby). Bo Derek's a 10, you're a 15."

A tall guy is next in line, and says he's Dunkin' Dave.

"I'm all-airport," he concedes, a reference to the name Vitale has given to players who look like they're good basketball players in street clothes but don't measure up on the court.

Vitale receives lots of suggestions from fans. One Indiana student tells him to come up with an "all-Visa team . . . they take the charge."

"I like that," Vitale says. "I may use it on the air. But I get the credit, baby."

He sees another attractive woman standing in line. "I want her up here. Get the blonde to the front.

"My wife doesn't mind (him flirting). She knows I'm ugly; nobody likes me."

Wherever he goes, impersonators show up. One Hoosier fan is standing to the side reeling off many of the popular Vitaleisms.

"I'm taking off tonight," Vitale says. "You're doing the game.

"But I get the check, baby."

A guy considerably overweight lays a book on the table. "Hey, it's a member of my wide-body team," Vitale says, laughing.

Some students become critical of Michigan Coach Bill Frieder. They mention something called the Frieder factor.

"What's the Frieder factor?" Vitale asks.

"He chokes," a guy replies.

The conversation then turns to the five worst coaches in the country, and they want Vitale's selections.

"Excluding Frieder," an IU fan says. "He's a given."

At 1:15 with close to 100 people still in line, Vitale is rushed out of the store and driven to Assembly Hall. After a 45-minute interview with the General (Bob Knight), Vitale expresses gratitude for some QT (quality time).

"I did it because I like you," Knight says.

Vitale's next stop is back to the hotel for some rest. By 6 p.m., he's downstairs in the restaurant, taking turns betweem eating, answering questions from two Indiana reporters and signing books.

For the 9:30 game, Vitale arrives at the arena more than two hours before tip-off. His first assignment is to tape his "College Basketball Report" for the next day's *SportsCenter* show.

Vitale gets teased endlessly by his co-workers about how many takes he needs for the three-minute segment.

Back in Knight's office a few hours earlier, he had nailed it with just one try, but the tape ran out 10 seconds before he finished.

Now, he must work with many distractions around him—fans entering the arena, cheerleaders practicing routines. All eyes are on him.

Little mistakes ruin several cuts. One time he says Norm Stewart instead of Norm Sloan.

"I'm sorry," Vitale tells Gaudelli. "Thanks for being patient."

Al, an assistant director, wins the pool. He had 17, and that's how many takes Vitale needed to complete the assignment.

A few minutes later, word comes down that Knight wants to see Vitale in his office.

Vitale enters the General's office, and Knight barks, "What are you doing here?"

They talk basketball for a while, and then Knight makes Vitale call home. Vitale is talking to his wife when Knight grabs the phone.

"Don't listen to that nonsense that he's sorry he didn't call," Knight tells Lorraine. "He was out here signing autographs, doing book signings, doing this, doing that and loving every minute of it. He's not fulfilling his responsibilities. He wouldn't have called if I didn't make him."

During the telecast, the crew puts on an impressive clinic in the art of setting screens. Vitale proves he's more than just a funny man with a nuts-and-bolts explanation.

The piece is labeled: "Sloan Screen 45."

Sloan wears No. 45 for the Hoosiers.

"No burn, all pain," Brando tells the viewers.

Vitale breaks in. "You stole my line. I said it at the production meeting this morning."

"You're both full of it," Gaudelli pipes in over the headset.

The idea was all Gaudelli's. Guess who didn't even like it at first? Remember, Dickie baby?

The game is another NC. Todd Jadlow, benched for the last couple of games, returns to the starting lineup, scores 32 points and gets 13 rebounds. Indiana cruises 104-89.

Late in the game, Vitale pleads to Gaudelli for some camera shots of signs in the crowd.

"Dick Vitale for president," reads one.

"Watch out George Bush," Vitale says on the air.

During a late-night drive to a hotel near the Indianapolis airport, Vitale can't stop raving about the General.

"The man's like a genius," Vitale gushes. "He said he had a feeling Jadlow now was ready to play and how they needed points inside. He felt that game they needed scoring inside that they (Iowa) were going to play tough on the perimeter people.

"I'm hearing this at 8 o'clock. Game's at 9:30. From 9:30 to 11:30, think what happened out there. Jadlow goes off for 32.

"I get letters from fans all over my case whenever I praise Bobby Knight. I'll tell ya, maybe I overdo it or whatever, but I'm just so enthralled with his stature.

"When he walks into the arena, it's like the president just walked right out of that locker room. Don't you feel that? The electricity. I felt it."

Vitale checks into his next hotel room at 1 a.m.

Sweet dreams about the General, Dick.

★ ★ ★

Tuesday, January 31, Indianapolis: A travel day. Vitale wears a warm-up suit to the airport for an 11:30 a.m. flight to Syracuse with one stop in Pittsburgh.

"My wife got all over my case this morning," Vitale says. "She thought at the end of the game (Monday) I got carried away talking about things not relevant to the game."

Vitale frequently shows a need to be reassured that he's doing a good job. When he started out at ESPN, he used to call one of his bosses at halftime every game to see if the telecast was going all right.

"Yeah, I think I am very insecure," Vitale says. "But maybe that's what drives me to success. I don't know if it's really insecurity as much as it's the fear of failure."

The plane ride is much too long for Vitale to keep from some more innocent flirting.

"If I were married to you," he tells a stewardess, "there's no way I'd let you out with all the vultures of the business world."

She makes the mistake of telling Vitale that her husband is a pilot.

"I hear stories about those pilots," he teases. "Yeah, I saw a pilot the other day that was married. Boy, I saw that ring come off his finger when the blonde came in the lounge, man. It was all over.

"And I think it was your husband."

The plane arrives in Syracuse about 2:30. Less than two hours later, Vitale is at the Carrier Dome to check out the Orangemen's practice. He roams around the court, picking up facts and anecdotes from coaches and players.

Villanova's team enters the dome about 6 p.m. for practice. Coach Rollie Massimino's first words aren't "Hello" or "How are you?"

Instead, Massimino says, "Where's the General? Where's the bleepin' General?"

Vitale makes plans to catch up to Massimino later in the evening at Grimaldi's, a popular Italian restaurant. A local radio station hosts an hour-long sports talk show from there starting at 7 with Vitale as a guest.

Fans can ask questions by stepping up to a microphone in front of Vitale's table. Rather than request Vitale's opinion, one young man runs off his personal All-America team.

"Who wants to hear your All-America team?" Vitale screams.

He then tosses one of his books across the room to the guy.

Vitale jokes with the fans endlessly. Once in a while it's misinterpreted, but most people seem to enjoy the needling.

Massimino arrives late at the restaurant. When he sits down to eat, Vitale interrupts everyone's dinner.

"I'd like to make a toast," Vitale announces. "Rollie, the only celebration you're going to have in Syracuse is the linguine you're eating now."

★ ★ ★

Wednesday, February 1, Syracuse, N.Y.: "You're going to shine my shoes and carry my bags tomorrow after we win," Massimino tells Vitale at a morning shoot-around.

Two security guards escort Vitale to the Syracuse student bookstore at 12:30 for another signing. Just like in Bloomington, a large crowd (400 or so) is waiting for him to take the stage.

"You guys better cheer like hell tonight 'cause I don't want to shine any shoes," Vitale tells the Syracuse fans.

Vitale fields many of the same questions from two days ago in Indiana.

"It gets old, but you know what?" Vitale says. "It really helps me in the telecasts because it's like cramming. It's repetition, and it starts staying in your head all the time. And you pick up a lot of goodies from the people, suggestions about different things."

For the third straight time, Vitale works a game that's over early. This one's all Syracuse, 90-57. Now shoes will need shining.

Vitale can't wait to get home. He has plans to take his daughters —Terri and Sherri, both avid tennis players—to the Davis Cup Friday in Fort Myers, Fla.

"I'm a nervous wreck every time I call home knowing my daughters are driving," says Vitale, who suffered several broken bones in a head-on accident two years ago.

Yes, there are times when even Mr. Upbeat has fears and worries.

After the Pistons fired him in 1979, Vitale had to pull out of a miserable period of depression.

"I felt sorry for myself, locked myself in the room, slept a lot, got hooked on "General Hospital." I just retreated. But then my wife said, 'All these banquets that you speak at to young kids, you talk about pride; you talk about not being a quitter and here you are rolling over when adversity sets in.'

"Sure, I have my down moments like anyone else. I think there's another side of me sometimes that people don't see.

"But when I'm in sports, that's a happy moment for me. All the enthusiasm comes flying out, I guess.

"God gifted me with enthusiasm. Why shouldn't I use that?"

The Legacy of Chris Evert

TENNIS

By *BARRY LORGE*

In the beginning, she was Chrissie, a pony-tailed schoolgirl from Florida who grabbed America's heart with both hands, the same way she hit her backhand. She grew up in the public eye and professional era—really the first player to do that—and became Chris Evert, the superstar next door.

She dated jocks, Hollywood hunks and a president's son, married tennis player John Lloyd and then former Olympic skier Andy Mill. She didn't like to be called a *femme fatale,* either, but she added sex appeal to women's tennis at a time when it needed it, without losing her image of innocent intensity.

Now, after 18 years of unparalleled consistency, she has retired, leaving a formidable record and a lasting legacy of style. Several generations of players imitated her baseline game, including the backhand. More important, she became the Portrait of the Athlete as a Young Woman. We watched her progress from enchanting princess to majestic monarch to grand dame, and through all the stages, she was an exemplary champion. Even at Sweet 16, she preferred to be called Chris because that sounded more sophisticated, but in our affections, part of her will always be Chrissie.

She burst into our consciousness in 1971. The women's pro tour was brand new. Evert reached the semifinals of the U.S. Open as an unseeded player, making three stirring comebacks against established women pros before losing in the semifinals to the champion she would succeed as queen of tennis, Billie Jean King.

Evert did not turn pro until her 18th birthday—December 21, 1972—because her father, a cautious, reserved public parks pro, wanted her to finish at St. Thomas Aquinas High School in Fort Lauderdale. But she clearly was the most likely to succeed in her class. She has earned more than $9 million in prize money, plus several times that in endorsements, and has done perhaps more than anyone to make women's tennis a respectable career—mostly just by being Chris Evert, consummate pro. Her 15-year rivalry with Martina Navratilova was the most glorious the game—or possibly any sport —has known.

More than any other player, Evert blended grit and grace and glamour. Her game was as conservative as Middle America; her professional persona as wholesome as apple pie; her contributions to governing the tour as solid as her ground strokes; and her after-hour style a jet-set fantasy. She readily admits that publicly and privately, she was two very different people, but she always was above the sleazy supermarket tabloids. When she let her honey-blonde hair down about her love life, it was in *Life* magazine, not *The National Enquirer.* She is really a *Cosmopolitan* woman, but you always expected to see her on the cover of *Vogue* instead.

Now she has retired from serious competition, reserving the right to make a cameo appearance now and then. The 1989 U.S. Open was her last Grand Slam event. She exited the same stage she entered 18 years earlier. "Win or lose, my last match would be sad for me because my career really started here back when I was 16 years old and I reached the semifinals," she said after losing to Zina Garrison in the quarterfinals.

Evert played 56 Grand Slam tournaments, reached at least the semis in 52 of them, won two Australian, seven French, three Wimbledon and six U.S. Open singles titles. Her overall record in the majors was 299-37. She thinks when people look back on her career, they will note her longevity and consistency, particularly in the big events. Her 125-match win streak on clay in the mid-'70s is a hallmark that most likely will never be duplicated. She internalized her competitive flame, letting us see the light primarily through laser-beam ground strokes, but she would like to be remembered as a champion who knew only one level of performance.

"I was in the Top Four for 18 years," she says. "I don't know if any player has done that. I am personally most proud of that fact. I wasn't a fluke. I didn't have three good years and then two bad years. I didn't have slumps. I think that shows something about the mental side of the game, the concentration and dedication I have. That's the most significant thing to me, because I'm not the most pleasing player to watch. I'm not a John McEnroe or a Jimmy Connors. They are flashy, brilliant showmen out there. I think I went about winning in more of a quiet fashion."

She went about leading in the same way. On the eve of her last Open, she was elected president of the Women's International Tennis Association (WITA) for a record eighth term.

Evert arrived with the Revolutionary War in women's tennis. King and eight other pioneers declared their independence from the male-dominated tournament circuit in 1970, just about the same time the 15-year-old Chrissie made a name for herself by beating Margaret Court, winner of the Grand Slam that year, on clay in Charlotte, N.C. The next year, Evonne Goolagong won Wimbledon at age 19, but did not play the U.S. Open; King won the tournament, but Chrissie stole the show. A star, and eventually an era, were born.

Holdovers from the "shamateur" days were in the forefront of the feuds and fights and lawsuits from which the women's tour was forged. "I call us the transitional generation," says King. "We did the trench work. Chris and Evonne were the first-generation professionals."

King was the firebrand reformer in the heyday of women's lib, playing and promoting the fledgling tour into prominence. She polarized the cause. Evert popularized it. She took the tour into the American mainstream and became its ultimate establishment figure.

"In my opinion, there have been two major people who had a political and emotional influence on the women's tour outside of what they did on the court," says Jerry Diamond, tournament promoter and former executive director of the WITA. "Billie Jean was the activist, the politician, the organizer. Chris became the standard-bearer. Billie was like the leader of the rebellion, and Chris the next president, who provided stability."

On the court and in other public appearances, Evert epitomized self-control, rectitude and diplomacy. "She's very gracious in most situations," King says. "She's calculated. She thinks before she speaks. That is the way she was brought up, the way her father is, the way she plays. She says and does the right thing, regardless of how she really feels—unlike me or Martina, who made waves."

Evert was seldom controversial, usually safe, steady, middle-of-the-road. In the board room, as on the court, however, she never shirked her responsibilities.

"It wasn't like I was going to play the tournaments and collect the prize money and not be involved in the decision-making or take an interest in helping make changes for the better," she says. "I'm proud of that because at certain times it does take away from your tennis, having these meetings during tournaments. But this way, you don't feel you're totally selfish, just taking the money and running. You feel like you're putting something back in the game."

Says Edy McGoldrick, who was director of women's tennis for the USTA when Evert came up and later was with the Women's International Professional Tennis Council: "That's a feeling the first group of women pros had, and passed on to Chris and Martina and Pam Shriver and their generation. It's a sense of responsibility and a P.R. feel that they had to keep selling the sport. I think the biggest plus for women's tennis was that the players stuck together, supported their association and made sacrifices to keep it strong."

Most experts agree that Evert set the example of how a professional should conduct herself. "Absolutely," says King. "No question." But, typically, Evert does not claim credit for that.

"I think the women tennis players are closer than the men, and they don't let each other get away with anything," Evert says. "If somebody is acting up on the court, one of the top players will have a talk with her, whereas in the men's game, it's more to each his own. You're not going to see a woman player ranting and raving on the court. You haven't seen it yet, anyway, and I don't think the women would let that happen because most of them are very concerned about the image of the tour, and fairness and being a good sport. It's not that they're never going to say a word or question calls. I question calls. But no one is going to get out of hand, because the women are pretty tough that way."

Evert always was pretty tough on the court, an uncompromising counterpuncher who responded to the challenge of Navratilova's superior athletic ability and serve-volley style by rededicating herself to a training regimen and coming back leaner and meaner. Evert maintained the mental tenacity that was her forte longer than any other champion.

"What's really miraculous is how long she was able to sustain that intensity and motivation," says Diamond. "There is something in the lady's psyche that I was never able to figure out, and I know her really well. She stayed with my family when she was a kid, I've been to both her weddings, and yet, there is a part of Chris that I don't think anybody knows."

Evert acknowledged as much in a first-person story in an August issue of *Sports Illustrated* that officially announced her retirement: "Because my father was my role model, I grew up with total seriousness all around me. But I love humor, and it doesn't bother me that the world doesn't know the real me. . . . Martina claims I tell the dirtiest jokes around—probably as a semirevolt against my strict Catholic upbringing. And when I've become angry in practice, every four-letter word imaginable has graced these lips."

Miss American Pie grew up, lived a la mode, became a worldly woman. Always, she was adored for her image, even if it was largely illusion.

"I was a normal teenager who liked boys and who liked wearing gold bracelets and earrings and nail polish and eye shadow." Evert says, recalling 1971. "I was just a teenybopper, going along with what every other teenager was doing. It was just normal for me, but it had such a big impact on the women's tour because most of the women were in their middle or late 20s, and the stereotype of the woman tennis player was pretty masculine-looking. . . . I wasn't trying to be a sex symbol, but I was trying to be feminine because that was part of me. My mother always used to make my lace tennis dresses and lace bloomers and put ribbons in my hair. I was brought up in a family where femininity was important, and I think that was part of my appeal. The image was slightly altered. I think probably a lot of young girls saw Evonne and myself and said, 'Hey, it's O.K. to be a woman athlete.' "

A lot of young players also saw Evert and thought it was fashionable to hit a two-handed backhand. Her father actually tried to change her to a one-handed stroke when she was 11 or 12, but says, "We'd finish practice and I'd peek over and she'd be back to hitting with two hands."

"Basically it's just an easier stroke to learn," Evert says. "A one-handed backhand, as a lot of one-handed players will tell you, takes years to learn. You can stick a racquet in a 6-year-old's hands and he can hit a two-handed backhand."

Not everyone agrees that one hand is better than two, either. Says Ted Tinling, aficionado of women's tennis for 65 years: "Her legacy is that we might have a few charming sporting players down the line because people remember Chris. She's a great role model—for the image she projects and for the backhand. I think there must be a million kids playing who wouldn't have played if they had defensive backhands. All the kids can attack on both wings now, and that wouldn't exist if it hadn't been for Chris."

Virginia Wade, the 1977 Wimbledon champion, looks at the new wave of young players in women's tennis—Steffi Graf of West Germany, Gabriela Sabatini of Argentina, Arantxa Sanchez of Spain, Yugoslav-born Monica Seles, Natalia Zvereva of the Soviet Union and 13-year-old Floridian Jennifer Capriati—and is optimistic about the mix of personalities and playing styles:

"In a way, it's much more promising now than a few years ago when the most promising players tended to be—now this is something that certainly is not supposed to sound in the least disrespectful—but the Chris Evert sort of clones. The reason I say that is because I have infinite respect for Chris. I think her greatest thing is really the mental side of it. Her greatness really comes from the head and not necessarily from the style of game she plays. So what happened was everybody copied the most obvious thing about Chris, which was her game. And what they couldn't copy was the thing that was her signature, which was her strength upstairs. So what you were doing was producing a whole flock of people playing from the baseline, not really playing very aggressively, and they didn't have the mental stamina she had. I think we're getting away from that now."

There was some apprehension that when Evert retired, she would leave a void that could not be filled. People wondered if TV and sponsorship revenues would decline when the women's tour had no native American star for the first time. Now most experts don't think so.

"The people who watch tennis are more or less diehards," says McGoldrick. "I don't think they care where the top players come from, as long as they compete in the U.S."

Diamond disagrees: "I think we desperately need a top American player if the WITA is going to keep its leadership role in the game.

Chris took up Billie Jean's position to keep the association strong, but I don't think the new players have much loyalty to the association."

To date, the young players poised to be the new rivals atop the rankings have not shown much interest in assuming the mantle the way Evert and Navratilova did. Evert sees that as a potential problem, too. "We hope it doesn't get out of control so that the European tournament promoters start to dictate how women's tennis is run," she says.

That may be why she accepted another term as WITA president even though she was retiring from competition. She expects to be on the scene, as spokesperson for the dozen companies she represents, commentator for NBC, and possibly as a coach.

"I would like to always be involved in tennis, and I'd like to come to the Grand Slam tournaments," she says. "That's important to me. I don't want to isolate myself entirely. I would be disappointed if in a couple of years my name completely disappeared from the face of the earth. I mean, you get used to a certain lifestyle. I've been famous since I was 16 years old. It would be sort of shattering if, in two years, I went into a restaurant and said, 'Chris Evert would like a table,' and they said, 'Who?' "

Little chance of that. A Madison Avenue survey a couple of years ago concluded that Evert was among the most recognized faces and admired names in sports. As Diamond puts it, "Chris is the personification of women's tennis. You say to an artist, 'Give me a generic sketch of a woman tennis player,' invariably he'll give you somebody who looks like Chris."

The superstar next door, with a two-fisted backhand. That is quite a legacy.

Inner Strength: Steve Largent's Farewell

PRO FOOTBALL

By *GLENN NELSON*

From the Seattle Times

Throw him a football. Watch his eyes widen as they fix on the point. He sees the ball floating like a balloon, as if suspended in time. This is an exercise he has repeated over and over again.

Focus and dedication.

Throw him a football. Allow him to observe the velocity and arc of the pass. With the ball in midflight, ask him to close his eyes. Watch him blindly extend his hands, where the ball eventually will find its haven.

Calculation and faith.

Such is the measure of an athlete who will end his career Saturday as the most prolific, most consistent and highest scoring receiver in the history of the National Football League. They also are the measure of a man, for a man and his game cannot easily be divorced. More often than not, as he plays, he also lives.

And this is true of Steve Largent, Seattle Seahawk.

The words used to describe him have spewed forth like credits after an epic film. Elegant, precise, honest. Sensitive, hard working, dedicated. Christian, husband, father. Football player.

Usually missing from the list are two words—tough and resilient. And their absence may be completely missing the point.

Two plays, two shattering moments of violence say more about Largent, his life and career, than perhaps any other.

The first occurred in Denver, September 4, the opening day of the 1988 season. In the third quarter of a game between the Seahawks and the Broncos, Largent runs a crossing pattern near the Denver 40. As he reaches for a pass thrown high by quarterback Dave Krieg, Bronco safety Mike Harden comes thundering from the middle of the field.

Harden throws a right forearm to the left side of Largent's face. The impact shatters Largent's facemask and a couple of teeth, jars him from consciousness and leaves him with a sprained left knee.

"When I saw that play on film, I wondered how Largent survived it," says Raymond Clayborn, a cornerback for New England the past 13 years. "Then, to see him come back the next week . . . well, that says a lot about the man."

The reprise came 14 weeks later during a rematch in the Kingdome. The Seahawks, leading 14-7 in the second quarter, have a third-and-one as Krieg launches a pass for Brian Blades. Harden intercepts the ball and runs up the sideline. Out of the end zone, Largent roars up the sideline and hits Harden so hard the ball pops loose. Largent recovers the fumble.

"That looked just like Steve," says Jerry Potter, Largent's Putnam City High School coach. "He was just a real aggressive high-school player."

Potter's favorite recollection of Largent's high-school exploits isn't a hit, however, or even a reception. It's a defensive play. Arch rival Ada High has driven deep into Putnam City territory. It attempts a pass. Largent picks it off at the 5-yard line and returns the ball 95 yards for a score.

"Except there was a penalty and they called back the touchdown," Potter recalls. "Well, the next play, they do the same thing. And Steve does it again. He intercepted the pass and ran it back 95 yards for a touchdown. Out of everything he did, that's my favorite Steve Largent story."

Largent takes a lick, returns to deliver one. Balance, through adversity. It is the storyline of his life.

To say Largent's toughness is strictly physical also would miss the point. More than anything, his is an inner strength, forged and fortified through personal turmoil. The abandonment by his natural father and a tumultuous home life with an alcoholic stepfather pushed him to three things in high school that would become the foundation for his life.

Football provided a focus. Terry Bullock, an A-student and cheerleader, gave him stability. Christianity became, as friend and former mentor Scott Manley puts it, "his personal gyroscope" and his essence.

So many turning points would follow, testing his faith, galvanizing his resolve: His release by the Houston Oilers, an acrimonious NFL players strike in 1982, the sudden death of a younger brother shortly afterward and the death of his grandfather.

Then came the watershed event of his life in 1985—an unplanned pregnancy, which produced his youngest child, Kramer, a victim of spina bifida, a birth defect.

The point is, Largent was not born to the Hall of Fame or the Man of the Year. He grew into the role, and the process was fraught with growing pains. For Largent, little came easy.

As his mother, Sue Stewart, says, "The one thing you can say about Steve is that he's always been able to bounce back."

★ ★ ★

"I'd do the same thing to get out of that situation. Football and baseball season were my favorite parts of the year because I could go to all the games. I also went to every practice. It was a way to be with my sons. That was the best thing about it. But it also was a way to avoid what was waiting for me at home."

—Sue Stewart, on the childhood of her son, Steve Largent.

★ ★ ★

Every week, the nine-year marriage of Sue and Jim Largent fell into the same routine. On Monday mornings, Jim, a traveling salesman, would kiss Sue goodbye, then hit the road for a week. He'd return Friday nights, kiss her hello, go to bed, sleep in, then spend the weekend playing with his three sons—Steve, the oldest; Doug, 2½ years younger, and Jeff, the baby.

One week, 30 years ago this coming May, was different.

"When Jim came back that Friday night, he seemed a little strange," Largent's mother recalls. "When I woke up the next morning, he had showered and was getting dressed. That was odd. I asked him what he was doing. He said he was going downtown to get a divorce. At first, I thought he was kidding, but then I saw he was serious.

"I'll never forget that day. It was the day before Mother's Day."

Steve Largent was only 6 years old.

That summer, the shock had almost dissipated when Sue Stewart peered out a window. A group of boys walked by; they were wearing Little League baseball uniforms. She decided Steve should join them.

"I thought it would be neat for Steve because, at that time, it was something he needed," she says.

As therapeutic as sports became for her sons, she knew they needed more. When she met a civil servant with the U.S. Air Force, she sensed he was the missing ingredient to her family. He was, after all, steadily employed and seemed to interact well with her sons. Two years after her divorce from Jim Largent, she married John Cargill. Three years later, they had a son, Craig.

Necessity, however, masked some trouble signs. Cargill's job required mobility. During Largent's second year of junior high, the Cargills moved three times—to Austin, Tex., Sanford, Fla., and Albany, Ga. Largent spent his entire ninth-grade year in one place when he lived with Stewart's parents.

The Cargills finally settled in Oklahoma City by the time Largent entered Putnam City High School. By then, the constant movement had affected Largent's personality.

"Steve was a typical, attention-seeking high-school kid," recalls Terry Largent, who first met her husband in a 10th-grade Latin class. "He was a smart aleck, a funny guy and not concerned at all with academics. He was a guy looking to make his way into a group of friends. Because he moved around so much, he was new to the school and not established with people."

There also was trouble at home. Largent's family had become dysfunctional. Cargill was able to settle in Oklahoma City because the Air Force had forced him to resign his post. John Cargill was an alcoholic.

"There wasn't any physical abuse," Sue Stewart says. "It was more mental and verbal. John would get drunk and throw things. There were times when the ashtrays were flying by my face so fast . . . and that, of course, would start arguments. And John was jealous of the boys. If they cuddled up with me, he'd call them names, call them sissies or momma's boys."

Stewart, who divorced Cargill and remarried, adds, "Sometimes I look back and wonder why I put up with all of that. But I had to. Steve's dad didn't pay much child support. I had four children to worry about. I felt I had to stay in the marriage, as bad as it was.

"Still, I regret it. I took a lot of the kids' happy years away from them. I look at Steve and Terry, and see what they have with each other and their family, and I wish I could've given my kids that."

In a way, she gave them something else almost as valuable. In Steve Largent's case, the personal turmoil presented an opening which, with her encouragement, he seized. Without it, his life may have turned out entirely different.

★ ★ ★

"I remember the day Steve came home and told me he wasn't going out for the high-school football team. A lot of people told him that he was too little and too slow and that in high school, they cut people who aren't big enough and fast enough."

—Sue Stewart, on her son's start in football.

★ ★ ★

Too small, too slow. The words have echoed throughout Steve Largent's football career. If he had listened to anyone but his mother, he may only have had to endure that criticism once.

"Steve had this friend with a motorcycle and wanted to hang around with him for a year and maybe try football the next season," Sue Stewart recalls. "I told him it would really break my heart if he quit. Well, he changed his mind and every day he would come home and tell me, 'Well, I didn't get cut.' "

As Little League had before it, high-school athletics presented a solution to Largent's personal problems. For one thing, they kept him away from a deteriorating home life. For another, they became a source of self-esteem.

"Football was a real focus for me," Largent says. "My self-worth was established on the athletic field. It was the one thing I felt I could do really well. So I spent a lot of time trying to hone the skills that I had. In large part, my life revolved around that."

Largent threw himself into sports. He turned the belief that he was too small and too slow into an edge. His coaches found he was willing to do anything they asked—often more. Early on, Largent was switched from running back and thrown in with a bulging group of receivers. Jerry Potter figures that Largent and quarterback Tony Brantley worked on 200 to 300 pass plays a day during the offseason.

"He's the most determined guy I've ever known," says Neil Dubberstein, one of Largent's first high-school friends. "All you'd have to do is tell him what he couldn't do, and that's why he'd do it."

Largent's determination didn't just help him overcome his perceived physical limitations, it helped him leap other, more prohibitive hurdles. It was rare for a sophomore to start for the largest high school in Oklahoma, but Largent did. The talent pool was so large at Putnam City High that it maintained two junior-varsity teams, but Largent started at receiver *and* cornerback.

Sometimes, Largent's drive bordered on the maniacal.

"One game, he got kicked above the elbow and the next day his arm had swollen up like a balloon," Dubberstein says. "He looked like Arnold Schwarzenegger on one side and me on the other. His family doctor told him his arm was broken. He went to the team doctor and was told it was just a bruise.

"Steve, of course, listened to the team doctor. They just taped that bad arm to his side and he played two games with one arm without missing a beat."

Competition was fierce enough, but Putnam City High School also was blessed with an abundance of great athletes while Largent was there. Pat Ryan, a quarterback for the New York Jets, was just a backup to Brantley, who went on to play for Notre Dame. Alvan Adams, who had a long National Basketball Association career with the Phoenix Suns, led the Putnam City basketball team. The high school baseball team was led by Ryan, a shortstop, and Bob Shirley, who went on to pitch in the major leagues.

And Steve Largent, who was both an all-state receiver and catcher during his senior year. He was good enough to attract a rare offer of a full-ride baseball scholarship from Oklahoma. Largent opted instead to catch passes in the wide-open offense at Tulsa.

"I told him he was making a mistake," Dubberstein says. "To be honest, Steve wasn't that dominant a high school player and I thought his size would limit him in football. I told him that if he wanted to make something of his life, he should play baseball at Oklahoma."

To the chagrin of NFL defensive backs, Dubberstein was wrong.

★ ★ ★

"I call him the Albert Einstein of pass receivers because he's always coming up with some kind of new space-age route I've never seen before."

—Lester Hayes, former Raider cornerback, on Steve Largent.

★ ★ ★

The year was 1979. Largent was only three seasons removed from being cut by the Houston Oilers for being too small and too slow. The Raiders' Lester Hayes was emerging as one of the most feared defensive backs in the NFL. This was to be the start of one of the game's greatest on-going personal duels.

As Largent burst up the sideline on a go-route, Hayes worked him out of bounds with a shoulder. Quarterback Jim Zorn's pass was high and inside. As the ball reached the end of its flight, Largent leapt over Hayes, nearly riding the Raiders' helmet.

Somehow, his arms intertwined with Hayes', Largent caught the ball, the momentum carrying him out of bounds. In mid-air, Largent managed to adjust his body so he crashed shoulder-first into the end zone to claim the touchdown before the rest of him landed out of bounds.

Ask anybody about Largent's best catch, and this is the one they are most likely to mention.

"It was an amazing catch," says New England veteran Raymond Clayborn, who's seen it on film. "Lester was considered the greatest cornerback in the game. And no one was doing Lester like that at the time."

Hayes, who retired in 1986, doesn't remember the catch. But he remembers clearly the first time he laid eyes on Largent in 1977.

"I laughed at him," Hayes recalls. "He didn't look like a receiver, he looked like an insurance salesman. I thought, 'I should be able to dominate this guy.' But I'll tell you what, he is God's gift. I've covered everybody in the NFL. All those high-tech speed guys. But I never covered anybody who gave me as many problems as Steve Largent did."

Perhaps the most amazing thing about that 1979 reception is that Largent can recall little more than getting up afterward, laughing. Maybe also that Hayes joined in the chuckling. But how he did it, Largent can't remember.

Apparently, Largent already had reached some kind of pass-receiving nirvana, lending credence to Zorn's assertion that his friend developed all his skills and moves within the first four years of his career.

They were four years of improvisational theater, with Largent and Zorn in leading roles for an expansion Seahawk team. The Seattle offense revolved around a sprint-out and a scramble series, catering to Zorn's preference for being on the move and allowing Largent to carve intricate routes. Zorn-to-Largent, the most prolific battery in the team's history with 455 connections and 49 touchdowns, was a perfect match.

Not an entirely natural one, mind you. Zorn figures the two worked 20 to 30 extra minutes after practice at least twice a week. They also practiced an hour or two daily during the offseason. As impressive as his physical regimen may be, the crux of Largent's well-known work ethic may be mental.

"Steve is the most well-prepared football player I've ever been around," says John Becker, Seahawk offensive coordinator and receivers coach. "He studies more film than most quarterbacks at a lot of other places."

"That's obvious," San Diego cornerback Gill Byrd says. "Sometimes it seems like he knows what you're running almost before you do."

Over the years, Largent has trained himself to focus on the point of an approaching football, a drill suggested by a skeet and trap shooter. He's also practiced catching the ball with his eyes closed. While that sounds like a circus trick, the skill comes in handy when sight lines are blocked by the kind of traffic Largent has attracted.

Largent's legendary diligence has created an almost stereotypical myth that he simply outworks everyone else. Which isn't true. Central to the myth is the matter of Largent's speed—or lack thereof.

The first game plan Clayborn ever saw on the Seahawks described Largent this way: No speed, but has all the moves. Able to catch the ball in a crowd. One of the true great receivers.

"People always said he was a slow white boy with a lot of moves," Clayborn says. "I found that to be totally untrue."

Albert Lewis, a seventh-year Pro Bowl cornerback for the Kansas City Chiefs, came to an even stronger conclusion:

"Steve Largent was equal in value to his team as an O.J. Simpson or a Jim Brown was. Without the ability to complete passes to Largent, people could shut down Curt Warner. When you drew up a game plan against the Seattle Seahawks, Steve Largent was the one guy you had to have accounted for."

In reality, the myth is a half-truth, one that Largent has helped perpetuate by steadfastly guarding his 40-yard times. According to Potter, his high-school coach, Largent possessed "under 4.9" speed at Putnam City High. By the time he led the nation in touchdown receptions two years running and even at the Houston Oiler training camp, Largent's time had improved to about 4.6 according to Jerry Rhome, who coached him at Tulsa and during his early years with the Seahawks.

"That's not blazing speed," Rhome adds, "but he had good speed and great quickness to make up for it."

Hayes says, "Steve was the Caucasian Clydesdale. When I faced him in Oakland or L.A., I was OK. But on AstroTurf, he would just abuse me. When he made his breaks on AstroTurf, he was a 4.4 guy, not a 4.6 guy. I would just watch him burst. I could feel the explosion. And I would think, 'Maybe the NFL should check his urine. He's an android. I don't think he's human.' "

After 14 seasons, Largent will have caught more passes, caught more touchdown passes, caught passes in more consecutive games and accumulated more 50-reception and 1,000-yard seasons than anyone in NFL history. Certainly, if all it took was good-enough speed and outstanding quickness, moves and body control, hours on practice fields and in film rooms, there would have been scores of Steve Largents. At least, more than one.

What separates the truly outstanding athletes from the rest is an almost inexplicable special quality. For Largent, it's inner strength.

"Steve has for football the same kind of feeling Donald Trump has for the business world," Becker says. "He's so intuitive."

Largent's inner strength does not defy explanation. It can be argued, and has been argued, that he had it all along. That adversity led him to discover, then acknowledge it. And that further turmoil helped him nurture it.

It is clear to those who know him best. As Zorn puts it, "Steve's spiritual walk has deepened."

★ ★ ★

"He was this little funny guy, who giggled and tee-hee'd and cut up with the rest of them in the back row. I never knew if anything stuck or took."

—Scott Manley, on Largent's days with Young Life, a nondenominational Christian organization for high-school teenagers.

★ ★ ★

It still surprises a lot of people, his mother among them, when Steve Largent speaks of himself as "flighty, surfacy and goofy" during his formative years. But Neil Dubberstein can vouch for him.

"He was a wild man," he says. "He could cut up with the best of them. He was the kind of guy who, if you said, 'Largent, I'll give you a quarter if you throw a rock through that window,' you'd be paying out that quarter so fast. He'd try anything once—within reason.

"A couple guys Steve hung out with in the ninth grade might have spent some time in prison later on. The kind of things they did back then was a lot of what Steve was leaning toward when he met Terry."

Ah, Terry. Everyone agrees that nobody has had a more profound effect on Steve Largent's life than Terry Bullock, an A student and cheerleader at Putnam City High. She was yin to Largent's yang. Stable family, disciplined, self-assured—Terry seemed to have almost everything Steve didn't.

When Largent began spending his time off the athletic field with Terry and the Bullock family, things changed. His grades. His outlook. Even, his personality.

"Terry is real consistent in her character," Largent says of his wife. "She's a real honest person. Back then, I was a people pleaser. I wanted to be accepted. But she just had this real security about who she was. From the beginning we just molded together so well."

Terry's influence allowed Largent to accept what he considers his greatest gift—a Christian way of life. Scott Manley, then the director of Young Life's Putnam City High branch, was uncertain of Largent's acceptance back then. It became apparent years later.

"The difference between Steve Largent and you and me," Manley says, "is if somebody he respects told him that if he did something, something positive would come out of it, he'd concentrate and do it. Whether it's finances or family or football, he tries to figure out where the truth is, and what principles are involved, and he commits to it."

Largent says, "The thing that's helped me more than anything is realizing that I'm a child of God. That's where your self-worth comes in because it's established by something somebody has declared you to be. To me, that's truth and that's real and that's something to hold on to. It can't be shaken by your performance on the field, or at home, or in the community."

The truth didn't always hit Largent like a bolt from the heavens. Most of the time, it was masked by some significant, often detrimental, event. The discovery process strengthened his commitment.

His release from the Oilers in 1976, for example, was a stinging rebuke that prompted much self-reexamination. Still, the blow was salved by his trade to the Seahawks. Even more so, the winter of 1982-83 was what steered Largent firmly away from the fleeting, often superficial, instant self-gratification of pro football.

Midway through that season, NFL players walked out over negotiations for a new collective-bargaining agreement. The strike polarized the Seahawks.

"That was one of the most difficult years of my life," Largent says. "The strike caused a lot of animosity between myself and a lot of my teammates. It made me reassess my relationships. That was when we decided to start spending our offseasons in Tulsa."

The Seahawks were Cincinnati-bound on Christmas to play a game the next day. It was then that Largent's younger brother, Doug, fell ill with encephalitis, an inflammation of the brain commonly referred to as "sleeping sickness." A week after Largent played a rescheduled strike game against Denver January 2, Doug was dead at 27.

"It was just one time in a series of events when I believe God was pointing out to me not to take anything for granted—especially the ones you love," Largent says. "After my brother died, the one thought I had was that I really wished I could hug him and tell him I love him. But he was gone.

"This is something I need to be reminded of every day of my life—that you just never know. There are no guarantees in life."

The message was reinforced a year and a half later, when his grandfather, Stan Sorenson, died of stomach cancer. He was perhaps the closest Largent ever came to having a father figure. Still another year and a half down the road, the biggest turning point of Largent's life waited.

★ ★ ★

"It almost was like grieving the death of a child. You always have expectations of what your child is going to be like. Then someone tells you that your child will walk with a peculiar gait for the

rest of his life, that he may have problems controlling his bladder and other things. You think, 'This isn't the child of my dreams.' It's like all your dreams are smashed."

—Terry Largent, on the birth of Kramer.

★ ★ ★

It wasn't supposed to happen. Steve and Terry Largent had taken measures to confine their family to two sons, Kyle and Kelly, and a daughter, Casie. So they were shocked to learn Terry was pregnant with a fourth child.

Even more stunning than Terry's pregnancy was the fact that Kramer James Largent was born November 11, 1985, with his spinal cord and nerves exposed in a small sac at the base of his back. The birth defect, spina bifida, requires corrective surgery and typically results in mild or severe paralysis.

Terry was the first to come to terms with the tragedy. Steve, on the other hand, was devastated. There was confusion and anger. And so many questions.

"I couldn't understand why," he explains. "Why would God do that, not to me, but to Kramer? I wrestled with that. It never caused me to question my faith—like, does God really exist? Eventually, it strengthened it."

Finally over the shock, Steve and Terry Largent concluded that Kramer's birth held a significance beyond their initial comprehension.

"We feel he's a special little gift from God," Terry says. "He's our only child who was not planned. He doesn't really look like either one of us at all. And, from the beginning, he's had a real sweet temperament."

With Kramer came a fundamental change in his parents. His birth instilled in both a greater sense of compassion. Before, they'd empathize with the plight of others, but could dismiss minor tragedies as just that—minor. From experience, Steve and Terry Largent now understand the magnitude of such events.

Kramer's birth prompted his father, already a willing benefactor for such charities as Children's Hospital, March of Dimes and United Way, to step up his community work.

"Having gone through something like that has helped me understand what others are going through," he explains. "When I call people to offer encouragement, they obviously recognize my name. More important, they know I've been in their shoes. My heart aches for them, and they recognize that."

Others who have benefited from Largent's involvement include Focus on the Family, the Spina Bifida Foundation, United Cerebral Palsy and Boys Village, a Christian-based organization that provides care for abused and neglected boys. Last year, when he was named the NFL's Man of the Year and won the inaugural Bart Starr Award for his community work, it was estimated that Largent raised or donated between $85,000 and $100,000 for charities.

"Steve Largent is just one of those amazing people," says Mary Ann Ranta, of Children's Hospital. "Whenever something comes up where we'd really appreciate his involvement, he's always been there for us. He is such a hero to so many people, one who is so genuinely the way he really is, and people sense that."

That quality is just one, but perhaps the most important, manifestation of the Largents' "special little gift from God."

★ ★ ★

"Football helped me establish a false self-esteem. Fortunately, I was able to perpetuate it. Over time, I was able to say to myself, 'This stuff isn't all real. In terms of life and society and contrbutions to mankind, what are you really doing that's significant?' You have to come to a point where you say, 'I'm just a guy.' The reality is, when I'm gone, somebody else will be in my locker and he'll be just another guy."

—Steve Largent, on his NFL career.

★ ★ ★

This just-another-guy syndrome has provided a mixed bag for Steve Largent, albeit one he encourages.

For one thing, it probably has prevented him from getting his just due as an athlete. That's partly because he will end his career without having played in a Super Bowl. But mainly because he lacks the hyperbole of most marquee athletes, Largent has not been celebrated in the national media until recent years and has not become a household name.

What Largent has inspired in his colleagues and counterparts is less awe than respect. The response to Largent's retirement by Kansas City's Albert Lewis is fairly typical.

"I'm definitely going to miss him," Lewis says. "When I came into this league, there were two receivers I knew I had to play well against if I was going to be one of the best—Largent and Charlie Joiner. Steve Largent has given me the greatest competition over the years, and I'm the better for it. I owe that to him.

"He's the kind of guy you love to play against. You love to play him for the competition, not as someone to get even against. And when he's not playing against you, you root for him. That's the kind of guy he is."

Lester Hayes recalls meeting Largent the first time in a noncombat arena. It was the 1981 Pro Bowl, and Hayes was touched by the way Largent interacted with his family. Immediately, Hayes says, he developed a special feeling for Largent. From then, the two fierce rivals on the football field began sharing meals and fishing trips off it. All the while, Hayes' admiration grew.

"People talk about Steve not playing in a Super Bowl, but that wouldn't have been his greatest accolade," Hayes says. "Remember, I have two Super Bowl rings, and I had to fight my way through Seattle to get them. I think that, in the Year 2040, I'll face Steve again—in the Heaven Bowl. That's the day Steve will receive his

Super Bowl ring from the ultimate owner, and that's God. That's the most important and most appropriate honor he'll receive."

So it is his family, friends and community—those who can best appreciate what he has overcome to get this far—who prized Largent's final days in the NFL like treasures from a lost civilization. Sue Stewart, for one, twice has taken a leave of absence from her job. She and her husband have lived in the home of former Seahawk Dave Brown during the past two Seahawk seasons to be close to her son.

"I was there when Steve ran onto the field for the first time," she explains, "and I want to be there when he runs on for the last time."

Scott Manley says, "When Steve retires, there will be a void. We will all be diminished a little bit." Yet Manley and those who know Largent best say the void will be theirs and not Largent's. They expect Largent to continue to flourish after football because he has positioned himself to do so.

Through adversity, Largent established diversity in his life. Concluding his devotion to football was "unhealthy," he taught himself to rely less on the sport for personal nourishment. Over the years, Largent has carved out of his athletic commitments the time for a weekly date with his wife and a weekly family night. Football, Largent found, he could live without; God and family, he could not.

If asked about the major disappointment in his life, Largent doesn't mention the Super Bowl. Rather, it is his perceived shortcomings as a father that vexes him most.

"Someone once said you only have enough patience for one less child than you actually have," Largent says. "I think I might have only enough patience for two less. That frustrates me. I'm not where I'm going to be as a father. I tell my kids that all the time. When I pray with them at night, my prayer is that the Lord will make me a better dad."

So walking off a football field for the last time Saturday night will, in a sense, be a release for Largent. An opportunity to concentrate on real priorities. And a challenge. Another challenge.

"People have been asking me how I want to be remembered and I always feel like we're drawing up an epitaph," Largent says. "But I'm not dying, I'm just moving on to something else.

"I've always been the kind of person who views things as half-full instead of half-empty. So instead of focusing on the fact that my football life is dying, I'm excited about what's coming next. I can't tell you what that is right now, but I can't wait to get to the corner, look around and see what it is."

Brophy's Last Brawl

HOCKEY

By *TOM HAWTHORN*

From Toronto Life Magazine

The ice at the old hockey arena in New Haven, Conn., was surrounded by a heavy wire fence. No one knows if it was there to keep the players from the crowd or the crowd from the players. The local citizenry had a habit of sneaking forks into the building, and when the opposing team trooped onto the ice, fans would stab at any backside within reach. The skaters developed the habit of parading with their sticks held high.

It was a tactic they had already perfected in games during which, typically, more punches were landed than goals were scored. "You could go to New Haven on a Sunday," John Brophy remembers, "and spend a long fucking night that had nothing to do with hockey."

Hockey has been Brophy's life. His classrooms were snake-pit arenas in decaying industrial cities, his teachers the hard men who knew the brutal ways of survival in a life in which even the pettiest of disputes was settled with fists, or worse. Brophy took to heart what he learned. But when he was finally blessed with a hockey job better than anything he ever allowed himself to imagine holding, the same lessons would doom him, for by then no one would be able to understand.

Brophy was a favorite target on the carnival circuit of the Eastern Hockey League. He carved the mark of Zorro on more than a few opponents and he took no guff. After his hair faded prematurely, he came to be called the Gray Ghost. It was said he rarely finished a game without blood running down his face. After one particularly rambunctious scrimmage, someone climbed the fire escape behind the shameful old building in New Haven. The intruder peered through a window that looked down on the visiting team's locker room, saw Brophy in the shower, levelled his gun and fired.

After the bullet finished ricochetting, Brophy's teammates lifted their heads to see it resting at the feet of the Gray Ghost. Some say he laughed. It was not yet John Brophy's time.

What would be Brophy's final stay of execution came on the first Monday in December. He was expected to be fired as coach of the Toronto Maple Leafs that day, so more reporters than usual attended the team's daily practice. Borje Salming, the veteran defenseman, leaned over the boards to whine, "Why don't you guys ever come here when the team's winning?" As he skated away, someone taunted, "When was that?"

National Hockey League coaches are hired to be fired. Still, that final reprieve from Harold Ballard left Brophy in a giddy state. He tossed off nervous one-liners. A few days earlier, he had suffered an ugly gash when he walked headlong into a girder at the Los Angeles Forum. "I tried to commit suicide," he joked, "but I guess I started too high."

He might have said he started too late.

In typical Pal Hal fashion, Ballard was incapable of replacing the coach without first humiliating him. But if Brophy was galled, he never let on. After decades in hockey's backwaters, Brophy was not about to squander the break of a lifetime.

★ ★ ★

It's tempting to see John Brophy as a cartoon character. After all, he spent 3,593 minutes in the penalty box, which is just a fighting major and a roughing minor shy of having watched 60 complete games from the sin bin. He played at professional hockey's bottom rung and he did whatever had to be done to keep his job.

That he survived as Leaf coach for as long as he did was a source of wonderment to many. Few expected he would even make the big time. "If you ever asked anybody who the least likely person would have been to become a coach in the NHL," says sportscaster Eli Gold, "everybody would have said Brophy."

You can read the story of Brophy's 56 years on his face. It has been caressed by more than a few hockey sticks, and it is a mug that has eaten its share of knuckle sandwiches. He sports a scar on his right cheek as long and deep as the Strait of Canso. His hair, which started turning gray when he was 16, is now as white as his language is blue. He roars invective between expletives, all coming in the clipped cadence of the Nova Scotia town he left four decades ago. Words spill from Brophy in an ever faster jumble until he sounds like John Turner on bennies.

He has spent many a late night retelling war stories with his cronies. Still, it takes some coaxing these days to get him to recount the days of busted heads and battered bodies. "It's not even worth talking about," he says in a sputter. "Are you digging up all that bullshit about the Eastern League and all those places? Nobody remembers that world now. Nobody understands that world. You got to be careful about what you're saying about my whole life. I could go on and on and on about being the most penalized player in the fucking world—and it's true—but it's not worthwhile."

Brophy's exploits in the league that was a pacifist's nightmare have long been part of hockey folklore. "In the Eastern League," says Gold, "if the folks didn't see a bench-clearing brawl, they'd want their money back." Brophy's adventures among the desperadoes and outlaws were the inspiration for the madcap Paul Newman movie "Slap Shot."

"We had teams sometimes where you didn't have to worry too much about home games," Brophy says. "You won them all. No one was gonna come in there too brave." The same rule also worked against his side. "I know we used to go into Syracuse some nights when Ronnie Ingram was there, you knew half your team quit around four o'clock in the afternoon. They weren't up to taking what they had to face." New Haven once hired the amateur heavyweight boxing champion of Canada just before a big grudge match against Brophy's Long Island Ducks. "He didn't exactly come there to rush the puck, I'll tell you that."

The closest Brophy got to the big leagues was when he broke an NHL player's leg during an exhibition game.

This was not quite the life Brophy had dreamed of when he listened to Foster Hewitt calling Leaf games on the radio every Saturday night. One of eight children, he lost his mother before he started school. Since his father was often away working on the railway, he was raised by an uncle. Brophy left home in Antigonish at 16 to play pro hockey, spending his summers working high steel, helping to build the Verrazano-Narrows Bridge in New York City before going north to Labrador to put together the hangars in Goose Bay. He made as much or more each summer as a construction steelworker, but stuck with the game because he loved it and because he didn't relish working atop some bridge in winter.

So he plied his trade as a defenseman in the Eastern League for 21 years, riding the bus from Commack, N.Y. to Jacksonville, Fla., from truck stop to greasy spoon, season after season. He played in southern cities where crackers would get down on hands and knees to marvel at the indoor ice, and he played in towns where the team bus would need a police escort to the county line. It wasn't much, yet he had to fight to keep it.

Owners had their choice of third-rate players to stock their teams. "If you didn't fulfill your job, if you didn't do it properly, you were no longer there," recalls John Muckler, an Edmonton Oilers coach who started out with Brophy in Baltimore in the mid-50s. "There was a man waiting to take your job. That in itself provides motivation." Brophy made up for his many shortcomings as a defenseman by playing with the ferocity of a madman. "When I played, if you didn't win, if you didn't spill your guts out every game, you were gone. Hell, back in them days, three bad *shifts* and you were out."

One common Brophy opponent was Don Perry. Pals off the ice, more often than not they were pugilists on it. "You would have to fight him over and over," recalls Perry, who outweighed the daffy Duck by 25 pounds. "Whatever it took to get things done, he didn't mind doing."

Once, Brophy went over the edge in an infamous stick-swinging brawl with Bobby Taylor, a football flanker who moonlighted as a hockey player in winter. "It was just an absolute war, like somebody was going to die," Perry says, his voice dropping to a hush. "The sticks were shattered all over the place, and they were trying to spear each other with what remained. They were cut badly. It was the bloodiest event by far that I've ever seen."

Brophy and Perry were teammates with Long Island the time Jackie Leclair of New Haven clipped Brophy in the face with his stick. Brophy vowed revenge. As word of the promised donnybrook spread, every seat and all the standing room inside the large Quonset hut that was home to the Ducks in Commack was filled.

Perry arrived at the rink to find Brophy stewing. "Don't you go get mellow on me now," Brophy told him. Perry said, "No, I haven't forgot." They sat down and taped their hands like boxers. Coach Muckler walked in, took one look at what they were up to and left. Thirteen seconds after the puck was dropped, Brophy and Perry had decked Leclair and one of his teammates. The bloodied New Haven team left the ice, got on the bus and went home. Muckler had to call the riot squad to clear angry customers from the building.

Brophy's playing days ended in Cherry Hill, N.J., where he shared an apartment with future NHLers Curt Brackenbury and Jack McIlhargey. Brophy's room was a closet off the kitchen. He had a mattress on the floor and his clothes overhead. It was not a lot to show for 21 years of hockey.

A coaching career came next. Brophy finally got to see all the leagues he'd never reached as a player: the Southern League, the Central League, the American League, the North American League, the World Hockey Association, the NHL. His first big break came in 1978 with the Birmingham Bulls (nee Toronto Toros) of the WHA. He was handed a team of highly paid veterans surrounded by a goon squad hired to protect the merchandise in what is generally recognized as the toughest team in hockey history. Muscle was provided by the felonious likes of Dave Hanson, Jeff Carlson and Steve Durbano. (Hanson and Carlson, incidentally, were members of the cast of "Slap Shot".) "If you can't beat 'em, beat 'em up," was the unofficial motto of the Bulls, and the mill workers of Magic City adopted them as their own. They played "Dixie" as an anthem, while fans waved Confederate flags and let out wild rebel yells.

In Brophy's first full year, however, team owner John Bassett Jr. had to sell players to NHL clubs to stay solvent. "If the price is right," Bassett said, "everything's for sale except my wife and four children." Brophy was left with the shell of a team. "Every day, Bassett would come in and say, 'Well, I didn't want to do this to you, but I've sold Linseman to Philadelphia for X dollars.' The next day, he came back: 'Well, I've sold Langway to the Montreal Canadiens.' Napier went to the Canadiens. So, Jesus, there's two more. The next day, there's Garrett gone to the Hartford Whalers. Every day he'd come in and say, 'I hate to do this to you. . . .' "

The Bulls roster was filled with unwanted free agents, tired veterans and a half-dozen teenagers who were ineligible to play in the NHL because of their age. Some said the Baby Bulls, as the team was dubbed, would never win a game. But Brophy proved he could inspire young players, filling them with the same sense of fierce loyalty that had been his hallmark all those years. The Baby Bulls, including future NHL stars Rick Vaive and Michel Goulet, missed the playoffs on the final day of the season. Brophy was named coach of the year.

★ ★ ★

Brophy's reputation as a hard-nosed taskmaster of the old school preceded him to Maple Leaf Gardens. He was known in the minors to have kicked rowdy players off the team bus in the middle of winter, or to hold a grueling practice immediately following a loss. In a rage after one bad game, he put his fist through a bus window. "I think he'll be a great man for discipline," Ballard said. Others predicted his Simon Legree tactics, so successful in handling teenage players in the minors, would fail miserably when used on the pampered elite of the NHL.

The new coach even called his team the Big Blue, an old-timers' tag from the glory days. The players were far too sophisticated to pay heed, even after Brophy bromides became a staple of Leaf practices. "If that's skating, your mother skates better," he would yell. "Take off your helmet, I think your head's clogged."

Brophy felt a player could be unworthy of wearing a Leaf sweater and he believed in the legend of the Leafs, but the players harbored no such illusions. To them, the sport is just a business.

To their coach, it's a primal struggle. He passed on a few tricks of his trade to the defensemen in a memorable practice soon after he became coach. His field of expertise has been the etiquette of clearing an opponent from the front of one's net, so he placed his players in the slot and chopped them down one by one. With his stick he poked Chris Kotsopoulos in the belly, probed the back of Jerome Dupont's knee, smacked Valmore James's shoulder then swept his feet out from under him. James got up and was promptly knocked down again. The coach then stood with his stick between the legs of dutiful Peter Ihnacak, who, instead of skating away as any sane person would have done, grimaced in anticipation of an upward tug that never came.

The more mature the players, the more they resented the

tongue-lashings and lumberjack lessons. As far as they could see, Brophy wasn't doing his job. Where other teams had set plays to rush the puck under different circumstances, the Leafs played hockey's equivalent of football's desperation call, "Everyone go deep." Throughout Brophy's tenure, the Leafs were stumblebums on the power play. When pressed in their own end, they often floundered about in a panic of uncertainty.

Brophy did not become coach because of his brilliant stratagems. He had won the boss's eye with his adherence to such values as discipline, loyalty and diligence. Not surprisingly, many are seen wanting according to the dictates of a code tempered in the blast furnace of the Eastern League. Once, a Moncton-born player on a rival team took a poke at a Leaf with his stick and, when challenged to fight, curled up on the ice, protected by his helmet. Brophy was disgusted by the display. "Look at that Charlie Bourgeois, turtling up like that. He's a disgrace to the Maritimes." Brophy became a coach by turning the Charlie Bourgeoises of the world into scrappy hockey players.

He has little patience for slick playmakers who avoid the heavy going of the corners, so it was sayonara to the swift but fainthearted Russ Courtnall (23 goals last season) and hello to Montreal tough guy John Kordic (two goals). The Leafs are so enamored of Kordic, with his doughy boxer's face, that he has been given sweater number 27, which once graced such stylish players as Frank Mahovlich and Darryl Sittler. Kordic responded to the honor by using his stick to perform radical rhinoplasty on Keith Acton of the Edmonton Oilers, an operation that netted him a 10-game suspension.

The Leaf brain trust under Ballard has long valued toughness over skill. Talented young rear guards had to learn the essential trade of rushing the puck by watching their opponents do so. If they messed up, they got another Brophy tantrum.

The players finally mutinied at the end of last season. "We'd all like to go out and shoot him between the eyes," one anonymous Leaf said. Salming blamed the coach for the team's turmoil and lackluster performance.

Brophy brooded over the revolt of the off-season. "I learned my lesson last year," he admitted last November. "At least I hope I did. You say some things sometimes that you wish you had back, that's for sure." Players were not publicly ridiculed this season. They still lost, of course, a team of inept enforcers and crowd pleasers.

Watching his somnambulant squad fritter away game after game frustrated Brophy. In the end, he could not inspire them. "The only thing I'm sorry about here is that I failed," he said the day he was fired. "I think I tried, but it didn't come off." He never understood why well-paid professionals could not be motivated to play hard for 60 minutes when a lug like himself had only kept his spot on pro hockey's bottom rung by being the toughest SOB ever to lace a pair of skates.

★ ★ ★

The return of the Stanley Cup is the eternal hope of long-suffering Leaf fans, who last celebrated a championship in Centennial Year. Vincent Damphousse, a talented center now in his third season with Toronto, had not yet been born. "They don't know," Brophy says. "They don't understand. How could they?"

What the players know only too well is that there is little sense in busting a gut over a meaningless 80-game season when the 20th-place team in a 21-team league can still make the playoffs, a trick the Leafs pulled last season. They know that whatever it was that fuelled John Brophy for all those years in the minors doesn't apply to them. They would never know the kind of loyalty that led Don Perry to tape his hands like a boxer when his friend had a score to settle.

So when George Armstrong, the captain of four Cup-winning teams in the 1960s, reluctantly replaced the white-haired hellion five days before Christmas, the club continued its losing ways. Ironically, the new coach does not believe in coaching. The easygoing Chief suffers from ulcers, and the Leafs are a team known to give them, so he immediately handed the reins to Brophy's faithful assistant, Garry Lariviere.

The team has kept on losing. When this season ends the day after April Fool's, the Leafs may qualify for the playoffs. If so, the Carlton Street cashbox will be filled for a few more money-making dates. Players and coaches will mouth cliches about playoffs being a new season. They will speak of pride and desire. They will help fill the owner's pockets before going down to defeat, then repeat the same sorry performance next season.

If the team is seen by many as a public trust, it can also be said that the coach is seen as an expression of the civic character. Brophy, the hockey savage from the Maritimes, could never meet the standard. He was a come-from-away with the audacity to believe he could infuse his charges with as great a desire to win as he had himself.

But Brophy never understood that hockey had changed. His players never understood that, even after riding the bus for 21 years, a survivor like Brophy gets just one shot at the big time. And when that time has come and gone, what sense do you make of a lifetime of having been beaten up and shot at? Only the Gray Ghost knows, and he's not saying.

Follow the Bouncing Balls

by Louis DeLuca of the Dallas Times Herald. When action on the field stopped because of a rain delay, DeLuca's camera went to work, creatively capturing the idle exploits of the dugout-confined Texas Rangers. The photo was shot during spring training in Plant City, Fla. Copyright ©1989, Louis DeLuca, Dallas Times Herald.

Man Down

by Brian Peterson of the Minneapolis Star Tribune. Minnesota wide receiver Anthony Carter, helmetless and obviously in pain, lies at the feet of conquering Detroit Lions defenders after taking a crunching hit during a 1989 National Football League game. Copyright ©1989, Brian Peterson, Star Tribune.

54
CARTER
81

After 10 Days of Pain, Let's Resume Series Gracefully

BASEBALL

By *MARK PURDY*

Let's do this gracefully. Tonight, we go back to Candlestick Park —either in person, or on television, or maybe just for a few seconds in our minds, at 5:04 p.m. Please. Let's do this gracefully.

That is not my phrase. It was first used a week ago by Fay Vincent, baseball's commissioner. He said the World Series would be resumed in time, if it could be accomplished "gracefully." Later, he decided tonight was the time.

It is not fair that the World Series and the earthquake became linked in the public consciousness—if it had happened a week later, no one would have connected the two—but that is the hand fate dealt. The Series and quake are forever linked.

And now, beginning this afternoon, fate gives the Bay Area a chance to complete the last chain in that link. Let's do this gracefully.

I know what we don't need. We don't need goofy posters at the ballpark making stupid puns about the earthquake. And we don't need ABC to come on the air with something like this: "*Well, that takes care of the earthquake highlights, and we'll be back with the starting lineups after this word from Budweiser.*"

The folks at ABC say there will be no such trivialization or exploitation of the quake and its victims. They'd better be right. There will be so much subcutaneous drama in these remaining games, no extra commentary will be necessary.

The Giants and A's—simply by holding their shaken families in the moments after the quake, let alone visiting homeless shelters—already have experienced more emotional swings than any other Series teams in history. I don't imagine we'll ever again hear quotes from baseball players like the ones of the past 10 days.

"It's almost in bad taste to come out here and do this," A's shortstop Walt Weiss said at the team's first workout after the earthquake, "but as professionals, we have to. Time will tell how it looks."

Initially, it didn't look so swell. Playing baseball with dead bodies still being pulled from the ruins seemed in dreadful taste. But waiting the 10 days, until the funerals were finished, has been a needed show of respect. We have a chance to play it out gracefully.

But only if we take advantage of that chance. A week ago, I thought the Series should have been canceled. My idealistic notion was that by doing so—by calling it off after two games—baseball's record books always would pay tribute to the quake victims. Now, by playing out the full Series, it won't look much different. But anyone who examines the records will know—and the A's manager, Tony La Russa, finally convinced me that resuming the Series after a mourning period was no crime.

"If someone could prove to me that we're hurting anyone by playing these games, then I might agree that not playing was appropriate," La Russa said. "I think it's clear that the celebration isn't going to be the same, whichever team celebrates."

We all need perspective, though, not just the players. In the nervous moments after the quake, as I interviewed Giants officials outside the team's locker room in the parking lot—with uneasy players gathering up their uneasy families to leave the stadium—someone tapped my shoulder.

"Could I borrow your pen?" a stranger asked. "I want to get Robby Thompson's autograph."

I wanted to slug the guy. I can only pray that no drunken fan yells, "OOO-REE-BAY!" during tonight's moment of silence.

Let's do this gracefully. There should be no fear in going back to Candlestick. I am sure of that. It will be very spooky to sit again in my second-deck press seat tonight, but I am not afraid. Whatever happens in the next few days, Candlestick still gets my Series MVP award. An architect friend worked out the formula for me. If 60,000 fans were in the stadium, then Candlestick's girders were supporting almost 10 million pounds of people during the quake.

Ten million pounds, yet it held. It should handle any aftershock. Funny. Only architects used to think about that. Now we all do.

After the moment of silence tonight at Candlestick, the crowd will be asked to sing the song, "San Francisco," from the old Clark Gable movie. Let's do it gracefully, if we can. Let's not make the sing-along an "Up With People" solution to our problems. In the movie, the song signified a happy ending to the audience. We don't yet have that happy ending here. We shouldn't pretend otherwise.

Face it. Most of the people singing tonight at Candlestick probably didn't suffer any serious loss in the earthquake. How will those people singing "San Francisco" strike those watching the game on television from a Red Cross shelter? I don't know.

But I also don't want to be a Scrooge about it. If you are going to the game tonight and they ask you to sing, sing gracefully. However, also bring something to drop off at one of the earthquake relief booths that will be set up outside Candlestick. Those booths may be the most graceful part of the Series. Major league baseball announced a $1.4 million donation to quake relief Thursday. Players are making their own donations.

My hope is that for once, a major sporting event such as the World Series will be played without the unctuous importance that tends to rightfully disgust non-sports fans. My hope is that the players perform well but stay cognizant of their small place in the overall picture. My hope is that no one in the winning locker room says: "We overcame a lot of adversity to get this trophy." Not with the adversity so many others here have had to face.

My hope is for a Series with heart, not hype. We've got a chance to see that in the next few days. Let's do this with grace.

The Dean

COLLEGE BASKETBALL

By *JOHN HAWKINS*

The 90-mile bus trip from Winston-Salem to Chapel Hill was no joy ride for a young University of North Carolina basketball team the night of January 6, 1965.

The Tar Heels had been swamped by Wake Forest, 107-85, their third consecutive loss. The season before had ended with a 1-5 stretch. And Dean Smith, 33, in his fourth season as coach in a program with high expectations, felt the heat.

By all accounts, Smith said nothing on the ride home. When the bus wheeled onto campus, the usual group of 100 or so students was waiting. Only this time, instead of pleasantries, there was commotion.

"We want Smith! We want Smith!"

From a nearby tree, a dozen or so students were hanging Dean Smith in effigy. In 1965, nobody was stopping them.

"The one thing I remember about that was that we were grumbling, too," says Bob Bennett, a junior guard that season. "He was starting a bunch of different combinations, constantly experimenting. . . . And we were wondering what was going on.

"But when we got back and the students were doing that, well, Billy Cunningham just jumped off the bus, ran at the tree and tore the thing down. And there was silence. The crowd started to disperse. It didn't come to us all at once, but later, we all wished we'd done what Billy C did. It was the single most important thing emotionally that I'd ever seen."

The folks who wanted Dean Smith's scalp in 1965 named a building after him in 1985. You could say, with great conviction, that public opinion has changed.

His teams have won 25 or more games in 16 of the past 22 years and 82 percent of all games the past 20 years. The Tar Heels have been ranked in the top 10 in every final Associated Press poll since 1978. They have won nine Atlantic Coast Conference tournaments and have reached seven Final Fours.

That UNC's arena is the Dean E. Smith Center—the Dean Dome for short—is testimony to his stature as a legend. He entered this season with 638 victories; he could pass John Wooden (667) in March. If he coaches until the end of the century, he should easily pass Adolph Rupp (875) as college basketball's all-time winner.

He has coached 34 men who have played in the National Basketball Association or the old American Basketball Association, 13 lawyers and 11 doctors. He has tutored a slew of coaches. Of the 168 players who lettered for him, 164 have graduated. Close to half (73) have done post-graduate work.

There are reasons why.

"The bottom line is values," says Mitch Kupchak, Class of '76, now assistant general manager of the Los Angeles Lakers. "The way he treats people. The way he respects players. The creativity aspect. The intensity."

There are detractors. Virginia coach Terry Holland once said, "There is a gap between the man and the image he is trying to project."

On a lighter note, Holland named his dog Dean Smith because, he said, the pooch wouldn't stop crying. And one of the best Carolina jokes these days is that only Dean Smith could hold Michael Jordan under 20 points every night.

That says something about Smith, too. The System comes first at North Carolina, not the superstar. And certainly not the coach, a man whose prodigious success at turning groups of young men into winners on and off the court is surpassed only by an almost apologetic sense of humility.

What follows is a look at the man who created and sustained such ideals—through the eyes of the people who once played for him. Let it be known that after the students hanged Dean Smith in effigy on that January night, the Tar Heels soon went on a seven-game winning streak. And two years later, Dean Smith was in his first Final Four.

"I think we realized that night how special he was," Bennett says.

★ ★ ★

There is a deep pause on the other end of the telephone line. "The rules are stated very clearly up front," says Charles Shaffer, Class of '64, now an Atlanta lawyer. "To be late for a team meeting or a bus is to be very selfish. And selfishness was a direct violation of everything he coached. And, of course, it was a direct violation of the total team concept."

Smith is a big fan of concepts. The total team concept. The good shot selection concept. The whole defense concept. "An individual has to submerge himself to the complete concept of concepts," Shaffer continues. "But in my time there, I can never remember any time that somebody did something that ever got him visibly angry. Not that I remember."

You come to play for Dean Smith, you follow the rules, and you win. You graduate, and you get a good job. And when you leave, you have his respect. No excuses. No strings attached. It is one of amateur sport's most consistent agreements. You will adhere while you're there. No excuses. No strings attached.

"Oh, he can get angry," says Lee Dedmon, Class of '71, now a high school principal in Gastonia, N.C. "But he gets angry at groups, not individuals. He'll bounce a piece of chalk off your head if you fall asleep watching a game film, though."

Every former player confessed to one constant: They had *never* heard Dean Smith use profanity. In turn, you don't cuss around Dean Smith. It's one of the rules. Positive thinking is another one. Smith doesn't deal in criticism, particularly on the court. Kupchak said Smith "can throw chairs with his eyes." He is speaking of the notorious stare.

With the System comes unabashed equality. Team managers are treated the same as Jordan. When Cunningham was a preseason All-America selection as a sophomore, he carried the film projector on the road because the senior scrub had done it two years earlier. Remember the "Blue Team," that celebrated reserve squad that spelled the starters throughout the '60s and '70s? Pure fairness, pure Dean Smith.

"Everything is so structured, so laid out," says James Daye, Class of '86 and now a high school coach in Elizabeth City, N.C. "It's almost impossible to make mistakes when everything is made so clear up front."

Smith coached at the Air Force Academy before taking a job as an assistant to Frank McGuire at UNC in 1959. The military experience and his degree in mathematics at the University of Kansas (Class of '53) are staples in his life. Practices are regimented by a stopwatch. Drills often last three minutes and 20 seconds, not three minutes or five minutes. And don't stand around.

"The practice outline is incredible," says Bruce Buckley, Class of '77 and now a lawyer in Charlotte. "There is not a wasted second in an hour and a half. At first, you think it's too much detail. But in a bigger perspective, you realize how important it all is."

If you want to be a scoring champ, don't come to Carolina. It has been said that Smith doesn't recruit players; he selects them. This is true.

"His operation runs like a Swiss clock," says Dennis Wuycik, Class of '72 and now running an ACC newsletter in Chapel Hill. "Time is always given top priority. The System has been good to him. He speaks in reverence of it."

★ ★ ★

If discipline and democracy dominate a player's Carolina years, graduation acts as a transition. "As soon as you put the ball down, it's like night and day," says Bennett, a Los Angeles lawyer. "If you feel at a distance while you're playing, it's supposed to be that way. But when you leave . . . the guy has helped I don't know how many people."

Smith's loyalty to former players is endless, but his sense of commitment goes deeper than just lettermen. While at Kansas, he was coached by an assistant named Dick Harp. Harp later worked for the Fellowship of Christian Athletes, but fell upon hard times a few years ago. Smith brought Harp back to the game and made him his administrative assistant.

He has gotten jobs for scores of people, written hundreds of letters of recommendation and probably acted as a reference for every guy who knows him. But Dean Smith cringes at the thought of taking credit. His credo: "The players win games, I lose them."

The Dean Dome? "I think he was overpowered by the community," says Wuycik. "He feels very strongly about the players being instrumental in the success of the program, and this Taj Mahal is testimony to it."

But naming it after a person who's still alive? Whose office is inside? "It rankles him," says Bennett. "We are forbidden to call it the Dean Dome."

It's not so much modesty as it is privacy, say some. Smith does not like personal kudos. Remember—individual achievement is not part of the System. This is a man who keeps to himself. A previous marriage left him swimming in bad publicity. Only church, his golfing foursome and basketball "family" penetrate his shell.

"He has been so revered, perhaps unfairly," Wuycik said, "that his life pertains to overkill."

Criticism has come and gone. He was maligned for containing Jordan, a talent whose NBA accomplishments speak volumes. He was chided for signing a junior college transfer in the early '70s, and when that player (Bob McAdoo) left after one season. He is currently feeling the brunt of having not won an ACC Tournament since 1982.

Of course, they were calling for Dean Smith's head back in 1965.

"He sends us the blue book (Carolina's media guide) every year," says Kupchak. "He attaches a personal note to every one, and everybody who played for him gets one. That's a lot of people in 28 years. He sent us all a book a friend of his wrote recently, and the same personal touch was there. I know they didn't just go to the pros. Do you think all coaches send personal Christmas cards to guys who played for them 20 years ago?

"I mean, how many guys would do something like that?"

The Longest Ride

HORSE RACING

By *WILLIAM NACK*

It happened so fast that even today Robbie Davis has trouble sorting out the whole haunting nightmare: the terrible fall and the vision of the silks flashing beneath him, the sound like a water balloon bursting at his horse's feet, his own screaming voice, the sight of the dead jockey, and then his hiding like a child in the darkened broom closet in the first-aid room at Belmont Park.

On the afternoon of October 13, 1988, in the fifth race at Belmont Park, Davis, atop Drums in the Night, was moving down the backstretch of the turf course and sensing in the hollow of his bones that he could not have been in a sweeter spot on this great green earth. "It was a beautiful, gorgeous, perfect day," Davis says. "There's nothing like a fall day in New York, you know, and I had won with my horse the time before and I had all sorts of horse under me."

Davis had never been riding better. With almost three months left in the year, his mounts had won 231 races and $7,154,435. He was the sixth-leading jockey in the nation in money won and was, at that moment, sitting just where he wanted to be. Drums in the Night was trailing the leaders but running strong against the bit in the 1 1/16-mile allowance race. "I was next to last," says Davis. "I was staying down on the inside, saving ground and waiting for some running room. I was waiting for the real running to start. Then all of a sudden. . . ."

Davis saw the horse directly in front of him—Mr. Walter K., with veteran jockey Mike Venezia up—stumble suddenly and veer to the right, out of Drums in the Night's path. Instinctively, Davis took hold of his horse, waiting to see what would happen in front of him. "All of a sudden I seen the jockey pop up right in front of me," he says, "and

I look straight back to see which way he would go, so I could miss him. I didn't want to move until he committed himself in one direction or the other. All of a sudden he lost his balance—it happened so fast, I didn't know who it was—and he kicked off the left side of his horse, and he went under my horse. My horse tried to jump, but it was too late. He clipped him and stumbled. The jockey's head was right in the path of my horse, right underneath! I looked down and seen him under me, and my horse scissored his head with his back feet. Shattered his skull."

Davis screamed, "Oh, my God!" He looked back and saw the body lying on the grass, motionless in the sun. Caught in the hot whips of panic, Davis came undone. He looked over to his left and saw jockey Nick Santagata, and he hollered, "Nickie! Who was that? I just killed him! I just run over him. Who was that?"

Santagata glanced at Davis over his shoulder. "Venezia!" he shouted.

The two men raced together for the far turn. Davis screamed again to Santagata: "I killed him! I *swear* I killed him. What do I do? Do I ride? I can't believe it. Nickie! What do I do?"

Santagata never answered, and together the two men drove their horses home. Drums in the Night finished fourth, and as Davis pulled him up at the clubhouse turn, he looked over his left shoulder and saw the ambulance already out on the backstretch. Venezia had been killed instantly, the blow from Drums in the Night's hooves having struck his head so sharply that it dislodged his right eye. But as Davis slowly walked his horse back to the unsaddling area, he didn't know that. He prayed, "God, I know I busted something, but I just hope he's OK."

Davis dismounted and took the saddle off Drums in the Night and studied the horse's feet. "They were beautiful horse feet, so dainty," says Davis, "and he stood there so kind, the horse did, and there were no marks on him, and he was just a beautiful black horse with nice perfect feet, and I'm looking down and saying, 'These are the feet. Why these feet? Why this horse? Why this?' "

Davis walked slowly back through the passage under the grandstand and down the stairs to the underground maze that leads to the jockeys' room. When he got below, he saw the ambulance sitting in the service tunnel, Pinkerton guards all around it, and he began hollering at the driver and the guards, "What the hell are you doing here? Get him to the hospital! What are you waiting for? Why are you leaving him here? Get him out of here! Out! Now!"

In a daze, Davis walked toward the ambulance, but someone stepped in front of him. "Don't look," the man told him. "Please, Robbie. Don't look."

Suddenly there was a commotion on the other side of the ambulance, and Davis saw jockey Angel Cordero Jr. arguing with the guards. Cordero's voice was resounding in the subterranean tombs of Belmont Park: "Hey! Mike was my friend. You can't tell me I can't look in there. You can't tell me what to do!" The guards let Cordero approach the vehicle. All his life Davis will remember the moment, that singular look on Cordero's face as he peered inside the ambulance. "He looked ghostly, pale and white, like he'd aged five years all at once," Davis says.

Davis had to see for himself. He pushed past the guards and looked in the back window of the ambulance. The horror was entire. "He's lying in there on a board," Davis says. "With his head turned away from me. I peeked in. All I could see was blood so thick on his face, and he was lying there motionless. I thought, Oh, no. It can't be!"

Davis bolted for the first-aid room, opened the door of the broom closet and closed it behind him, leaving himself alone in the sudden dark. He fell to his knees. His whole life flashed past him, as though it was *he* who was dying, and in a way he was. "It was flashing and flashing and flashing," Davis says. "If it wasn't one thing flashing, it was something else. All the violent things in my life came back to me. I was on my knees, and I was gripping my fists and saying, 'God, why me? Why does this happen to me all the time? Why do I have to take the pain all the time? Why so much pain?' My whole life was flashing."

Flashing back to those afternoons, so rich in an oily aroma that he can smell them now. Back to when he was 4 and was sitting on the gasoline tank of his Uncle Tim's dirt bike, holding on to the handlebars as he and his uncle roared along at 60 miles an hour among the rock-encrusted hills outside Pocatello, Ida. Back to the day he got the call at Eddy's Bakery, where he was stacking bread, and found when he got home that Uncle Tim, who had been like a father to him, had died of carbon monoxide poisoning in a mining accident. Back to the night that his best friend plunged to his death when the friend's truck rolled off a 60-foot cliff into a cemetery on the east side of Pocatello. Back to his own aborted suicide attempt, when at three one morning he screeched his light-blue 1968 El Camino to a stop just shy of the tree he had been aiming for at the end of Kinghorn Road. Back to the fights at home between his mother and his stepfather Thomas William Darner, the sound of the ashtray smashing through the television screen, and the nights he hid in the closet or under the bed or covered his head with a pillow and screamed to muffle the noise of the violence. Back to his terrorized childhood and the sexual abuse he suffered at the hands of his stepfather. Back to all those years of biting anger, self-loathing and shame that had sprung from that abuse, the dark little secret of his life.

★ ★ ★

After Davis had spent a few agonizing minutes wrapped in the blanket of darkness within that closet, there was a knock on the door. Davis saw a man step forward in the ray of light. Davis was weeping. The voice said, "It's OK, Robbie. It's OK. There's nothing you could have done. We just watched the films. There's no way you could have avoided it."

Davis was inconsolable, and in a state nearing shock. "He was white," says his valet, John Mallano, who had opened the closet door. Almost immediately, Davis began to shear himself of his past. After undressing in the jockey's room, he told Mallano, "Throw everything away. Throw my boots away, my pants, my T-shirt. Everything I was wearing. I don't want these clothes around me ever again."

The next day, after a memorial service for Venezia at Belmont Park—at which Davis fell sobbing to his knees—he quietly told his wife, Marguerite, "Let's go get my hair cut. Maybe I'll feel better." So he had the barber "cut all that old stuff off," he says. "And I cut all my nails down."

His moods swung between sorrow, depression and remorse, and at times he appeared as frail and helpless as one of his three children—Kristen 3, Jacqueline 2, and Robbie Jr., then an infant of two months. He refused to attend Venezia's wake—"I can't do it," he told Marguerite—and so she went in his place. "When I left the house, he was sitting in the rocking chair in the bedroom, clutching the baby's blanket," she said.

All that week Davis brushed off repeated entreaties that he ride again, refused to talk to most of those who called and at night swam in and out of turbulent sleep. One night Marguerite awoke to find him mumbling and sweating in his sleep. The nightmare played and replayed like an old black-and-white movie. "I kept seeing it over and over," Davis says. "Mike kept falling off in front of me. Then the other riders started falling off in front of me, and I started getting paranoid in my dreams."

After Venezia's funeral, in Westbury, N.Y., on October 17, which Davis did attend, he finally settled on what he had to do. His former agent, Lenny Goodman, had been begging him to keep riding. "It's like falling off a horse," Goodman had told him. "You got to get back up and ride right away. You've got to put this behind you!" But Davis wasn't buying that. He had another agenda, the hidden one that had been haunting him. And so, a week after the accident, Marguerite found him frantically packing all their belongings—winter and summer clothes, books, tapes, pictures, VCRs, golf clubs, dirt bike. "I knew exactly what I wanted," Davis says. "But I was in a frenzy, I was hysterical."

"What are you doing?" Marguerite asked.

"I just want to get out of here!" Robbie said. "I want to escape for a while. Take a vacation. I want to go home. I want to get back to myself. To my roots."

So, at age 27, riding high in his prime as one of the leading jockeys in one of the richest venues of American racing, Davis packed his family and their belongings, aimed his Suburban truck west and hit the gas. Until last week, to the dismay and confusion of all his friends, Davis did not ride in another horse race. True to his word, he did go home again.

Pocatello lies in the fertile Snake River Valley in the foothills of the Rocky Mountains in southeastern Idaho, just above the western wing of the Caribou National Forest. It was there, in that one-time railroad tent town that's now a trade and industrial hub of 46,340 people, that Davis was born and raised. He barely knew his natural father, who left his family to get a job and never came back. "He hitchhiked and ended up in Oregon," says Jana McOsker, Robbie's mother. "He just left me there"—with Robbie, then 2, and his sister, Jodi, an infant.

Theirs was a hardscrabble existence. McOsker went on welfare and worked around town as a bartender, a waitress and a cook. The kids lived itinerant childhoods, moving from one place to another, and Robbie attended practically every grade school in Pocatello at least twice. "I'd show up, and they'd say, 'Hey, he's back again!' " he says. McOsker says they usually packed up and moved when the rent came due. "I'd move in with my brother until I got another check, and then I'd move into an apartment," she says.

At an early age Robbie began making money. When Jodi lost two fingers in a washing machine wringer, Robbie went to work at a gasoline station next to their house, cleaning out the bathroom and putting the oil cans away at closing. He was 5 years old and earning 50 cents a night. "He earned 12 dollars and bought her a tricycle when she was in the hospital," McOsker says. At other times he sold Kool-Aid on street corners, and he spent his summers pushing a power lawn mower, the gasoline can swinging from the handlebars, around Pocatello. He washed dishes and bussed tables at a restaurant after school. He hawked the *Idaho State Journal* on the street. He gave his mother money for gas and groceries. "He once had a garage sale and sold all of his toys so we'd have money," she says. "You wouldn't believe this boy. He was special."

His teachers remember him as a sensitive, polite, hardworking lad who was particularly devoted to his sister. "A real likable kid, the kind you just like to be around," says Del Hildreth, Robbie's homeroom teacher at Irving Junior High School.

★ ★ ★

Hildreth had no idea what Robbie had endured: the unspeakable instances of sexual abuse he had suffered for four years in the 1970s at the hands of Darner. In 1976 Darner was convicted of sexual assault and served three years in the New Mexico State Penitentiary at Santa Fe. McOsker says today that she didn't know what had been going on in her house until she found photographic evidence of it and brought charges against Darner. Today, she lives with the remorse. "I am very ashamed and don't know what to say," she says. For years Davis told no one about the abuse and it became the central, gnawing secret of his life, until it ultimately surfaced as a primary force that drove him from New York.

By the time he reached the end of the 10th grade at Pocatello Senior High, Davis was entertaining thoughts of suicide. As with many abused children, his sense of self-worth had broken down, and with that came the onset of his chronic depression, his anger turned inside out. "You're made to feel like the lowest thing on earth," he says. "I've been so low at times that I've sat on a curb and felt that was where I belonged. I felt like a bad person. That's the way you feel." His best friend, Jeff Lindauer, had just died, when his truck dropped off that cliff. Davis was stung by guilt over that, too. "Just a month before, I had showed him how to get up there," he says.

He started drinking vodka and dropped out of school, in which he saw no future. "A kind of waste," he says. "I had already grown up a long time ago. I hated myself for whatever happened in the old time. I just didn't have no use in life anymore."

One evening, in aimless despair—"I was *so* depressed, you know," he says—he backed up the El Camino on Kinghorn Road, dropped it into gear and set sail for that big tree. Headlights on, he barreled toward it through the darkness. He doesn't know why he hit the brakes, but he did, locking the drums with a screech. "I slid to a stop about a foot away," he says. "Something touched me. I didn't want to die, and I hit the brakes and I set there, it was three o'clock in the morning, looking at the tree, just crying. I didn't have a dad. . . ."

McOsker has known a lot of men in her life—she has been married eight times, twice to the same man—but none of the men she brought home became a father to the boy. Instead, Davis found his surrogate in Tim Lords, his mother's brother. Uncle Tim was his mentor, his teacher. "The father that I never had," Davis says. "He taught me everything."

Uncle Tim's death in a freak mining accident in 1979 left Davis grieving as he never had. "That was devastating," he says. "It was so unbelievable. I would throw rocks at trees for hours. I was crazed." But Uncle Tim had left him far more than grief and summer memories, as things turned out, and the most valuable gift of all was an abounding love of racing and speed—those hair-blowing, rock-climbing, wind-in-your-face ascents up mountain trails to a freedom Davis had never before known. He vividly remembers when he was 4 and Uncle Tim would take him riding on the dirt bike. "He went so fast I couldn't breathe," Davis says. "Took my breath away. Sixty miles an hour. We'd fly over jumps, climb mountains. We'd hit something and he'd hang on to me. I wasn't afraid of anything."

At 15 Davis got his first dirt bike—he had saved the money while working at a pizzeria—and he rode it every day. For the deeply scarred young man, that dirt bike meant escape, a way to get away. "I could ride up to 40, 50 miles a day," Davis says. "I loved it. It was my first love. The wind and the mountains and the freedom! I was so comfortable with it." He dreamed of one day being a professional dirt-bike racer, and he began entering small events in and around Pocatello. He won a few races, he says, just amateur stuff: "All I got was trophies."

The 5-foot-1 Davis soon found that he could race for more than that at Pocatello Downs, the local racetrack that was part of a county fair circuit for quarter horses and thoroughbreds. He was almost 19, working at Eddy's Bakery, when a co-worker and part-time horse trainer, John Dalkey, urged him to come out to the Downs and learn to be a rider.

"I thought, 'Hey, I can do that!' " says Davis. Soon he had quit his $250-a-week bakery job and hired on as a groom at $65 a week, first with Dalkey and then with veteran trainer Marv Whitworth, who became the surrogate father he had been looking for since Lords had died. That summer, 1979, Davis mucked stalls and slipped into the game as easily as a pitchfork into a bed of straw. He quickly learned how to ride and then really went to the races in 1980, when he rode his first winner, in a 220-yard dash for Appaloosas at the fairgrounds in Burley, Ida. He still gets a rush, recalling the race.

"Oh, god," Davis says. "Out of the gate it was like a dirt bike coming out of the hills off a jump—voom! Like a dragster coming off the line, with the front wheels coming off the ground. He was really a fast horse. God, what a blast!"

Davis loved his work and threw himself into it, wanting to be a jockey more than anything he had ever wanted in his life. "You'd tell him to be at the barn at four o'clock in the morning and he was there at four, waiting for you," says trainer Lynn Bowman, who employed Davis then.

"You could set your watch by him," Whitworth says. "I never had a boy so dedicated or want anything as bad. He had ambition. You had to be around him to see the intensity. And what an athlete! A natural—his balance, his coordination on a horse, and real fine hands—and he never, never abused his mount in any way."

Whitworth and Davis grew so close that until very recently Whitworth was the only person with whom Davis had shared the secret of his past. "It makes your gut crawl," Whitworth says.

That fall Davis packed off to a quarter-horse and thoroughbred ranch in Southern California. He got his seasoning there, riding and exercising 22 horses a day all winter, but what he really learned was what he wanted to do with his life. The inspiration dawned on him the day he visited Santa Anita Park, the Taj Mahal of California racing. In the spring, with the Idaho racing season coming up, Davis announced he was going to ride in California. Whitworth told him to stay one more summer in Idaho. "You're not ready for California," Whitworth said.

Of course, Davis stayed in Idaho. He was the leading rider that summer on the fair circuit—at bullrings in such places as Idaho Falls and Blackfoot—but when the fall came, there was no keeping him in the bushes. In fact, he was gone for good, heading for the thoroughbreds, the big time. He tried his hand with a trainer at Turf Paradise in Phoenix and won four races there, and followed the trainer when he moved to Louisiana Downs. But he languished there for months, unable to get mounts. He had begun his one-year apprenticeship in

May of '82, after he had won the fifth race of his career, but he went nowhere with the "bug"—the weight allowance granted to apprentices—in so provincial an outpost as Shreveport. One afternoon, jockey Sam Maple told him that he ought to go to New York. "They'll ride you with the bug in New York," Maple told him. "You might not stay when your bug is over, but you can make $100,000 there as an apprentice."

That's all Davis had to hear. A few days later he was edging his El Camino across the East River and onto Long Island. He hired himself a hustling agent, Steve Adika, and together they lit up the tote boards. They very sight of mammoth Belmont Park, with its sweeping grandstand and infield and its 1½-mile oval, left him in awe. He climbed on his first mount in New York, Commanche Brave, on September 2, 1982. "I walked out of that paddock to the track and it took my breath away," Davis says. "I thought, I'm here. This is it."

Commanche Brave, a 20-1 shot, won that race, and it was not long before Davis was the hottest bug boy in New York. At Aqueduct that winter, he was the leading rider in races won, with 51. He won his first stakes race, the Lucky Draw, on Rock Lives, in February of 1983. He won some 170 races as a bug, all but 17 of them in New York and New Jersey, and made more money than he had ever dreamed of seeing. When he lost his bug on May 28, 1983, he found that Maple had been right. "I had $100,000 in the bank," Davis says. "Cash! I was ready to come right back to Pocatello. I was going to be the King of Pocatello! I was going to have the nice car and the boat and take all my friends fishing."

He did nothing of the sort. Instead, he went back to work. There was the inevitable lull in his action after he had lost his weight allowance, but Adika pestered trainers to give Davis a break. Six weeks later, sure enough, they started lifting his leg again. "Steve pushed and pushed us to ride him," says trainer H. Allen Jerkens. So, unlike most hot apprentices who lose their bugs and disappear, Davis stuck in New York. Of course, it was more than just Adika who did it. "Robbie learned as an apprentice how to rate horses," Jerkens says. "Through the years, guys who learn to rate horses keep going. Guys who don't learn, don't do anything after they lose the bug."

His early triumphs notwithstanding, Davis lived a difficult life in New York. He usually kept to himself. "God, it was lonely," he says. "I'd win a $75,000 stake and come home to an empty house. What a cold feeling. You tend to be a loner when you have such shame. There was so much shame there. When I skated, I always skated alone."

Davis roller-skated often in New York, as he had as a kid in Pocatello, and on one Friday night in the spring of 1984, at the Roller Castle in Elmont, N.Y., a pixieish blonde introduced herself to him. They skated couples. He had always been afraid to date, insecure and wary as he was, and there was an awkward moment when he took her hand and said, in his first words to her, "Boy, you got rough hands! Been digging ditches or something?" Marguerite Hoveling, who did a lot of yard work, liked him anyway. "He was shy and polite," she says. They have been together ever since. They got married the next February—they had their kids one-two-three—and shared the months during which Davis moved in among the leaders of his profession. He made money whip over stirrup in New York and earned the same kind of reputation among horsemen there as he had in Idaho—as a friendly, polite, personable young man with a quick, pearly smile and no apparent demons driving him. "I put on a good front," Davis says. "I didn't want anybody to see through me."

What they would have seen last summer, had they been able to see through him, was a man increasingly in turmoil. "I was like a time bomb," he says. "I was very, very depressed. I kept all my anger in. You build up a lot of anger. You can be in a great mood and all of a sudden you think of something that happened, and it just turns everything. Then you're mad at everything. . . . I hated myself. I could never do enough or accomplish what I wanted. I was always mad at myself and at other people. I used to build up a big hate for people, and it hurt inside."

And it was all a secret, down at the deep root of the rage, a secret unshared for years even with his wife. "It was always there," he says. "It was just grinding at me: 'You've got to tell her, you've got to tell her,' I'd say to myself. 'No, she doesn't have to know this. It'll hurt her too much.' " He envisioned her leaving him if he told her of his past, running to her mother's Long Island house with the kids, telling her mother, Hey, this guy was sexually abused, he's a complete wacko!

He didn't know how to handle his turbulent emotions. Last summer he felt them mounting. "It was getting worse and worse," he says. "I was getting meaner and meaner, angrier and angrier. For no reason whatsoever, I'd fly off the handle. I was a real crybaby in the jocks' room; things would happen to me in a race and I'd scream and holler at the other riders. I was getting scared of myself."

Davis was carrying all that unchecked baggage from his childhood when, on that fine October afternoon, Venezia fell in front of him, Davis peered into the ambulance and then ran off to hide. As his life flickered before him in that closet, the scenes of violence and abuse, something in him seemed to die. A kind of serenity came over him, as if the accident, in catharsis, had suddenly slain all the old torments in his life. "It pulled a trigger," he says. "It shot off inside me and went through me. I never loved people more in my life than that moment right there. All the hate I had for everybody, it just all went away."

★ ★ ★

With that began the craving to head home. Davis says, "It's hard to explain, but there was something pulling me back to Pocatello—to my values. I was packing too heavy a load. There was too much I had to get off my mind."

There was that delicate matter of unburdening himself to his wife. They drove to Edwardsville, Kan., and spent two months, off and on, with his mother and sister. They spent $85,000 on a huge motor home. They took a skiing trip to Colorado before Christmas, and then one night, after all those years of keeping it in, Davis finally let it out, first telling Marguerite of the deaths of Lindauer and Lords and how hard it had been growing up and how low he had been at times.

"I took a lot of abuse when I was young," he said.

"What kind?" she asked.

"Sexual. I was sexually abused by a man my mother was married to. . . ."

It was easier than he had thought it would be. They talked about it into the night. "It just flowed out," Davis says. "We were both crying. She was so understanding. We tied the knot that much tighter. She held me all night and we went to sleep. It was such a relief. It was like a new beginning."

On Christmas Day, Davis talked to Lenny Goodman by telephone—he had taken over the rider's book early last year—and Goodman reminded him that Gulfstream Park was opening soon. Davis was not ready. "Only millionaires take off like this," Goodman said. "You're taking the longest vacation in history!"

Speaking to one of America's leading riders, a 27-year-old whose mounts had amassed lifetime earnings of $37,382,325, Goodman may have been right. But Davis was still too involved in sorting things out and looking for answers, unfolding his childhood bit by bit to his wife, and just being with his family and wheeling around the West. They finally came to Pocatello on January 10, hooked up at Sullivan's motor park and lived there for nearly two months. They never connected their telephone—a blessing, what with all the people looking to talk to Davis—but you could reach them here and there if you tried. At the laundromat on Fifth Avenue. At the home of Bonnie Lords, Tim's widow. At the Whitworth home in Inkom. At the ski lodge at Pebble Creek. At the home of Buddy Jones, an old pal from the days when he and Davis worked at the bakery. At the skating rink. At the Downs for the races on weekends.

The Davises remained in Idaho until one snowy morning in early March, when he and Marguerite suddenly decided to leave. They drove west, through Las Vegas and into Southern California. Robbie was itching to ride again.

The old nightmares were gone. Davis still occasionally thought about Venezia, a gentle, soft-spoken man who, like Davis, had been an apprentice sensation in New York, in 1964. Davis recalls spending hours with Venezia after the races, talking about life and their kids. Venezia left a wife and two children when he died, at age 43—a son, Michael Edward, 15, and a daughter, Alison, 8. "I think about him, not every day, but every once in a while," Davis says. "I don't dwell on it. I still feel a little hurt over it, but there ain't nobody on earth who can change it. I think about his kids, his son and daughter, and I feel that they were lucky they got to know him."

Nor do the memories of the accidents haunt Davis as they did immediately after the mishap, when he blamed himself "totally." Totally? Oh yes. After all, Davis says, Drums in the Night had natural early speed, but he had chosen to take him back, leaving him behind Venezia and Mr. Walter K. down the backstretch. If *only* he had sent Drums in the Night to the lead. . . . If *only* he hadn't shown Lindauer how to get to the top of the cliff. . . . And if *only* he had been bigger and stronger he might have been able to strike back at his stepfather. . . .

Which is what he thinks he may have finally done, symbolically, on that day last October. "That makes sense to me," he says. And sense is what Davis is still trying to make of what happened to him five months ago. It was a confusing, chaotic, desperate time in his life, and he has not yet fitted all the pieces together. Clearly he had passed through a purging experience that frightened and humbled him, but ultimately lifted him.

And where he found himself on the hazy, sunny afternoon of March 8 was in the jockey's quarters at Santa Anita racetrack. It was nearly three o'clock. He had just slipped into red-white-and-blue silks and was waiting for the fifth race. He would ride a 15-1 shot, Hickory Crest—his first mount since the accident and his first for his new agent, Jeff Franklin, whom he had hired only five hours earlier. (During Davis' months of inactivity, Goodman didn't take on a new client.) Davis had been touched by the warmth of his welcome in the jockey's room at Santa Anita—the home of such riders as Chris McCarron, Laffit Pincay Jr. and fellow Idahoan Gary Stevens, who won the Kentucky Derby last year on Winning Colors. "They came over and shook my hand and gave me a hug. Chris was very comforting," said Davis as he sat and felt the anxiety mounting.

"Boy, I have butterflies like crazy, but it feels good to put the silks back on," he said. "It's like I've got the bug again, and this is my first mount."

He rode Hickory Crest like a jittery young apprentice too. Heading into the far turn, lying fourth, the filly suddenly kicked into gear and took off, nearly running up the heels of the horse in front of her. Davis, noted for his silky hands, snatched Hickory Crest back too hard, causing her to throw her head in the air. To make matters worse, just after they straightened out for home, he dropped his whip. They finished fourth. "Whew!" he said. "Old fumble-fingers. I'm a little embarrassed. My hands got all tangled up. I felt like a bug boy again. But everything will come back to me."

It began coming back in the next race, in which he finished a solid third aboard Swifterthanthewind, at 8-1, in his only other race of the day. "My hands were normal," he said. Davis appeared tired but relieved as he emerged from the jockeys' room at the end of that first day back, to find Marguerite and the kids waiting to greet him.

Even the fans were glad to see him. "Welcome to Santa Anita," one horseplayer said, reaching to shake Davis' hand.

So it was here, at the foot of the San Gabriel Mountains, that Robbie Davis ended up—after fleeing New York, after weeks of traveling the Northwest, after months of tortuous journeying through his conscience and his past. There he was after his two rides, standing near the paddock in blue jeans, as the bugle sounded the call to post for the eighth race and the horses strode through the sunshine onto the track. This was his world, a world of silks and starting gates and powerful thoroughbreds pounding for home.

"It's been a long, long road back," Davis said. "Longer than anyone can imagine."

Field of Freedom

GENERAL

By *JOHN MEYER*

The third baseman leaves his crutches in the dugout and he kneels on the infield, using a fish net to handle ground balls. His name is Randy Milliken, and he has cerebral palsy.

He is replaced after one inning by a teammate who uses a lacrosse stick to help him make the long throw to first. His name is Curt Garrett, and he has rheumatoid arthritis.

In the third and final inning, Garrett gives way to Jeff Harring, who roams the corner in a wheelchair because he has curvature of the spine.

Their teammates have an assortment of physical handicaps. One has a wooden leg. Another has arms so short that his hands appear to be attached to his shoulders. Another has arms no bigger around than broomsticks, and he catches the ball with his cap. Still another swings the bat with his one good arm—and hits home runs. The catcher rolls the ball back to the pitcher, because the pitcher can't move too well.

Many of the spectators watch with lumps in their throats.

These are the Freebirds, a team for the physically handicapped in Lakewood's Special Populations Softball League. That's right, the Freebirds.

"What's the freest thing in the world? A bird," says Garrett, one of the team's founders. "It can go anywhere, it has no barriers, the sky's the limit. That's what our goal in life is."

There are 15 teams in the Friday night Lakewood league, the only one of its kind in the area. There are three divisions of competition, and most of the 200 or so players in the league are mentally handicapped. The Freebirds stand apart, however, because their handicaps are mostly physical.

★ ★ ★

Garrett, 29, has had rheumatoid arthritis since he was 16 months old. He was wheelchair-bound until the age of 15, when artificial hips gave him some mobility. He and Joe Lujan founded the Freebirds five years ago because they felt the physically handicapped were being ignored.

"We just knew, growing up, that there weren't a lot of recreational opportunities for the physically handicapped," said Garrett. "There's a lot of things for the mentally handicapped, such as Special Olympics, or for spinal-injury individuals, the wheelchair sports. But the rest of us in the middle have been left out."

They've found a place with the Freebirds. To watch them is to be humbled.

"The Freebirds have a lot of courage," says Larry Sidebottom, a paraplegic who runs the league from a wheelchair. "These guys are out here with crutches and wheelchairs, playing on dirt, running from base to base, hitting the ball, catching fly balls. I give them a lot."

The coach, Lou Blackshere, is able-bodied.

But his brother, Ed, suffers from rheumatoid arthritis that stunted his growth.

Growing up, they shared a bedroom, and it was Lou's job to help Ed get dressed for school.

They are very close.

"I was the logical choice to coach," said Blackshere, "because I can deal with the handicapped. I grew up with my brother. It's not all that strange for me.

"But a lot of people (spectators) do leave with a different feeling."

"Goosebump City," one called it.

★ ★ ★

Some of the images are hard to forget.

Right fielder Ron Schultz is "the one with short arms," as his mother, Joan, puts it.

"He was just born that way. They never found out why."

Schultz generates power at the plate by holding the bat against his chest and swinging his upper body.

To pick up a bat discarded by the plate, he has to lie down with his chest pressed to the ground.

He uses a chest pad to smother fly balls.

But Schultz's teammates call him "Wheels," because he's the fastest guy on the team.

"I'm just a normal person," says Schultz, 26. "Everyone has some handicap—some show and some don't. Every person has their own special thing they can do to help the team."

Anybody who watches the Freebirds leaves with two vivid mental pictures. One is of Schultz.

The other is of Randy Milliken, the third baseman with a fish net.

"I have a problem closing my fingers, with eye-hand coordination, and reflexes with a glove," says Milliken, 31.

"So I just tried the net, tried different sizes, and that was it."

Milliken usually gets around on crutches, and he uses them to run the bases.

But he shuns them at third, kneeling to keep his hands free.

"To be able to catch the ball and pull it out and cock and throw to the next person," Milliken explains.

"Randy's probably got the most determination of anybody on the team," says Blackshere. "He gives 169,000% every practice and every time I put him in a game, in every situation. He's just really competitive and he does not like to lose."

"It's a great opportunity to play," said Milliken. "For me, the biggest thing is you learn about winning and losing in life. And when I go into a job situation and things go bad, I can draw an analogy to what I would do if I was six runs down in a softball game."

"That guy really amazes me," teammate Tom Kaluza says of Milliken. "I amaze myself, too."

★ ★ ★

Kaluza also suffers from celebral palsy.

He could have wound up in a full body cast for the rest of his life, if not for a lot of determination—by him and his family—when he was growing up.

Kaluza skis, plays basketball, runs in the Georgetown-to-Idaho Springs half-marathon every year and plays a variety of positions for the Freebirds.

Lujan's cerebral palsy is more severe than Kaluza's.

When he runs, he looks as if he's about to fall down at any moment, but he manages somehow to remain upright. He plays first base and he does not like to be told what he can and cannot do.

"Last year I slid into home plate and had to have 23 stitches," said Lujan, 30. "My mom and dad told me, 'No more ball.' You've got to deal with that, because you gotta do what you want to do."

"Most of our lives, society and a lot of people tell us we can't do stuff," said Garrett. "To be able to come out here and do this is such a confidence builder for everybody."

But this isn't Special Olympics, where everybody gets a hug and a pat on the back and there are no losers. The Freebirds recently blew a 13-1 lead, losing 14-13, and they were mad in the aftermath.

Garrett figures you can't win if you can't lose. "One of the problems I have with Special Olympics is that Special Olympics has always been about participation," Garrett says. "It's a problem a lot of handicapped people have, you were always taught that you weren't allowed to fail. Real life isn't like that. I don't care how mentally handicapped a person is, somewhere in their education they have to be allowed to lose."

It can get complicated like that, as complicated as running the basepaths with crutches. Or it can be very simple, as simple as a brother's love.

But in the final reckoning, the Freebirds are really just like any other softball team in town, playing for the same reasons. "You forget who you are," says Lujan, "and you just play."

A Real Yawner

by Tom Reese of the Seattle Times. There's no doubt that the life of a professional golfer is fun and full of excitement, but there are those times when everything starts to drag. Senior PGA Tour veteran Arnold Palmer was caught by the camera in one of those moments during 1989 competition at a Seattle stop. Copyright ©1989, Seattle Times.

Bush League

by free-lance photographer Richard B. Gentile. Although he might not have been the hardest-throwing lefthander to take the mound on this day, President George Bush was a big hit among Baltimore baseball fans. The occasion was Opening Day 1989 and Bush delivered the ceremonial first pitch before the Orioles-Boston Red Sox game at Baltimore's Memorial Stadium. Copyright ©1989, Richard B. Gentile.

Coming to America

GENERAL

By *JAN HUBBARD*

From Newsday

Each word was formed carefully and spoken deliberately. For Sarunas Marciulionis, it was the oral equivalent of an infant pulling himself from the ground to his feet and taking that majestic first step. English was very new and foreign to Marciulionis, but he was also introducing a friend to a very important person and English—no matter how primitive—was required.

Marciulionis was trying to communicate with Golden State Warriors Coach Don Nelson on the telephone and he was about to hand the phone to Rima Janulevicius, his friend and translator.

"Coach Nelson," Marciulionis said slowly, "I . . . give . . . you . . . my . . . friend . . . Rima. . . . I . . . want . . . you . . . touch . . . her."

Janulevicius burst out laughing and grabbed the phone. "Forget that, Don," she said. "He means you can keep in touch with me."

Perhaps Marciulionis will tell that story in 20 years to members of his national basketball team. And perhaps he will speak fluent English and the members of the team will understand every word he says. For by then the story of Sarunas Marciulionis (pronounced Sha-ROON-us Mar-sha-LOAN-us), the first player from the USSR to sign with a National Basketball Association team, will have been told many times in his native Lithuania, one of 15 republics in the Soviet Union. And Lithuanian children will know that one of the major obstacles faced by Marciulionis was the language barrier, which limited his ability to communicate with his coaches and teammates—not only posing problems on the court but making it difficult to enjoy all of the newfound pleasures of America.

So perhaps one small part of the dramatic evolution taking place in professonal sports will be a meltdown of the language barrier.

"Right now, there is a tremendous boom of the English language in Lithuania," Marciulionis said through an interpreter. "It (his presence in the NBA) might be an additional stimulus. But it goes beyond language. In many cases, diplomats have failed to establish the human contacts and athletes have made up for them. Athletes are better ambassadors. Many people are not represented through diplomatic channels, but are represented by athletes. I feel that I am an ambassador of the Lithuanian people, who are not represented diplomatically."

★ ★ ★

In what might be called the internationalization of American professional sports, foreign athletes such as Marciulionis are coming to the United States in growing numbers to join American basketball, hockey, football and baseball teams. At the same time, American professional teams increasingly are competing against foreign teams and making appearances abroad. Borders that formerly served as barricades protecing our national sports against foreign intrusion are now being crossed as regularly as goal lines. Perhaps most startlingly, many of the foreign athletes playing here are from the Soviet Union and other Communist countries. And there is no way of knowing how many of these athletic developments will find parallels in the worlds of politics, government and human relations.

"The danger in relating sports to a bigger subject is the exaggeration," says former Montreal Canadiens goalie Ken Dryden, now working on a book and a documentary for the Canadian Broadcasting Corp. examining the sports relationship between Canada and the Soviet Union. "But sports is the metaphor. It is the most vivid example we have."

Marciulionis' goal of using his expertise in sports as a political tool is nothing new.

In some cases, at least, developments in sports have clearly presaged events in other arenas. There was, for example, the heralded Chinese diplomatic initiative known as Ping-Pong diplomacy. In April, 1971, a U.S. table tennis team was unexpectedly invited to play in China. The team received a warm reception. A year later, as a direct result of the Ping-Pong initiative, President Richard M. Nixon made his historic visit to China. When Jackie Robinson broke baseball's color line in 1947, he may not have set any legal precedent for later court-ordered desegregation, but he certainly helped influence the climate that made possible a broad spectrum of civil-rights advances.

Evidence of the growing internationalization of American professional sports abounds. Consider this:

Last month, during the National Hockey League preseason, the Washington Capitals and Calgary Flames toured the Soviet Union. Four Soviet teams will visit North America during the regular season, which begins Thursday. And each of the 21 NHL teams will play a Soviet visitor at least once. At least six Soviet players, including two for the New Jersey Devils, are expected to play in the NHL. These developments, of course, have resulted at least in part from a relaxation of political tensions between the USSR and the West.

The Boston Celtics played in an international exhibition tournament in Madrid last year, and the Denver Nuggets will play in a similar tournament in Rome this month with the champions of Europe (a Yugoslavian team), Spain and Italy.

During the summer of 1988, the Atlanta Hawks played the Soviet National team three times in a tour of the Soviet Union. Next year, two NBA teams may open the regular season with a two-game series in Tokyo. And, in addition to two Soviet players who will play in the NBA, which opens its season November 3, there will also be five players from Yugoslavia, another NBA first.

It is not a one-way street. Danny Ferry, who graduated from Duke last spring, was the second player taken in the 1989 NBA draft. But he chose to play in Italy, where he will earn more than $1 million, instead of for the Los Angeles Clippers. Ferry said part of his motivation was that he wanted to learn about a different culture.

The National Football League will start a spring minor league in 1991 (the World League of American Football, or WLAF) with franchises in London, Frankfurt, Milan, Barcelona, Mexico, Canada and six U.S. cities.

And in January, a group of Christian major league players will go to Moscow not only to conduct baseball clinics but also to promote Christianity in the offically atheistic Soviet Union.

Athletes from all over the world have mixed in other sports—track, golf, tennis. But there has been nothing comparable to what will take place regularly during this NHL and NBA season—players from the Soviet Union and North America playing for the same teams and sharing the common goal of jointly winning a championship.

The possibilities are intriguing. What if Marciulionis or Alexander Volkov of the Atlanta Hawks makes the winning field goal in the seventh game of the NBA championship finals? Or what if Viacheslav Fetisov or Sergei Starikov of the New Jersey Devils makes the key play that leads to a victory in the Stanley Cup series? Imagine fans of the American home team high-fiving and slapping each other on the back and screaming, "I love those Russians. Great players. Great country."

What next? There are rumors that a Soviet basketball player will sign a letter of intent with an American college team, which means he would pursue an American college curriculum. It will be interesting to see how he does on his first American history test. Bill Wall, executive director of the Amateur Basketball Association of the United States, suggested that the infusion of Soviet players into the NBA and NHL will have widespread ramifications. Interest created by professional sports should stir the curiosity of younger fans. "It could lead to cultural and educational exchanges," Wall said. "What better way for college and high school kids to learn about foreign cultures? The educational implications of all of this are mind-boggling."

The Soviet Union recently began playing baseball, primarily because baseball will be an Olympic sport in 1992. Anytime a gold medal is up for grabs, the Soviet Union is reaching.

Contemplate this scenario: Cuba is a Soviet satellite country. It does not allow its players to leave the country, but major league scouts say there currently are Cuban players who not only are capable of playing professional baseball but also capable of becoming all-stars. So it is logical to assume that in the next few years Cuban players and coaches will be invited to conduct clinics and teach in the Soviet Union, and Soviet baseball players will go to Cuba for training. And in two decades, who knows? Perhaps a Soviet first baseman will sign with the New York Yankees.

★ ★ ★

For those tempted to question how far the internationalization process has actually come, it is necessary merely to recall what befell Alan Eagleson when he tried to arrange the first hockey exhibition series between Canada and the Soviet Union in 1972. Eagleson, executive director of the NHL Players Association, was told that he could not begin negotiations with the Soviet Ice Hockey Federation because it was necessary to have an official of the Canada Amateur Hockey Association present. Then he was told the NHL president, Clarence Campbell, had to be present. Then he was told a meeting could take place only in Moscow.

"I just got stalled and stalled and stalled," Eagleson said. "So I called our (Canadian) ambassador in Moscow, and he said, 'Alan, they read everything that goes through the telex. Come up with something imaginative and put it in a telex to me.' So I wrote a telex and said, 'Dear Mr. Ambassador. I've been invited by the Soviets but they will not meet with me. They said they could only meet with Mr. Campbell, the president of the league. Please advise the Soviets that Mr. Campbell is the representative of the capitalist owners. I represent the workers.' I had a meeting with the (Soviet) Ice Hockey Federation a few days later." Today, Eagleson says, the Soviets are much more accessible. "Now, they don't care," he says. "They say, 'Who's got the most money?' "

★ ★ ★

The 1972 Canada Cup was a sobering experience for North American sports fans because the professionals from Canada, the motherland of hockey, were unable to win the eight-game series against the Soviets until the last minute of the last game. That gave the NHL four victories while the Soviets, who began playing hockey in 1946, won three times and one game was tied. The Soviets were considered "amateurs" but it was apparent that in 1972 their best players were among the best in the world. They have remained so ever since.

But they were not allowed to compete regularly against the best —those in the NHL—until 1989. That presents an obvious question: Why now?

"That is a direct result of (Soviet President Mikhail) Gorbachev's policies of *glasnost* and *perestroika,*" said Dr. Henry Morton, chairman of the political science department at Queens College and author of "Soviet Sports," a 1955 book. "Before Gorbachev, it was not really possible."

But *glasnost* and *perestroika* have had a remarkable impact throughout Soviet society, and sports is only one small part. It seems that, almost every day, something incredibly different happens in the Soviet Union. And, to be incredible, it needn't be a Communist Party conference at which the current regime is subjected to public denunciation.

During the summer, heavy metal groups played a concert in Moscow. As for sports, the International Management Group has signed a contract to build the first two golf courses in the Soviet Union and will also open an office in Moscow.

The NBA will televise 17 games to the Soviet Union on tape delay this season. They are expected to be viewed by an average of 60 million persons per game, and all will have commercials for Mastercard and Coca-Cola.

Money is not the least of the incentives for the Soviets in such enterprises. "Everybody has been told they have to be self-supporting," said Robert J. Osborn, a Soviet scholar who is chairman of the political science department at Temple University. "Overall, the system is encouraging organizations to do things that will bring hard currency into the system. So it's no surprise if the state's sports committee has deals that are going to bring in hard Western currency. They are going to do it. They can keep a portion to spend again for their own purposes and they have to trade it in for rubles, which is usually the case. So, if there are big sums of money involved, the money incentive really plays a role."

And there have been big sums of money involved. NBA executives have indicated that about 75 percent of Marciulionis' yearly salary of $1.3 million and Volkov's $675,000 will go to various Soviet sports and government authorities. And perhaps the biggest deal was the $5 million paid by an Italian soccer team for the services of Alexander Zavarov in the summer of 1988. Reports in the Soviet Union indicate Zavarov's Soviet team received $2 million, the government received $1 and *Goskomsport,* the national sports federation, got $2 million. Zavarov received only housing costs and an allowance. In the Soviet Union itself, however, sports are heavily subsidized. And, in the past year, major changes in the Soviet Union have permitted athletes to keep more of their money.

★ ★ ★

"It reflects an overall loosening of the climate in Soviet society," Dr. Morton said. There are other motivations. In May, professional basketball players were approved for participation in the Olympics and other international competition, meaning Marciulionis and Volkov still will be able to play for their national teams.

Most of the elite hockey players who will play in the NHL are older. The next Olympic Games are in 1992 and, by then, Fetisov and Sergei Makarov of the Calgary Flames will be 33 and Igor Larionov of the Vancouver Canucks will be 31.

"When you've accomplished the things all of them have—gold medals in the Olympics and world championships—then there is only one other thing: the National Hockey League," said Lou Lamoriello, general manager of the Devils. "And, unless they are given the opportunity, they may not want to go any further, and I think the Soviets recognized that when they lost a couple of people who would have liked to play in the NHL and could not."

One who retired relatively early was goaltender Vladislav Tretiak, such a great player that he will this month become the first Soviet inducted into the Hockey Hall of Fame in Toronto. Tretiak was 32 when he retired in 1984, and NHL executives say he lost interest in playing because he felt he would never be allowed to play in the NHL. If Fetisov, Makarov and Larionov experienced similar feelings and retired, they would be of no benefit to the Soviet Union in the 1992 Olympics, anyway. By allowing older players to leave, the Soviets are sending messages to their younger players that, if they play hard and are successful, they, too, can one day play in the NHL. And perhaps such a policy will discourage defections of younger players such as 20-year-old Alexander Mogilny, who got in touch with the Buffalo Sabres in defecting. At his first press conference in Buffalo, Mogilny said he felt there was "no chance" that he would be allowed to play in the NHL, so he left.

★ ★ ★

One day in August, San Antonio Spurs assistant coach Gregg Popovich was driving through the streets of Corpus Christi, Texas, where he had gone to conduct a basketball clinic. Seated to his right was Zarko Paspalj, one of the initial group of Yugoslavs to sign with NBA teams. The radio was on, and Popovich wasn't paying attention to Paspalj until he began hearing Paspalj singing along with the song on the radio.

"All of a sudden, Zarko's over there singing, 'Nights in White Satin,' with a Yugoslav accent and I couldn't believe it," Popovich said, laughing. "I said, 'Zarko, who is that?' And he said, 'Moody Blues.' "

Popovich told that story while making a comparison between players from Yugoslavia and those from the Soviet Union who are entering the NBA. The Yugoslavs, along with the Soviets, are the next best group of basketball players in the world after the Americans. Since the Yugoslavs and the Soviets are both coming into the NBA for the first time, there is a tendency to lump them together.

They share some common traits. They are from Eastern Europe.

Unlike other foreign players in the NBA, they have never played for American colleges. They are being allowed to leave their countries and play in the NBA, in part, because of the new Olympic rule that will allow them to return and play on their national teams.

Some, such as Marciulionis, Volkov and Yugoslav center Vlade Divac, who has signed with the Los Angeles Lakers, have only begun taking English lessons. All are sufficiently accomplished basketball players to make their national teams outstanding. The Soviet Union won the Olympic gold medal by defeating Yugoslavia, which won the silver.

But Yugoslavs can become irritated when mentioned in the same sentence with the Soviets. Although still socialist, Yugoslavia hasn't been a Soviet satellite for more than 40 years—something the Yugoslavs say is commonly misunderstood.

"All people think Yugoslavia is part of Russia," said Dino Radja, a 6-10 forward who will play for the Boston Celtics and began learning English when he was 12. "That is not true. It is something between East and West. We are in the middle between Russia and we are not good like America." Radja plans to make that known, which is another fascinating part of foreign players coming to America: geography lessons.

Radja figures that if the Yugoslavs are successful in the NBA, "Maybe now people will say, 'Where is Yugoslavia?' And they will look on the map and see where it is," he said. "And maybe people will go visit and see what it is like."

When Popovich was trying to get Paspalj to sign with the Spurs, he went to Zagreb, Yugoslavia, where the European championships were being held.

"Most people think of Romania, Bulgaria and Yugoslavia as Eastern Bloc countries," Popovich said. "It's a mistake in Yugoslavia's case because they're not like the others. Zarko's team was Partisan Belgrade. The name comes from the Partisans during World War II. They helped the Americans. They would hide them and get them food. They're very pro-American.

"I walked through Zagreb, through the back streets, with some of the people I got to know there and it's like a time warp. It's like the 1950s. There are outdoor cafes. It's like the beatnik time. All the young people are there, and on one side of the street you hear Billie Holiday and Johnny Mathis, and on the other side you hear Otis Redding and the Four Tops. It's American music and it's everywhere. It's not like you walked into Prague, Czechoslovakia, and it's gray and black and people are totally ignorant of what goes on outside the country."

Popovich's ability to persuade Paspalj, a free agent, to sign with the Spurs was a result of an extraordinary background. Popovich, the son of Serbo-Croatian parents, majored in Soviet studies at the Air Force Academy, took four years of Russian and served part of his tour of duty in Turkey on the Soviet border. He had a job so sensitive that he prefers not to discuss it.

Paspalj learned Russian well enough to teach it to children for six years. He also speaks some English. Popovich's parents never taught him Serbo-Croatian, which is spoken in Yugoslavia, but he knows a few words and he has retained some of his Russian.

"As the years go by, you get worse and worse," said Popovich, who once was head coach of a small college and has been with the Spurs for two years. "But with what I know of Russian and what Zarko's taught and the little bit of Serbo-Croatian that I know and the little bit of English that he knows, we had a lot of fun communicating. If there had been anybody around that knew any of the languages, they would have been cringing."

Inevitably, the foreign players' presence will result in a mixture of politics and sports. When Marciulionis arrived in the United States in early August, he said he preferred not to talk about politics, but that he hoped his presence in the NBA would help teach Americans the difference between Russia and Lithuania. Each is a republic in the Soviet Union. Lithuania, however, was independent before being annexed by the Soviet Union in 1940. Lithuanians often are insulted when they are called Russians.

"I want to educate people and show them that is not so," Marciulionis said. "We have nothing similar in culture or language. There are about one million Lithuanians in America who are first, second and third generation. As we in Lithuania fight for our own Olympic committee and economic sovereignty and our own basketball federation, it is a very big statement to tell the world that it is a Lithuanian who is playing in the NBA. Not a Russian and not a Soviet. I'm a Lithuanian."

Marciulionis won't have far to go to begin educating Americans. Don Nelson, his coach, regularly refers to him as a Russian.

★ ★ ★

Although Soviets are new to North American professional sports, foreign players are not. Jackie Robinson's breaking of the color barrier opened the door for black and Latin players to play major league baseball.

Foreign players have been in the NHL for more than a decade, and as many as 30 Swedes, Finns and Czechs will be on NHL rosters this season.

For the last three years, Houston Rockets center Akeem Olajuwon of Lagos, Nigeria, has been the first-team All-NBA center. And players from Sudan, West Germany and the Netherlands will play in the NBA this season.

Soccer-style kickers have dominated National Football League place-kicking for so long that it seems ancient history to remember that the first was Hungarian-born Pete Gogolak, who played with the Buffalo Bills in 1960.

The foreign influence on the four major professional sports that have originated in North America has nothing to do with lack of talent in America. It simply is an indication that certain select players from foreign countries, including the Soviet Union, are among the best in the world. But they make up a small group. This season, only two of the 324 players in the NBA will be from the USSR.

Understandably, there has also been an American influence on foreign countries that play American sports. Players who were not quite good enough to play in the NBA have been able to compete in Italy—and maintain a high standard of living—for more than a decade. And leagues in Spain, Greece and Israel also pay six-figure salaries.

But much more is to come.

In 1992, many of the restrictions and regulations in the European Common Market will be removed. The 12 member countries will, in essence, be one economic unit. And there will be a great deal of competition for the sports dollar and franc and pound and lira and mark.

"All of the American businesses are making plans to be over there, and all of the European companies are consolidating," said Tex Schramm, the former Dallas Cowboys president who will direct the WLAF spring league. "So, from an economic standpoint, it is the ideal time to go over because of this influx of international money."

Also, many countries have deregulated TV. The number of stations has increased in Europe. There is even an all-sports channel in England. More channels will be created.

"They've been moving away from the state-owned into the private sector," Schramm said. "So they feel there is going to be a tremendous need for programing in the next five years. Sports has always been the forerunner for programing."

The Common Market and the proliferation of TV stations explain why the NFL minor league will be in Europe, where Schramm predicts there eventually could be 14 spring football teams. Could a fall league be far behind?

But beyond the mere European presence lie more intriguing possibilities. Obviously, wealthy men will own the television stations. How long will it be before they become aggressive in bidding for NBA teams, which are popular all over the world? How long will it be before a wealthy European in, say, Milan offers $150 million for an existing NBA team? Does the team move? And then is the NBA forced to expand to have a European division?

NBA Commissioner David Stern has consistently maintained that the NBA is not interested in European expansion, but he is not so adamant as he has been in the past. "That is not our intention," Stern said. "We have no plans in that direction. We'll just continue working and see what happens."

But Stern recognizes how popular basketball has become during the '80s. At the beginning of the decade, there was talk of several NBA teams folding or merging. But in the last two years the NBA has added four new franchises at $32.5 million each, and franchises have recently been sold for as much as $70 million. This year, NBA games will be seen live or on videotape in 70 countries.

"If you had asked me in 1981 what did I think about adding four expansion teams, I would have laughed at you," Stern said. "So I have learned in life, and especially in basketball, not to make any projections five or six years out."

Eventually, the form of professional basketball and hockey competition could change. "Looking into a crystal ball," Washington Capitals General Manager David Poile told the *Washington Post* last spring, "I see the Stanley Cup champion playing the world champion in a seven-game series to be viewed by a Super Bowl-size audience all over the world. At least that's something we can hope for."

★ ★ ★

And now that many of the barriers to professional sports have been removed—even to the extent that players from communist countries can pursue capitalist activities such as shoe contracts—talent scouts will become even more aggressive in attempting to find players. The Warriors and Hawks were so aggressive when vying for the services of Marciulionis, a free agent, that they continually bumped into each other all over the world. They saw each other in the Frankfurt airport, at the Olympics in Seoul, South Korea, at tournaments in Spain and Yugoslavia and once even met in Marciulionis' living room in his apartment in Vilnius, Lithuania.

"I've been to Lithuania five times and I've been to Hawaii five times," said Hawks General Manager Stan Kasten. "And frankly, I prefer Hawaii."

But Kasten admits that will not slow the Hawks' pursuit of foreign players. The Hawks have been the most aggressive NBA team in seeking foreign talent. They own the rights to players from Italy, Yugoslavia, Greece, Argentina, Spain, the Soviet Union and China.

The temporary hardships basketball and hockey executives may have endured in seeking Soviet players, however, were nothing compared with what baseball scouts have encountered. Major-league teams have aggressively sought players in Central and South America, regardless of the risks. Texas Rangers scouting director Sandy Johnson once flew into Bogota, Colombia, got into a cab, and did not make it out of the airport because the cab was taken over by a group of youthful guerrilla fighters.

"Luckily, I had my scout with me," Johnson recalled. "He said, 'Don't worry. Play it cool. They just want to use the radio in the cab. This is kind of a normal thing.' But I said, 'Yeah, the guy up there is about 17 years old and he's got an itchy finger on the gun.' "

Johnson was not harmed but was spooked all night by the sound of soldiers running through the hotel hallways. "Most clubs will go to almost any length to get a player," Johnson said. "If you can get a player who can turn your club around, it's worth it. A lot of times when you go on a trip like that, you expect something. You just have to have confidence in your scouts in that country that they can handle those things. But it is different. It is a little strange to watch a baseball game inside barbed wire with soldiers around you."

★ ★ ★

Ken Dryden predicts that one day the sports exchange between North America and the Soviet Union will be complete. One day, perhaps an NHL player will play for a Soviet team—obviously not for the glamour or income but for the educational experience.

Dryden nearly became the first to do that in 1979, when he enlisted the support of various Canadian sports and government authorities in an attempt to help him play one year, after his NHL retirement, with one of the four Moscow teams in the Soviet league.

He conducted extensive research into what it would be like to live in Moscow for a year with his wife and two young children. He knew it would be difficult, especially for his family, but his wife was willing and he found the prospect of living in the Soviet Union fascinating. "To spend a year living somewhere else and the kind of intense, involved experience that it would mean . . . learning 100 things a minute. It would have been great."

The request eventually was rejected by the Soviets, and Dryden speculated it was because "there were great risks involved. Some were my risks, but to a great extent they were Soviet risks. Here they were actually confronted with someone who was looking to live in Moscow. From their side, they could see somebody who might not have a good time and might come back and tell about it or somebody who would leave in the middle of the year and that would be an embarrassment. Even if the Soviets could fulfill all they could fulfill, but they weren't up to what we thought they were up to, they would take the black eye. It was just far easier to say no."

Under Gorbachev, however, black eyes—which are only temporary, anyway—no longer seem to be feared. One of the remarkable results of openness is fewer restrictions on the media and free speech, and athletes have been quick to exercise their newfound rights.

Larionov and Fetisov publicly feuded with Soviet national hockey coach Viktor Tikhonov. World chess champion Garry Kasparov regularly attacks Goskomsport in Soviet publications and accuses the "bureaucrats" of financial underhandedness.

"The bureaucrats at Goskomsport don't want to give up their power because sports is what feeds them, and it feeds them very well," Kasparov said in an interview in the Soviet publication Ogonyok in March. Kasparov occupies such a singular position that he has been allowed to become more forceful. Since he is a world champion of an individual sort, he cannot be replaced. He has not only been able to speak out but also to sign endorsement contracts, including one for a club soda. That was a first for a Soviet athlete.

If Soviet authorities are to continue permitting such freedom, then perhaps the next intrepid North American hockey player who makes a request similiar to Dryden's will be allowed to play a season in the Soviet Union. Kevin Lowe, a defenseman for the Edmonton Oilers, has in fact expressed interest in doing exactly that. If it does happen one day, that will signal another change, or perhaps advancement is a better description, of relations between the United States and the Soviet Union. Even though the subject is sports and not nuclear disarmament, government cooperation is required for what is currently taking place with Soviets playing in the NHL and NBA.

"In order for anything like this to occur, you have to have total cooperation," said Lamoriello. "You're dealing with passports, visas, countries who have not experienced anything with reference to the specific situation of athletes."

If sports is an indicator, then perhaps that cooperation will eventually be extended to other areas, not only between the United States, Canada and the Soviet Union, but also the rest of the world.

But, of course, that will happen only if Gorbachev remains in power or if his policies remain intact. If Gorbachev loses power, there is no intelligent way to predict what might happen—not only in Soviet sports, but in Soviet life as a whole.

Still, Dryden said that what is happening in Soviet sports right now is significant, although he also said there is a danger of exaggerating the importance of sports. In working on a book and a television documentary, Dryden has spent much time seeking a credible perspective.

"Sports, very simply, is part of life wherever it happens to exist," Dryden said. "Nothing more, but nothing less. Sports is going to be performed according to the styles, standards, expectations, rules and regulations of a certain place at a certain time. And so you can look around and see how baseball is being played in the United States in 1989, or football, or anything else, and I think it does tell a big story about a lot of things, whether it's a sports business or kids or parents or communities.

"And so when you get into things like the Soviets and their decision to allow these players to come and play in North America, you look at the story and it comes from somewhere. It comes out of conditions in both places, particularly those in the Soviet Union. It says something about the country and the relationship between those who are here and those who are home and where all the power lies. And, yes, absolutely, there is certainly something happening."

Ryan Strikes Milestone

BASEBALL

By *MIKE LOPRESTI*

Number 5,000 came as so many had come before, on a fastball barely seen, impossible to hit.

The Texas Rangers' Nolan Ryan rode into history on the wings of a 96-mile-per-hour heater Tuesday night, taking Oakland's Rickey Henderson with him.

"I'm relieved it's over," Ryan said after fanning Henderson to open the fifth inning for his 5,000th career strikeout, a peak no other man has approached. "When I came out here tonight I drove by the ballpark. That shows you where my mind was. I had to turn around and come back."

Ryan (14-8), who needed six strikeouts to get to 5,000, fanned 13 in a five-hitter but still lost, 2-0.

The Rangers looked awful, with five weak hits and two errors. Winner Bob Welch (14-7) struck out nine in pitching the first eight innings and Dennis Eckersley finished for his 26th save.

What could be more typical than that of Ryan's career, so full of strikeouts but never full enough of victories?

When Henderson missed, a packed Arlington Stadium crowd of 42,869 exploded in noise and a thousand points of light—camera flashbulbs.

"To tell you the truth, I'm honored," Henderson said. "Maybe I'm not in the record book the way I wanted, but I'm in the record book."

On Monday someone asked Ryan, 42, what he would do when the Big K came.

"Nothing," he said.

That's nearly what he did. He walked around the mound, shook hands with his infielders and tipped his cap twice. Someone threw the ball out to keep. Henderson waved to the crowd.

Then Ryan went back blazing his strikeout trail. A single and error gave the A's a run and their 2-0 lead, but before the fifth was over Ryan struck out Ron Hassey and Dave Henderson. Hassey gave him 226 for the season, a Texas club record.

Ryan struck out the side in the sixth, making it five in a row. Nobody knows how far Ryan can go. He left the park with 5,007, No. 1 on the all-time list by nearly 900 over Steve Carlton.

It was a torrid night punctuated by several standing ovations. The crowd stood when Ryan loosened up and stood when he took the mound with the temperature at 95.

Ryan's night began inauspiciously, with a Henderson double to center, but then the K's began to come. Jose Canseco, fooled on a curve in the first inning. Dave Henderson and Tony Phillips in the second. Rickey Henderson and Hassey in the third, when the Athletics also scored a run.

So history was ready for Ryan and his unwilling accomplice.

"I don't envy the person," Ryan had said Monday. "But somebody's got to be it."

Fate marched down the line like a platoon sergeant looking for a volunteer. Fans stood with cameras ready to flash on every pitch with two strikes on the board.

Terry Steinbach? The count went to 3-2, but Steinbach twice fought off fastballs and fouled them away. Then he walked on a pitch just outside.

Walt Weiss? The count went to 2-2. More cheers, more flashbulbs. But Ryan missed with a curve to go 3-2 and Weiss bounced to short to end the fourth.

Henderson opened the fifth. Two fastballs were called for strikes. Then two balls, a foul, and another ball on a curve that just missed.

Then catcher Chad Kreuter called for the fastball. A catcher putting down one finger to Ryan is like the soldier loading the cannon.

Next came Henderson's whiff.

Then the roar.

Then the short celebration.

"If you had asked me before the game what pitch I would have wanted for 5,000," Ryan said, "I would have said on a fastball swinging. That's what got me to the majors."

Then Carney Lansford stood in and it seemed half of Arlington Stadium got up to finally go to the bathroom.

A taped message from President Bush was played in the sixth. "Well done, my noble friend," Bush said. Ryan hardly noticed. His team was behind.

What about 6,000?

"I don't think," Ryan said, "that I'll be around."

Thompson's Attack on Prop 48 is Wrong

COLLEGE BASKETBALL

By *RON RAPOPORT*

From the Los Angeles Daily News

We must say this much for John Thompson. When the man is wrong, he is wrong.

And in the matter of his intention to boycott Georgetown's basketball game against Boston College Saturday as a way of protesting the NCAA's recent strengthening of Proposition 48, Thompson is as wrong as he can be.

He is not charging racism, Thompson says, because "if I jump up and down and holler racism, everybody will lose sight of the issue and focus on the words." Others have not been so reticent, however, notably Temple Coach John Chaney, who has called the NCAA a racist organization and Proposition 48 a racist rule.

But let us ignore Chaney's rhetoric for the moment and let us accept Thompson's challenge to focus on the issue. The defenders of Proposition 48 can ask for nothing more.

Proposition 48 requires that any college freshman receiving an athletic scholarship must post a score of at least 700 on a standardized test called the SAT that is given to high school seniors. Opponents of the rule complain that black students are at a disadvantage when they take this test because it contains an inherent cultural bias against them.

★ ★ ★

This is very probably true. Schools in poor neighborhoods where many black children grow up are notoriously deficient in teaching the skills required on tests like the SAT. But there is something else that is also true. That score of 700 is so ridiculously low, so easy to achieve, that the term cultural bias loses all relevance.

How do I know this? Because I took the test just for fun a few years ago and, although my math was a little rusty, I did pretty well. Not fair? Well, how about this, then. The sixth-grader living in my house took the test, too.

How did she do? Not very well, of course. She was in the sixth grade, for goodness sake. But she did do well enough to qualify for an athletic scholarship if she had been old enough and if she had had a hook shot.

Now this girl was no more ready to go to college than she was to go to the moon. But she was able to break 700 on the SAT. Is it too much to say that any high school senior who cannot do at least as well on a standardized test as an 11-year-old girl has no business going to college? I believe that it is not.

Proposition 48 is really not so much a requirement as it is a message. If you want an athletic scholarship, it tells high school athletes, then sit down and study. Pay attention in class. Learn how to get some meaning out of what you read. Learn some math. It's an easy test, nothing you can't handle, but you have to do a little work.

The real racists, it seems to me, are those who tell black children that they are too dumb, too backward, to score 700 on the SAT. The real racists are those who tell black high school students that no matter how hard they try they cannot achieve the test scores of a bright sixth-grader.

★ ★ ★

Which brings us to the real scandal concerning black athletes in America's colleges today, the one you do not hear so much hollering about. It does not concern those who fail to enter, but those who fail to graduate.

Harry Edwards, the professor and black activist whose credentials on racial matters are not in dispute, once pointed out that no more than 14 percent of the black athletes entering college received their degrees in four years. After six years, the number was up to just 30 percent.

What this says is that big-time collegiate sports chews up the black athletes—and many of the white ones—who are unprepared for academic life and spits them out. Education is not the issue here or the colleges that enroll athletes would see that they learn something.

"The joke is on the black athletes," Edwards has said. "They're going to bring them through with no support system and no standards, take their football from them and send them back on the street. It's the slave mentality. Why should the slave master give the slaves shoes, housing and adequate nutrition when there's an unending supply of more slaves building up in the system?"

These are harsh words, to be sure, but they are no more harsh than the cries of racism hurled at those trying to establish the most minimum admission standards for college athletes.

John Thompson can boycott all the basketball games he likes. Up in the stands or on the bench, he is simply wrong.

Stroke of Genius

COLLEGE SWIMMING

By *MARK SHELTON*

Two duties that Jim Steen delegates to others in his capacity as head swimming coach at Kenyon College are, first, changing light bulbs in Ernst Natatorium, where the Kenyon Lords (10 national swimming championships in a row, and counting) and Ladies (six national swimming championships in a row, and counting) regularly swamp their opponents. Second, he delegates the drawing of blood samples from the earlobes of shivering, dripping-wet college swimmers. He delegates the first task because, after all, he can't do *everything;* he delegates the second because delegating allows Steen to sit at the keyboard of his Apple computer and enter the data gleaned from the blood samples the instant they become available. "Sure, we do a lot of things that a lot of swimming programs don't do . . ." Steen says, drumming his fingers on the countertop and doing his best to wait patiently as Assistant Coach Todd Clark meticulously pricks the ear of freshman swimmer Mary Hooker, and transfers a few drops of blood into a slender glass tube.

". . . Like blood-lactate testing," Steen continues, staring at Clark as he inserts the glass tube into a slot on the machine that performs an analysis of the blood sample, and presses a button, ". . . but"—Steen, still staring at Clark (who has learned to remain absolutely oblivious to the hard-eyed scrutiny he gets whenever he is charged with doing something that produces data, data that Steen seems to need so intensely that he looks as though he is about to begin hyperventilating), poises his fingers over the keyboard in the classic touch typing position—". . . we do it in the context of a normal collegiate experience."

A number appears on a little red screen on the blood analyzer, and Clark looks at it for a moment. "OK," he says, "Mary Hooker," and he pauses; Steen looks as though he will faint with frustration: He *knows* who Mary Hooker is, he wants to know the *number.* Clark relents: "Three-point-eight."

Steen has the "three" and the decimal point entered into the computer before the words are fully out of Clark's mouth. He punches the "eight," hits a few more keys, and then stares at the screen as the computer collates this information. The computer, in addition to all the frills that computer salespeople are able to sell to people bloodthirsty for data, has a software program that makes it work faster. Such software is appropriate for no one more than Jim Steen. "I am probably," he says, fingers pounding the keys, "the worst person to have a computer. If there's something we can monitor, we monitor it." He punches a button. "And then it goes in here." The screen dissolves, and the printer begins to print out a complicated-looking chart with Mary Hooker's practice times, lactate test results, daily and weekly workout goals, peaks, valleys, plateaus, strategies for training—a blueprint for her next month in the pool. Todd Clark pulls the page from the printer and slips it into a clear plastic bag, like a sandwich. He seals the top, hands it to Mary, and sends her on her way. Then he sticks his head out the office window, which opens onto the pool deck, and shouts at Dave Wenz, who is midway through the timed sprint that precedes the ear-sticking. Clark gives him an earful. "Jeez," Clark says, half to himself when Wenz is out of earshot. "What a *lousy* turn." He heads out onto the deck to shout again.

At a college like Kenyon, this all seemed something more than incongruous. Kenyon is an assertively high-toned, militantly liberal-arts, quintessentially eggheaded place, draped in social history and overgrown with ivy, nestled in the tiny village of Gambier. It has all of 1,550 students, many of them from prep schools with three last names. It's common for some of the students to have three last names, too. Kenyon has a bookstore that is to the college what bars with live music are at other schools—a magnet for students. It is a truly incredible bookstore, open from 7 a.m. until 11 p.m., 365 days a year, a bookstore where it's possible—probable—to overhear conversations about, simultaneously, European monetary policy, the French Revolution, the Imagist poets, and the urban poor. On the racks in the bookstore sit copies of the most literary of literary quarterlies, *The Kenyon Review.*

One expects that fingers poised over a Kenyon computer keyboard with the heartfelt intensity displayed by Jim Steen would belong to someone editing a poem, rather than monitoring a swim team, someone with a fanatical interest in James Joyce, rather than someone with a fanatical interest in the level of metabolic waste products in the blood of swimmers.

On the other hand, much of the swimming world knows Kenyon College only as the most successful and winningest collegiate swim program in history, and Jim Steen as the most successful swim coach of any era anywhere, and to heck with *The Kenyon Review*—everyone who is familiar with the smell of chlorine knows about Kenyon. They know about swimmers like Jim Born (Kenyon '86), who won 17 NCAA swimming titles—second only to Olympic champion Pablo Morales. They know about Patty Abt, class of '87, who won 23 NCAA swimming titles—more than *anyone*. They know that Kenyon outscored the second-place teams on both the men's and women's sides at the NCAA Division III Championships in 1989 by more than 100 points. Most even know that Steen has since 1976 coached more than 100 All-American swimmers at Kenyon, swimmers who earned nearly 1,000 All-American designations, a human wave of Jack—and Jill—Armstrongs. People who know swimming know Kenyon; people who know high-quality education know Kenyon. But not everyone knows about both, so Jim Steen is left to be a bridge between two worlds.

One world assumes that "a context of normal collegiate experience" includes, say, familiarity with poets like the late Robert Lowell (who went to Kenyon), and the late John Milton (who did not, but probably would have liked it, since he was a swimmer of some note); another world assumes that normal collegiate experience includes the drawing of blood from the earlobes of swimmers en route to another pair of NCAA team championships. It is perhaps the strangest marriage in college athletics, as well as one of the most successful hyphenations of the words "student" and "athlete" in the history of the term: Every number associated with the team's athletic success is countered by a number associated with academic prowess. Sixteen national championship teams since 1980, for example, versus 14 NCAA post-graduate scholarship winners (no other school has ever had more than five post-grad winners in a single sport) since 1970. Swimmers with national titles and NCAA records, and swimmers who are fellows at the Center for Astrophysics. Sprint champions studying at the London School of Economics. Backstrokers in medical school. Breastrokers with Ph.D.s from the University of Chicago. Undergraduates like Meg Cary, who took last year off to get a master's degree from Tufts University and returns this year to complete a bachelor's degree in psychology—and to swim. She dabs a bit of blood off her ear, and notes that, after all, "swimming is, in large part, a *psychological* activity."

Sophomore backstroker Eric Chambers is also a psychology major, one, however, who describes swimming not as a psychological activity, but as "a sort of ridiculous sport, when you think about it." He saves the psychology for analyzing the team, and Jim Steen; in a clear example of identification with the aggressor, Chambers has developed the team's best imitation of Steen: Operatic gestures, a hard-eyed, intense stare, a scratchy, yet resonant voice—Steen's oratorical style, particularly when he gets going on something that inspires him, like blood-lactate levels or his souped-up computer, is reminiscent of Spencer Tracy playing an indignant lawyer, at once homey and electrifying; Chambers' rendition plays the voice as bordering on the fanatical, and thus sounds more like Robert Preston in "The Music Man." If psychology doesn't work out, Chambers could fall back on a stage career: " 'C'mon, Eric,' Coach will say," says Chambers, his arms waving as if to encompass all of Gambier, " 'I want to, uh, *empower you*!' " The voice is authentic enough that two freshman Lords peek around a bank of lockers, wondering who Steen is empowering now.

Jim Steen talks a lot about empowerment, about "creating programs and incentives and then allowing people to take charge themselves," which is how he rather modestly describes what he has done at Kenyon since 1976. "I don't want to be a *coach,*" he says. "I'm actually more of a manager; my role is helping people decide what it is they want to do, and creating an opportunity for them to do it. The lactate testing is *not* done for the purpose of winning another national title—we don't sit around talking for hours about winning the national championship. We do the lactate testing mostly for . . ." Steen sits for a moment and looks sheepish. "Well, the swimmers like it, because it really gives them a sense of what's going on with their training, but actually, I'd say we do it mostly for, uh, *me;* it's like having a computer on your desk: You have to figure out what it can do, what it can *really* do. Or like taking a class in a subject you don't know anything about. You can't do the same thing over and over and over again; I want to *know* what's going on, how things work, and I want to be surrounded by people who are stimulated by new things, who want to optimize their performance; the validation of what we do here isn't a string of titles; the validation is in what the people who win those titles *are.* They're . . . uh, *empowered.* There's really no other way to put it."

Steen is always quick to point out that Kenyon has a tradition as a swimming power dating back to the 1930s, when Charlie Imel was the coach and the swimmers wore long pants, and that the last time Kenyon lost a conference championship meet was 1953, when Steen was in very short pants. Tom Edwards, who coached for 10 years in the 50s and the 60s (and won the second through 11th straight conference titles) before becoming Dean of Students, still drops in at the pool regularly, and *he's* quick to talk about the tradition that existed before *him.* When he and Steen are together, they sound like Chinese diplomats, each going further and further in eloquent praise of the other. They make it sound easy.

Collegiate swimming might be ridiculous, but it's not easy, even at the small-college level. The NCAA has twice restratified the divisions in which colleges and universities compete in an effort to level the pool: Division I consists of thoroughbred swimmers on athletic scholarships from the big schools like Texas and Ohio State, swimmers who grow, impossibly, bigger and faster each year; Division II collegiate swimmers seem to grow bigger and faster each year, too, but the swimmers, like the schools, are smaller to begin with. Division III is where swimmers swim purely for love, because there are no athletic scholarships; they don't necessarily grow much bigger, but they have grown faster. Division III swimmers also face their first challenge when they're in high school, because they have to be *admitted* to places like Kenyon, or Denison, or the Massachusetts Institute of Technology, before they can swim. Division I champions tend to look like artists' conceptions of Perfect Athletes; Division III champions tend to look like college kids. In head-to-head competition, Kenyon beats its share of Division II schools, and can beat some Division I schools, but it's beside the point to say that they could not beat Division I champ Texas.

Which is not the same thing as saying that the Kenyon teams are any less remarkable; in fact, it's probably *more* remarkable, because of the rather rarefied environment that Kenyon's swimmers must inhabit scholaristically and sociocollegiately. Kenyon makes its meets with the big Division I schools interesting and competitive, which in terms of pure athleticism is a staggering accomplishment: They fare far better swimming against Ohio State than the Division III football champs would do lining up in Ohio Stadium. And the swimmers manage to do it at a place with a long history of nonconformism and free thinking and cultural arts, all the while being assimilated into the life of the college themselves; when the Lords and Ladies have a home meet, the stands are filled. Despite Steen's modest-sounding protestations, something happens at Kenyon when it comes to swimming, and something happens to the swimmers themselves. Take, for example, the Ladies.

When Steen arrived in 1976, there was no women's swim team at Kenyon; he organized it first as a "club sport," rather than as a varsity sport: That first year, with just the swimmers Steen could round up on campus, they were second in the Ohio State Small College meet. In 1977, they won the state meet, as they have won every state or conference championship meet since. In 1984, they won their first NCAA championship, and they have won every one of those ever since, too, accumulating along the way more than 90 All-American designations, 31 NCAA records, 60 NCAA individual and relay titles; in 12 years, they have come to dominate the sport as no other team in any sport has done in so short a time. Steen's explanation is that "the women borrowed a bit on the men's tradition at the beginning, before becoming fully enfranchised themselves."

Only at Kenyon, perhaps, can an athletic coach so casually use a word like "enfranchise"; it rolls as easily from the tongue in Ernst Natatorium as it does around the teapot in the Kenyon Bookstore. Steen is aware, of course, of this, of what he calls "the nice romantic notion of being the small school that wins the Big Meet," and he certainly uses that notion to good advantage, as he uses his blood analyzing machinery and his turbocharged computer. He speaks of a college administration that is supportive, but "supportive in a *cor-*

rect way, a way that understands an emphasis on quality. The College," he says, "is proud of the swimmers, but proud of them in the same way, I think, that it's proud of *The Kenyon Review,* in fact, we're not all that different from *The Kenyon Review."* Steen looks sheepish again. "I, uh, *like* that analogy; both the swimmers and the *Review* are aspects of the College that are *special,* that are distinctive, and distinctively Kenyon. I don't think it would disappoint the administration if we came in thirty-fifth, but I think they would find it very strange if we had a group that decidedly stood apart from the rest of the College."

Coaches, even those who compare their teams to venerable literary journals, are usually allowed a certain level of disingenuousness; that's one of the things that coaching *is.* What makes the Kenyon program so engaging, however, is the overriding sense that a coach who was *only* motivational and inspiring and upbeat—a Knute Rockne—would be driven mad by the batch of honors scholars and Rhodes candidates that plop into Ernst pool every day, articulate and questioning and curious about things they don't know about yet.

Steen has at tiny Kenyon College what many coaches think they wish they had: Athletes who *think,* and he's adjusted the program to exploit that characteristic and use it to motivate the swimmers, just as he's adjusted the program to exploit the more traditional motivations, like history and winning streaks and All-American certificates, which cover one entire wall behind the bleacher seats at the pool. Kenyon College provides plenty of traditional motivation for swimming excellence—would *you* like to swim on the team that ended the streak of 36 straight conference championships? Steen says they don't sit around for hours talking about winning the national championship, but that's mostly because they don't have to: Fully a quarter of the swimmers are honors students, and even the dullest Kenyon swimmer can count the simple Kenyon-purple banners that hang high above the pool deck, one for each national championship.

But the intellectual side, the cerebral challenges: Steen can say, as he sits in the pool office and watches the swimmers come in one by one to have blood samples drawn, that the lactate testing is really, uh, for him. And it probably is, to some degree. If that is the case, then a bonus of the lactate testing is that it requires each swimmer to understand, and participate in formulating, a highly complex and theoretical workout schedule, the epitome of individualized training. A Kenyon swimmer who understands the theory and practice behind lactate testing-based training is a Kenyon swimmer who has become at least as intellectually engaged by swimming as he or she is by Milton's "Sonnet on Swimming." It's sort of like Tom Sawyer's fence for Phi Beta Kappas; he catches them with bait he knows they'll lunge for.

So Steen draws on Kenyon's tradition of swimming excellence, and he draws on the intellectual engagement of an exceptionally high-quality group of student athletes for motivation. He says he's but a lowly managing editor of swimmers, while swimmers like Missi Nelson (another psychology major, another NCAA champ, another multi-All-American, and the 1989 North Coast Athletic Conference Swimmer of the Year) say simply that there's something about Steen "that makes people swim fast."

Finally, and just as engagingly, is another form of empowerment that Steen practices, one that has to do with life after Kenyon. He keeps the swimming alumni in close contact with the team and the swimmers; he solicits from them letters, letters for the annual Kenyon College swimming guidebook, letters for the swimming alumni's newsletter, letters this year, for example, from all of the team captains and co-captains from past teams that he could. He asked them to write letters to this year's team and share what Kenyon swimming meant to them. Almost all of them wrote, sending letters on letterhead from Fortune 500 corporations and emerging businesses; on letterhead from what seems to be every prestigious graduate, medical, dental, law and professional school in the country: University of Chicago, Case Western Reserve Medical School, Harvard, Cincinnati, Wisconsin. There are letters on the stationery of a panoply of physicians and lawyers in private practice. It is a stack of letters to make one quit slouching and straighten the creases in one's pants, a truly impressive collection. Near championship time, the letters were posted, so that the current Lords and Ladies could glean a bit of inspiration from Lords and Ladies past, as well as a subtle reminder that a world awaits beyond the smell of chlorine.

Did Steen, uh, solicit the letters *on* letterhead? His answer is absolutely deadpan. "Uh, now that you mention it," he says, "yeah."

A Struggling Hero: Killebrew Hits Hard Times

BASEBALL

By *JAY WEINER*

From the Minneapolis Star Tribune

Somewhere between fame and 50, Harmon Killebrew lost his way, his marriage and his financial security.

The only Twins player in baseball's Hall of Fame once owned this town and the hearts of Minnesotans. Now he is deep in debt, the victim of fraud, inexperience, poor advice and bad decisions.

Lifted in 1954 from the high school fields of tiny Payette, Ida., to the major leagues and stardom.

Killebrew is now 53 and struggling. Since his last at-bat in 1975, he has found that life beyond the stadium can be harsh.

He owes at least $700,000 to four banks, Calvin Griffith and Reggie Jackson. He owed $270,000 on his dream house on 19 acres on top of an Oregon hill when he stopped making the $2,500-a-month payments and the mortgage company foreclosed.

His auto dealership in Ontario, Ore., and a failed car leasing company in Bloomington pushed him close to bankruptcy.

He lives in a rented condominium in Boise, Ida. He travels frequently to sign autographs, earning up to $5,000 an appearance. His name, signature and wholesome image are his most valued capital.

His wife, Elaine, lives in Edina, separated from her husband after nearly 34 years of marriage.

"It's been a living hell. You have a lot of those days when you feel you're at the bottom," Harmon Killebrew said. "You get to feeling that sometimes you're out on that island by yourself. I don't feel anger, more sometimes frustration, sadness is another, loneliness is another one. . . . Stressful? That's an understatement."

He is determined to pay off his debts and has new projects, most of which he won't detail, to "turn things around."

"I want to say that maybe I've made some wrong decisions but I'm still an honorable person and I intend to take care of all of my obligations."

He is the fifth most prolific home run hitter in history. Nothing in Killebrew's 22-year playing career matched the pressure he faces today.

"In baseball, you pack your uniform in the clubhouse after a ballgame and you see it hanging up in your locker when you get to your next city," Killebrew said. "You pack your bag and your bag gets in your room when you get to the hotel. They pay for your meals, your hotel. When you're out and you're strictly doing it on your own, it's a different situation."

Now he confronts impatient banks in Minnesota and Idaho for defaulting on loans. Among his creditors are Midwest Savings Association and Marquette Bank, controlled by Twins owner Carl Pohlad.

He is the defendant in a lawsuit in California, brought by former star outfielder Reggie Jackson, for failing to pay a loan Jackson cosigned. That suit is on hold because Killebrew and Jackson have worked out a paycheck plan.

Jackson said, "Harmon's been at the bottom of the pit and he's climbing out of the hole. All he has left is his word and he wants to keep it."

Former Twins owner Griffith said Killebrew owes him $100,000 for a loan Griffith gave "three or four years ago" to cover Killebrew's taxes.

Griffith said, "It's a sad situation."

Yet Harmon Clayton Killebrew, the Minnesota sports hero, remains "Killer," your basic nice guy. At 6 feet tall and 197 pounds, he's 23 pounds lighter than during his final season, and two pounds heavier than when the Washington Senators signed him 35 years ago. Killebrew is warm to strangers who simply want to shake his hand. He's remembered fondly enough that television viewers from across the country paid $149.92 each to buy autographed bats during a home shopping network sale in July.

Killebrew seeks no sympathy. In 1974, when "Harmon Killebrew Day" was held at Metropolitan Stadium in Bloomington, he refused gifts, calling them "embarrassing." Instead, $10,000 was raised for charity.

"My feeling then was the people didn't owe me anything," he said. He frowns at the thought of $10 checks pouring in from supporters. "I don't want that sort of thing. I think I'm getting help from the people that can help me right now."

Those people are lawyers. On a recent afternoon, Killebrew was about to enter a meeting in St. Paul with his lawyer, Bill Tilton, and an attorney for Midwest Savings, to which he owes about $190,000. Killebrew and Tilton have proposed a payback plan. A hearing on the matter is set for September 13.

"No matter what, I've always been an optimistic person," Killebrew said. "I'm not a quitter. All my career I went through a lot of physical adversity, injuries. It's in my nature to be a battler."

In Washington, Minnesota and Kansas City, at first base, third base, the outfield and as a designated hitter, Killebrew became the most productive righthanded home run hitter in American League history with 573, driving in 1,584 runs, making it to Cooperstown in 1984.

His fame came during a simpler time in sports, when ballplayers seemed more like neighborhood drinking buddies than multimillionaires. Killebrew's annual salary topped out at $120,000 in 1972—a nice paycheck—but, accounting for inflation, about $350,000 in 1989 dollars, or $200,000 less than Twins outfielder Randy Bush's current salary.

In 1976, his baseball income stopped, but Killebrew remembers his exit from the field as smooth. His first job was a color commentator on televised Twins games. He received his securities license and became a partner in a Boise insurance and financial planning firm with former Idaho congressman Ralph Harding.

Killebrew said he practically welcomed the end of his playing days. "The last couple years that I played my knees hurt so bad it was painful to play. That's why these old-timers games are so difficult—because it hurts. People forget that's the reason we quit playing—because we couldn't play anymore. I'd had my day and my day was over."

Elaine Killebrew, who has known Harmon since both were 12 years old and growing up in Payette, remembers Harmon's passage from field to office differently. Nine months after the cheers ended, he reached 40 and she noticed a change.

"He was not handling (turning 40) well," she said. "He admitted to me he was really having a tough time. He had a tough time leaving baseball, too, even though he was having pain in his body. He didn't want to leave baseball. There was silence, a sort of underlying hostility (toward) everything, the children, me. He became noncommunicative."

He was facing his first financial crisis. A cattle ranch he bought toward the end of his career failed. Elaine said the family was forced to sell some of its investments. At the same time, she said, the house they were building on the hill wound up costing about $180,000, twice as much as expected.

"He had that feeling, 'I was successful in baseball. I can do it again,' " Elaine said. But her husband seemed a candidate for business failure. "He's always been the type of person whose niceness gets him used. He didn't want anybody to be displeased with him."

His reputation as a good fellow and sports hero might have attracted business partners, customers and bankers, but it took its toll on the Killebrew family, she said.

"We couldn't be left alone. It was difficult because his celebrity took him away from his children. I don't think it's good to put people on a pedestal and worship them as a hero. I don't think it's good for the person they make the hero."

As Howard Heminger, the Killebrew's accountant, said of Harmon: "he's great at hitting home runs and swinging a mean golf club, but he has no education in business."

Killebrew said he has been working since he was 12, that he was a straight-A student in high school and that he became a good insurance salesman. He disputes a suggestion that baseball somehow failed him by limiting his life experiences to locker rooms from the ages of 18 to 39.

"I think it's inaccurate to say I wasn't prepared for business," Killebrew said. Still, his history has been crammed with painful lessons.

"Who do you trust? Is that the TV show? I guess sometimes things happen to you and then you wake up and ask yourself, 'What happened?' It didn't happen overnight. It came over a period of time."

In one venture, Killebrew found himself in a criminal situation. In 1981, he and Harding entered into a relationship with California real estate developer Jack Franks. It was a giant step on Killebrew's increasingly shaky financial path.

The Killebrew-Franks deal involved a proposed development, called RM-18, on 157 acres in Rancho Mirage, Calif. The plan was to construct 18 luxury homes on each hole of a golf course designed by Robert Trent Jones Jr. Each lot was to cost $1.5 million and each house was to have at least 5,000 square feet.

Killebrew said Franks approached Harding to help recruit investors for the development. Killebrew's name was used to pique the curiosity of potential backers. For their work, Killebrew and Harding each received a $100,000 commission, and those "payments" were used to purchase their interest in RM-18.

In the end, there was no development and Franks eventually admitted diverting more than $1 million for his own use. He pleaded guilty to mail and wire fraud and served 60 days in prison.

"(Killebrew) was a victim, clearly a victim," said Los Angeles-based Assistant U.S. Attorney James Asperger. "He did get other people involved that he knew, but that is not uncommon in a fraud scheme."

After the conclusion of the legal proceedings, Killebrew and Harding parted ways. The two remained involved in a charity golf tournament in Sun Valley, Ida., until Killebrew pulled out of the event in 1986.

Killebrew said it wasn't RM-18, but his auto businesses that forced him to borrow money. He acquired a GM dealership in Oregon in 1984 and started a car leasing company in Bloomington in 1986.

He purchased the dealership, which sells Buick, Pontiac, Oldsmobile, Cadillac and GM trucks, without "knowing one blessed thing about auto dealerships," as Elaine Killebrew put it. "He had others manage the store. He turned it over to somebody else and walks away," she said.

Likewise, his Twin Cities car leasing concern was shut down in 1987 amid suspicion that an employee was writing checks for personal use. According to special agent Byron Gigler, the FBI looked into the matter but discontinued the investigation because of insufficient evidence. Heminger said Killebrew lost at least $100,000 on the leasing company, which went unsupervised by either Harmon or Cameron, the oldest of Killebrew's five children, who was another partner.

James Hanvik, the lawyer who helped incorporate the leasing firm, said, "I think it was one of those things his son (Cameron) sort of got him into, figuring (Harmon's) name would be magic."

There was no magic, only debt. Cameron said he, Harmon and advisers in Minnesota believed a leasing company would be "a perfect outlet" for the Oregon dealership. Instead, it became "a simple thing that went crazy," Cameron said.

Heminger said Killebrew's dealership was undercapitalized and had poor cash flow. Killebrew planned to have a wealthy partner in his leasing venture, but that investor pulled out, Hanvik said.

In Oregon, the dealership was running aground. Killebrew acquired it "quite by accident. I knew nothing about the automobile business and I must not know much now. A friend of mine owned a dealership there and he said, 'Hey, this one's for sale, why don't you look into it?' And I did. I should have walked away, probably. I wasn't capable and I didn't have the time, either."

Banks kept lending him money—some, it seems, because he was a former baseball star. "I would guess that a lot of people who are lending money to people with notoriety are buying an autograph sometimes," Heminger said.

Tilton said, "He was throwing good money after bad, hoping it would turn around."

Killebrew said, "I just made some bad business decisions. The automobile dealership, I don't know if you know anything about that business, but it's a tough one."

Killebrew borrowed $100,000 from Griffith in 1986 or '87 and has not repaid it, Griffith said. "He called me up. He said the Internal Revenue was on him. He said if he didn't pay up they'd put him in jail," Griffith said.

Records show Killebrew owed the IRS substantial amounts for his personal taxes and auto dealership and that most of the liens have been satisfied. Last week, records in the office of the clerk of Malheur County in Oregon showed that Killebrew's auto company still owes more than $10,000 to the IRS and $11,370 to the state of Oregon.

Killebrew acknowledged that he owes Griffith money, but would not confirm the amount. Of Griffith, with whom he had some well-publicized contract disputes, Killebrew said: "I think he gets criticized unjustly sometimes. I have a real soft spot in my heart for Calvin Griffith. Calvin has helped me, done things a lot of people don't even know and I appreciate it."

Griffith's arrangement with Killebrew was the least formal of a series of loans gone bad:

• On December 21, 1987, Killebrew borrowed $175,656 from Midwest Savings (then called Midwest Federal). By March 21, 1988, he defaulted. With interest, he owes "in excess of $190,000," according to documents in St. Paul federal court. Killebrew is pursuing a payback plan.

• On July 5, 1988, Idaho First National Bank filed legal documents stating that Killebrew and the dealership owe the bank $175,101.

• On July 20, 1988, Marquette Bank of Minneapolis submitted papers in Hennepin County District Court saying Killebrew owes $40,282. This loan was for the car leasing agency.

• On August 23, 1988, First Security Bank of Idaho told a district court in Idaho that Harmon and Elaine Killebrew owe $81,899, plus interest of $8.06 per day.

• On Nov. 17, 1988, Jackson sued Killebrew in San Francisco federal court. A year earlier, Jackson co-signed a promissory note allowing Killebrew to borrow $184,166 from Midwest Federal. Court documents say Killebrew paid back all but $47,716 of the loan. Jackson then completed the payments to the bank. But Jackson claims that with damages, interest and attorney's fees, Killebrew owes him more.

The two became pals in 1969 when Killebrew edged Jackson for the American League home run title, 49 to 47. Their relationship was more professional than personal, but in the spring of 1987, Jackson said, "I saw a friend in need. . . . I had the money, so I stepped up to the line."

Coincidentally, Jackson recently closed a Chevrolet dealership in Oakland, Calif., after his debt surpassed $1 million. He spoke from experience: "It is a very sophisticated business. If you're a novice you can be taken to the cleaners. People like Reggie Jackson and Harmon Killebrew who are not in that business can be taken advantage of because we come from baseball, where everything is black and white. You hit a home run because it went over the fence. You hit .270 because you have 27 hits out of 100 at-bats. Car dealerships are different. Most people are not afraid to take advantage of you. They figure you're Reggie Jackson, you're Harmon Killebrew, you've got it and they want some of it."

In retrospect, Killebrew regrets borrowing the money and getting into the auto business at all. The dealership has stabilized, however, since Cameron took over its management two years ago.

"The real lesson here is that a person who is a hero and celebrity like Harmon is basically trusting other people in the business world, where you have mutual things to contribute," Tilton said. "They have their skills, Harmon has his name and personality. It's one thing for Harmon to give his name. It's another thing for Harmon to be on the note for everything. Harmon took all the risk."

Compounding the business crisis was the July 1988 foreclosure on the Killebrew family home. To Elaine Killebrew, that was the final blow. The vacated house on the hill, she said, is "the symbol of a destroyed, split family."

To Harmon, the foreclosure was "just part of the whole situation. It was a tough deal, yeah. They just took the house back."

The foreclosure came a year after Elaine filed for divorce, citing "irreconcilable differences" and after Harmon moved out of their house. Elaine said she wanted to divorce Harmon because of his long-term relationship with his former secretary. Elaine said she became aware of the relationship in 1982 and that Harmon continues to travel to baseball functions with this woman friend.

Harmon declined to discuss his marriage or relationship. "Elaine and I are on good terms. We've had many years of happy marriage. I still have very, very deep feelings for her. I'm still close with my children. I prefer not to go into that."

Elaine said she hoped the divorce action "would wake him up. You can only take so much public humiliation." But on March 16, 1988, she withdrew the divorce petition. "Everything was so complicated with threatening bankruptcy and I just couldn't see that we could afford another attorney. Emotionally, I felt I couldn't handle it anymore." For now, the two are separated, with no legal proceedings pending.

Last September, after spending time with her three daughters in California, Elaine moved to an apartment near Southdale, to "rebuild my shattered life. I married when I was 19 and never worked. I spent my life raising kids and being his wife and supporter. . . . I was sitting in bed one morning, reading the paper, and I thought, 'I've got to go to work.' "

She scanned the newspaper classified ads and was hired as a "fashion consultant" at a women's clothing store. Harmon supports her with his baseball pension, which Elaine said is about $3,500 a month. "I couldn't survive without that. I'd be finished," she said.

Harmon Killebrew maintains that he is far from finished. He has been advised that declaring bankruptcy is the cleanest way to face his obligations, but he is proud and refuses to make that formal admission of financial defeat. "I see some light at the end of the tunnel," he said. "I went into this thing with good intentions and that's the way I want to come out of it."

His only real asset is himself. Last month he was in the Twin Cities to appear on the Cable Value Network's "Sporting Collections," the same show that last week featured Pete Rose. On this home-shopping program, Killebrew helped sell, among other things, an ironic memento: a ball autographed by Jackson and Killebrew for $59.94.

Killebrew has not placed his personal cache of trophies on the market, however. "If it meant my survival, I suppose I would take a hard look at it," he said.

During the past year Killebrew has been attempting to establish new businesses that will help him out of debt. His major venture, in its early stages, is the sale of a special edition bat collection. For $1,995, fans can purchase copies of the bats Killebrew used to hit his first, 100th, 200th, 300th, 400th, 500th and last home runs. Displayed in a handcrafted oak case, each bat is autographed and engraved with the date and the pitcher off whom the homers were hit.

Jackson is impressed by the way Killebrew has begun to tackle his debts. "I honestly felt that six months ago, a year ago, I was never going to see his money," Jackson said. "But now I think Harmon's going to make it. He's moving in the right direction. His only chance is if people give him a chance."

Heminger said, "I think the worst is behind. He's been through the troubled water. This, too, will pass. I think the people should trust him. He trusts them."

Said Killebrew: "I think I've learned that you've got to pay better attention to what's going on, that's the No. 1 thing. Sometimes when you find out, it's too late. I learned: Don't put yourself in a position where it's just you out there."

The thing is, his fame and reputation were established by standing out there, bat in hands, all alone, wearing No. 3, fourth in the batting order, the fate of the Twins on his shoulders, hitting a game-winning home run.

"I struck out an awful lot, too," Killebrew said. "Sixteen hundred and 99 times." He laughed at the memory of those swings and misses in the batter's box. "I always bounced back."

That's his current plan.

"I like happy endings," he said.

Manley: Crisis After Crisis

PRO FOOTBALL

By *TOM FRIEND*

Dexter Manley named a son after his favorite football player (himself) and a daughter after his least favorite football team (Dallas). The two children climb in his bed every night, grabbing for any available knee or elbow, tickling any bare skin, and Manley has particularly admired a bumper sticker sent to him anonymously in the mail.

"It Is Better To Build Children Than To Repair Adults," it said, and Manley slapped it on the rear of his Bronco truck.

Manley's own unsettling childhood, which included his being locked periodically in a closet and ignored in school, left him with the deepest of insecurities, and he has spent a good portion of his adult life immersed in personal reconstruction.

When drafted out of Oklahoma State in the fifth round by the Washington Redskins 8½ years ago, Manley had no sacks, no books, no wife, no culture, no cash, no couth. Today he has pretty much obtained all of the above, but now he has no football.

On Saturday, Dexter Manley, 31, was banned indefinitely by the National Football League because of three violations of the league's substance abuse policy, the last for testing positive for cocaine. He may apply for reinstatement in a year, but for now, he seems to have reached a personal denouement.

Based on his track record, he seems likely to clench his teeth and attempt a cleansing revamping of his lifestyle. It will not be his first comeback from crisis. He has yearned for public acceptance from first grade on, and has taken great lengths to make himself a better person in the eyes of others.

Manley recently thought it would make sense to take up tennis.

In a tight Lacoste shirt and shorts, he could cover the court well enough, but would usually mis-hit his makeshift topspin strokes. He needed every inch of his oversized, $500 boron racket, but at least he learned how to keep score.

In the showers of his tennis club, he met a mortgage banker, Chris Applegate, so tennis had served its purpose. Applegate offered him a job at his mortgage company, where Manley would help attract clients through his contacts in professional sports and—as a bonus—learn the art of closing a deal.

What drove Manley toward a non-football job? He said he had come to the realization that if his career ended, as Joe Theismann's had so suddenly, he'd better know something other than a pass rush stunt. He's said that's why he decided to learn to read at age 28.

Manley also traveled to France (where he wanted to eat french fries), and later planned visits to Japan (for sushi) and Egypt (for pyramids) and also his ultimate journey—to Africa (for a safari). He has had his children riding horses. He assumed this would grant them a better life than his own.

When his son was born, he said, "His name is Dexter Keith Manley II. He's not Junior. Just 'the second.' Sounds classier that way."

His wife, Glinda, learned she was pregnant the day of a Dallas Cowboys-Redskins Monday night game, so they named their daughter Dalis. "If we'd been playing Green Bay, her first name would've been Green Bay, her middle name Packer," he said. They spelled her name Dalis, rather than Dallas, again to be extraordinarily classy, Manley said.

Also, Manley said he enjoyed the Hazelden Foundation in Minnesota, where he underwent substance abuse rehabilitation in 1987 and 1988, because "it reminds me of Harvard Business School." Harvard apparently was his dream campus.

If ever he spoke at a public function, he needed to bring with him a sophisticated line. At a heavily attended, black-tie Touchdown Club dinner in 1987, he started a speech by leaning toward former secretary of state Alexander Haig nearby and said, "Before I begin here, I want to say one thing: I'm in charge here."

His own father, Carl, who died in 1977, was a man sturdy as can be, about the same size as Dexter today at 6 feet 3, about 250 pounds. Dexter was the youngest of four, and if he was naughty he would be led to a closet, where he'd be trapped beneath the trench coats. For fear of retribution, he never told his father about his high school marriage.

When he was arrested here in 1982 for impersonating a sheriff's deputy and altering a license plate, he said: "I come from a good family life, but maybe if my father was still here he'd be on me a little more. When he died, I had to learn right from wrong on my own. I had to take on a lot of responsibilities."

School, for Manley, was like a jail cell. An undiagnosed learning disability left him unable to comprehend teachers, who eventually banished him to a special education class. He remembers being teased—but of course not bullied—and says the catcalls of "You dummy!" have left scars that ache today.

By high school, his wonderful talent for football was noticed and cheered by all, and Manley gathered his self-esteem. By his senior year, he also found that some good could come out of lies and deceit. For instance, he has admitted wearing custom-made suits as an undergraduate.

"I'm not gonna say how I got them," he said. "It was my senior year in high school, so you put it together. I had 37 scholarship offers. So, that's how it works."

In college, his rage peaked. His brother, Reggie, was shot and killed in Houston over a money dispute, and he contemplated an all-out search for the killer. He was unable to do so because of a football injury. "Thank God I got hurt," he said later. "If I wasn't hurt, no telling what I would have gone home and done."

In an argument over a simple parking space, he fought two college students and got slashed in the cheek with a razor blade, a scar that remains front and center. By the time his professional career began, he found a new source for attention—the media. His colorful quotes were splashed all over the sports pages and broadcast over the airwaves.

- In 1982, when his contract was due to expire in a year: "I want to become a natural-born free agent next year."
- After wrecking his truck outside Redskin park in 1985: "Me and Riggo (John Riggins) are going to do a car commercial."
- After a particularly good game: "The three most famous people in this country are Michael Jackson, Prince and me."
- On what he thought of owner Jack Kent Cooke during a 1986 contract haggle: "A miser."
- On why he passed out in Georgetown in 1986: "I knew I was allergic to seafood, but I ate it anyway because I like it."

Now that he's out of the game, there is concern whether he can function with no one listening and recording. With all that publicity came fame and a million people offering advice. He trusted almost no one and is now on his fourth agent—Boston attorney Bob Woolf.

With his wealth and popularity, and the almost inevitable hangers-on all around him, there was the opportunity to drink and dabble with drugs. What led to his third violation of the league's substance abuse policy is unclear, but there were problems at home, he said, that led him to stay out all night four days before he tested positive the third time. Still, teammates wonder if he knew a positive test meant banishment, how could he succumb?

He didn't mean to.

He said before this season: "The older you get, you get a broader vision of what you can do. I've been playing football eight years, going into my ninth, and it's like I don't want to mess anything up because I want to take what I have and run with it. It's now that I'm beginning to appreciate what I do. When I was young I wasn't appreciative because I knew I had the ability, but now I appreciate it because it could be over like this (snapping his fingers).

"I think it's the suspension (30 days before the 1988 season). I don't want to mess up. I want to be the best person I can be. I've got to cultivate myself. I've got to find other things to do. I've got to discover who Dexter is. Because a lot of athletes don't really have an identity. When it's over, what will they do? You could be like Elvin Bethea, who killed himself.

"I'm 30 now. That makes me think. Hey, I'd like to play football until I'm 36. . . . I know what's at stake. One more strike and I'm out. I have to remember what I am. I can't sit down and think I can sit with my peers and drink a beer."

This latest failure was not about foolishness. Manley attended Alcoholics Anonymous programs for two years straight before his relapse. He had a "guru," Pham Chopra, who served as a guide and alcohol counselor. Manley carried around a frayed book called "One More Day," which contained sayings for every calendar day. On March 1 of this year, it said, "A man without a plan for the day is lost before he starts."

Now, he needs a new plan. But what becomes of the children?

Dalis has been in a leg cast since birth, born with no bone between her kneecap and ankle. Her father cries about it.

The other day, as television trucks waited outside Manley's house hoping for interviews, Dexter II, 5, played with a few of the cameramen. He had no idea why they were parked there, but inside the house, Dexter I was hurting badly.

Kareem: Leaving Legacy Of Consistency

PRO BASKETBALL

By ***PAUL ATTNER***

He waved to the crowd one last time, then left the court, his head slightly bowed, his pace quick, as if he was intent on removing himself from the spotlight as soon as possible. It was a walk he had made many times before, but this one was different. After 20 professional campaigns, Kareem Abdul-Jabbar had played his last regular-season game.

It is easy, of course, to call the retirement of any great player "the end of an era." But this time, it would be no exaggeration. Abdul-Jabbar may be the best player in pro basketball history. Certainly, a case can be made in his favor. And any time such a player leaves, the game itself can't ever be quite the same.

By playing so long at such an elite level, he gave fans a sharp picture of what can be produced by truly remarkable athletic ability combined with iron determination. There was never anyone quite like him before, not even Wilt Chamberlain or Bill Russell. And there is no heir apparent waiting to replace him. The National Basketball Association was once a center's league, but flash and pizazz have ended the big man's domination. And no one symbolized that domination better than Abdul-Jabbar, who gave his position grace, agility, quickness and elegance never before possessed by one man.

His Los Angeles Lakers teammates captured it best. For his retirement gift on this nostalgic April 23 afternoon in the Great Western Forum, they gave him a Rolls Royce. What else could a man making $3 million a year need? But just as appropriate, you don't send out someone like Abdul-Jabbar in a Cadillac or a Mercedes. Only a Rolls will do.

Abdul-Jabbar showed that a player could have magnificent individual statistics and still be such a significant team player that he can retire with six championship rings, possibly seven. Chamberlain had magnificent individual statistics, but titles eluded him most of his career. Russell played on 11 championship teams, but his statistics never came close to matching those of Abdul-Jabbar. For 20 years, Abdul-Jabbar had the best of both worlds.

"My legacy? That I played as well as I have for as long as I have," he said.

Remember, this man was voted Most Valuable Player of the playoffs both at age 24 and at age 38.

His accomplishments are, without question, awesome: a record 38,387 career points, 787 straight games in which he scored in double figures, a record six regular-season MVP player awards. Great NBA stars began and ended their careers during his reign. But he endured those flights, game-day walk-throughs and foul calls.

He never mesmerized fans. His style lacked flare, and his harshly cold demeanor erected a wall. Even the Lakers' fans never really adored him, not like they worship Magic Johnson or even Michael Cooper. That's what made Abdul-Jabbar's retirement ceremony so unusual. At last, after 14 years in Los Angeles, the player and the public gave each other a prolonged hug. The crowd gave him standing ovations, and Abdul-Jabbar responded with a rare hint of sentiment, almost breaking down in tears at the end.

This was the conclusion of a farewell tour that began in November in New York, where he was born and raised. That was a poignant time, too, and so was the ceremony in Milwaukee, his first NBA home. The Bucks gave him a motorcycle, and he was so stunned he didn't know how to respond. He had another surprise in Oakland, where the Golden State Warriors presented him with a sailboat. Again, he was shocked.

But the NBA, and the Lakers, indeed saved the best for last. He had entered the league with a head full of hair and an abundance of talent. Now, 20 years later, he stood before the Lakers' fans, his head bald, his talents depleted. But they didn't care. They knew this moment was special, and they made him feel comfortable and wanted. In turn, he wanted to reward them with a great final game, but all he could muster was 10 points. For once, his output didn't matter.

But statistics alone should never be used to measure Abdul-Jabbar's role in history. That would be an injustice, because, during his time in the NBA, he made contributions that extended far beyond the ability to shoot a skyhook.

Once athletic careers could be measured in a vacuum of sorts, isolated from the real world. So Babe Ruth was a womanizer and a drinker. So Joe Louis had a roving eye. The private lives of our sports heroes were just that—private. You could laugh about the gossip, but boys will be boys. What was important was how they performed at the plate or in the ring, not how they felt about politics or religion. These were knights on a pedestal, the idols of millions, the symbols of all that was good about sports and America.

Abdul-Jabbar began his pro basketball career with Milwaukee in 1969 amid a swirl of athletic change and turmoil. No longer isolated, sports became entwined forever with real life. Once athletes rarely questioned authority and only occasionally protested management's iron rule. Suddenly, they not only were challenging the system, but they also dared raise questions about inequities in society.

This was the era of the Black Panthers, Black Muslims, Abbie Hoffman and Yippies, violent Vietnam protests, Martin Luther King's death, ghetto riots and the 1968 Democratic Convention in Chicago. This was the era when Cassius Clay changed his name to Muhammad Ali and refused to go to war, a decision that so outraged the sports establishment that it cost him the heavyweight title. This was a year after two black American athletes had raised their fists in protest in the 1968 Olympics.

In a country entrenched in conservatism—Richard Nixon beat Hubert Humphrey to win the 1968 presidential election—sports stood as one of its most conservative elements. The rest of the world could be falling apart. Patriotism could be outmoded. But sports, that playpen of fantasies and childhood dreams, must not change. And anyone who challenged the essence of sports was the enemy. Into this atmosphere walked Lew Alcindor, twice the college player of the year, one of the all-time great pro prospects and as it would turn out, one of the pioneers of visible black pride in the NBA.

Twenty years later, it is hard to grasp the racial and social tension that plagued the United States in that era. Now we have soaring contracts and athletes on drugs. In Alcindor's rookie year, the very fabric of the nation was being shaken. People were fearful and angry, and they felt helpless. Just a year before, Alcindor decided not to play on the Olympic team, only to be told, on national television by Joe Garagiola, that if he didn't like his country, why not move? It took guts to be an outspoken black athlete, since such boldness was sure to create a barrage of racial backlash.

Despite his Olympic protest, there really was no reason to believe that Alcindor would become a towering symbol of black progress. He had been sheltered so successfully by John Wooden at UCLA that we didn't know much about him, although he was a star before he took his first shot in the NBA. We didn't know that he was quietly studying to become a Muslim after being raised a Catholic. We didn't know that he was angry at white America, unsure of the wisdom of Martin Luther King's teachings and confused about his role in society.

But this most private of men soon would have his life, like it or not, exposed for all to see—and many to hate. He had the guts, in 1971, to declare his religious conversion by changing his name to Kareem Abdul-Jabbar, which means noble, powerful servant. Although he was not associated with the radical Black Muslim movement, in the eyes of the sports establishment he was suddenly a radical. Later, Black Muslims would kill eight Muslims who were living in a house he owned in Washington. Still later, his religious mentor, who also lived in that house, would go on a rampage and take over three buildings in Washington, resulting in another death.

None of those episodes endeared him to the sporting public or to the people who wrote and broadcast sports news. Just like the country itself, the sports media of that era felt threatened by what was happening to athletes. They wanted to continue to report scores and heroics, not protests and politics. They wanted to praise stars, not hear their outspoken views. They treated Ali with contempt and Abdul-Jabbar with suspicion. They treated the NBA, with black athletes methodically dominating the sport, as a second-class citizen, not worthy of the same praise as the National Football League or major league baseball. In turn, Abdul-Jabbar viewed many reporters as racists and mudslingers. He decided to shut all of them out.

From that self-declared isolation, towering above everyone, grew contempt, mistrust and mystery on both sides. Abdul-Jabbar was already lugging around a truly heavy burden, because he was a dominating big man in a sport in which men of such size and ability automatically were considered goliaths operating with an unfair advantage. Players such as Russell, Chamberlain or Abdul-Jabbar might have been respected. But loved? Not really. And now one of these big men was defiantly snubbing his nose at society. Yet his incredible power of concentration allowed him to continue to produce on the court at a level rarely attained by any other player.

The way he played didn't help, either. He perfected what he candidly describes as an "unsexy" signature shot, a skyhook that was relentlessly, unemotionally and mechanically deadly. It rarely brought fans to their feet, but it sank like a sword into the body of opposing teams. Lost in all this was the fact that the skyhook required great athletic skill and precision, so much so that even now Abdul-Jabbar has no imitators. But he performed his chores in such a workmanlike fashion that the majesty of his weapon was overshadowed. It was just another reason to dislike him.

Maybe that's why Abdul-Jabbar's final season should have been called the peace tour. The NBA now has a love affair with the public. Abdul-Jabbar has been a foundation of its growth, a pioneer for modern athletes. He endured the sticks and stones so Julius Erving, Larry Bird, Magic Johnson and Michael Jordan could cavort in a much more positive atmosphere. Just think of how long he has been around: In 1969, Gale Sayers won the NFL rushing title, Joe Namath led the Jets to a stunning triumph over the Colts in Super Bowl III, Rod Laver won tennis' Grand Slam and the amazin' Mets captured the World Series. Harmon Killebrew and Willie McCovey were baseball's MVPs. So much has changed in sports over the last 20 years, yet Abdul-Jabbar has remained a constant.

Still, in his mind, he was not sure how he was viewed by the public. He made attempts to reduce the tension, starting with the 1983 publication of his autobiography, "Giant Steps," which revealed the warts and all. The acceptance of that book both shocked and pleased him, and he became a bit more open, a bit more willing to open the door and let others see his off-the-court life. But the farewell tour had risks.

"It was kind of like taking a chance," he said, "but you don't know until you find out. It was worth it to find out how people perceive what I have done."

He calls himself a villain, because for so long he has been the central reason his team has beaten other teams. But this villain—"the baddest among the bad guys," he says—received standing ovations throughout the league and was showered with gifts and love, even in cities like Boston and Oakland, where the passions ran deepest.

His brief thank-you speeches gave us a chance to sample his humor. Yes, this cold, sullen man can smile, even laugh at himself. The hostility and distance he had projected for so long was erased for a few minutes.

"It's been nice," Abdul-Jabbar said of his final season, still keeping his emotions under stoic control.

But the way his eyes sparkle, you know it has meant much more to him than just "nice," for even this proudest of men didn't want to leave the game he loved so long feeling hated. Earlier in the season, Denver Coach Doug Moe called him "a jerk," pointing out that other players, the fans and the media never really have liked Abdul-Jabbar very much. Rival players talk about how he never tried to be friendly. Abdul-Jabbar admits he could have done more earlier in his career to ease the animosity, but he had no time or interest then for what he considered public relations. Take me as I am, he was saying back then. Now, he is leaving on a kinder, sweeter, more proper note.

That's what makes the debate about his on-the-court performance this season so irrelevant. No question, his skills have deteriorated, but that has been happening for the past few seasons. He had already ceased to be a defensive force or a rebounder. But the Lakers would not have won the last two NBA championships without him, and he turned 40 and 41 during those seasons. At 42, he can still toss the skyhook, get up and down the floor and not embarrass himself. More important, if the Lakers were willing to pay him $3 million, why shouldn't he take it? And why not allow him the chance to have a public love feast before he leaves?

★ ★ ★

In 20 years, Abdul-Jabbar has earned and lost fortunes, seen his $1 million house burn down, his family estranged and his closest religious friends killed. He has had fights on the court, had his every move booed. He has taken drugs, trained with Bruce Lee, appeared in movies. He has been playing basketball since the fourth grade, and from the moment he began his high school career in New York as a ninth grader, he has been under public scrutiny.

The game itself long ago ceased to be fun. But he still respects it.

"As a professional life, this has been incredible," he said. "But it is tough, very competitive, a lot of stress, a lot of moments of extreme disappointments and frustrations."

And, of course, extreme triumphs—all those MVP awards, titles and records that may never be surpassed.

His final season forced him to open his mind to the past. The floodgates of memories revealed that Nate Thurmond was his most difficult opponent, that the 1985 championship victory over the Celtics was his proudest moment, that his ability to avoid crippling injury and stay in shape have allowed him to continue playing all these years. Of course, not even Abdul-Jabbar expected to be around this long. But the money was great, he was still better than almost anyone else and the team needed him, reasons enough to keep going.

He has never lost his social consciousness. His concerns now center mainly around fighting illiteracy and feeding the hungry. He will continue those efforts in his post-NBA life, which will include public relations work with an athletic equipment company and perhaps some acting and movie producing. He says he is content with what he has done and hopes he will be remembered as "a complete person who lived life as an intelligent human being."

No question, he says, the timing was right. "I would have been wrong to leave earlier, and certainly I shouldn't stay any longer," he said.

But he isn't quite finished. His coach, Pat Riley, wants one more supreme effort for the playoffs.

"This is the final stand of what could be the greatest team ever," Riley said. "He has to want to go out and endear himself to his image and legacy.

"His last walk on stage has to be as gallant and as heartfelt as it ever has been. He needs to go out with that kind of dignity, as a patriarch embracing his family."

Abdul-Jabbar listens to what Riley has said and silently absorbs it for a while. There is a weariness about him, the toll another long season has taken. But even now, the challenges are there. His work isn't finished, even after so many skyhooks and so many victories. You want him to say, "Hey, Riley, enough is enough. Leave me alone."

Instead, he finally looks up and says quietly: "I hope to be able to contribute something along those lines. I will pursue it."

For 20 years, he has been pursuing dreams. Soon, he can rest. And the NBA will never be quite the same again.

In End, Rose Not Bigger Than Baseball

BASEBALL

By *PHIL HERSH*

From the Chicago Tribune

"The prism through which I see things," A. Bartlett Giamatti said in a conversation earlier this year, "is the prism that understands baseball is an enormously important American institution with long and deep roots, whose purpose is to provide pleasure and fun for the American people, and whose integrity and authenticity are essential to provide that pleasure."

The relative importance of baseball and the enormous concerns for its integrity were never clearer than Thursday morning, when Commissioner Giamatti barred Cincinnati Reds manager Pete Rose from the game for life because he bet on his team. The national television networks interrupted highly rated morning game shows and talk shows for live coverage of the press conferences by Giamatti in New York and Rose in Cincinnati.

The *Cincinnati Post's* front page was headlined "ROSE IS OUT!" in red type of a size last seen announcing the end of World War II.

Baseball, Giamatti said Thursday, has "such a purchase on our national soul." Pete Rose, made a millionaire by baseball, gambled his soul on a game of chance for a few more dollars, and it has cost him dearly.

Baseball can live with artificial grass made of plastic, artificial bats made of metal and artificial bodies made of steroids. It cannot live with even the possibility of artificial results made of unholy alliances between gamblers and baseball men.

Judge Kenesaw Mountain Landis, the game's first commissioner, made that evident when he ignored a court's decision that absolved eight 1919 White Sox of conspiring to throw the World Series they lost. Giamatti acted similarly, his convictions of rightness no less than those held by Landis.

Baseball is richer for not compromising its rules, poorer for losing Rose, whose chances for early reinstatement seem unlikely. He was one of the game's best-liked figures, popular with fans and the media, as well as one of its greatest players. He was a man of mythic proportions in a sport with a mythology as complete as anything Homer created.

Like any myths, baseball's heighten the ideal at the expense of the real. Thus was Peter Edward Rose turned into a hero.

"The essence of baseball," Babe Ruth biographer Robert Creamer wrote, "is a small boy looking in absolute rapture at a grown man."

Rose was baseball to the generation that grew up with the game on television. His greatest glories were celebrated as the national pastime recaptured the nation's interest after the Vietnam War.

The country was captivated in 1978 by his two-month pursuit of Joe DiMaggio's apparently unbreakable 56-game hitting streak. Rose fell 12 games short but set a National League record.

America watched again as Rose, obsessed like Ahab, relentlessly pursued Ty Cobb's apparently unbreakable record of 4,191 major-league base hits, finally passing him in 1985 and adding another 64 hits for great measure.

And the nation followed every episode this year of the seven-month investigation into Rose's gambling, when each day seemed to bring new indictments against his character. Few other athletes, and no one but a baseball player, could have commanded such attention.

Rose's accomplishments and the country's sporting life seemed completely intertwined for two decades. The essence of his existence was baseball. Baseball is an essential element of the American social and historical fabric. A piece of Americana seemed torn apart as the country watched his life unravel.

We are confused by how to treat Pete Rose as a fallen idol, but that shouldn't be the question. The question should be why we ever worshiped him at all.

Even before his reputation was so clearly debased by the lifetime suspension, Rose was far from a behavioral exemplar. He was named in a paternity suit, accused of being a poor father by the children of his first marriage, guilty of choosing his friends injudiciously. Since the gambling problems became public, many of Rose's statements, including the latest, have been contradictions at best, lies at worst. Rose continued to insist Thursday that he had not bet on baseball. Commissioner Giamatti was convinced Rose had.

What of redeeming value was there about this man, other than his ability to hit a baseball? We admired him specially for that skill because of Rose's seeming lack of natural ability. It reinforced the illusion that baseball is everyman's game. It revived the frustration and fascination baseball brings to grown men who convince themselves that they, too, could have been major-leaguers.

Yet Rose managed to reduce himself below the dimensions of ordinariness that he overcame as "Charlie Hustle." Only hours after making the agreement that included his banishment from baseball, Rose was indulged in a carney hustle, hawking baseballs with his autograph for $39.94 on a cable-TV show. In his Thursday press conference, Rose apologized to baseball, the game, for being bothered by the problems caused by his lingering soap opera "You Bet Your Life." There was no apology to his wife or children or friends or ex-teammates or the players he managed for the problems he caused their lives.

Rose was as imperfect as Cobb, even though he was infinitely more likable. Cobb was truly a miserable human being: mean, misogynistic, an insulting, paranoid alcoholic in later life, accused and absolved of taking part in a game-fixing scheme.

Cobb also was in the initial group of five players elected to the Baseball Hall of Fame. The Hall, sanctum sanctorum, includes several unsavory characters, although none who had been banned from baseball. Whether that ignoble distinction will keep Rose from the Hall is uncertain. Giamatti exhorted those who will make that decision to wrestle with the distinction between life and art. In the attempt to do so, one recalls the 17th Century Italian painter, Caravaggio. He was a reputed pederast, an accused murderer forced to flee Rome and a painter of such surpassing brilliance that he is included in all pantheons of his art.

Rose's art was baseball. His offenses against life are not as serious as Caravaggio's. The main difference, of course, is that Rose may have committed crimes against art as well as life. His case could blur into details of when he gambled and on what.

The distinctions will be small, which Rose fails to understand. He thinks nothing he did after his playing records were totaled could deprive him of enjoying his twilight years with baseball's gods in Cooperstown. He may finally realize the difference between immorality and immortality is just one letter. The letter of the law. Major-league Rule 21, which forbids gambling on the game. Right there in black and white.

Near the end of the movie, "Eight Men Out," the story of how the 1919 White Sox became the Black Sox, the Buck Weaver character is talking with two young boys. Weaver, the third baseman, recalls the pure joy of hitting a baseball well: "When you can just feel that ball just give and you know it's going to go a long way. Damn if you don't feel like you're going to live forever."

It was once guaranteed that Pete Rose would live forever in the Hall of Fame. He was an authentic American hero of the authentic national pastime. He was. The game is.

A Big Divot

by G. Loie Grossman of the Philadelphia Daily News. Chris Patton, a 300-pounder out of Fountain Inn, S.C., brings up more than just his ball as he plays out of the rough during action in the 1989 U.S. Amateur golf championship at Philadelphia. Patton went on to win the prestigious event. Copyright ©1989, Philadelphia Daily News.

Web of Arms

by Albert P. Fuchs of the Knoxville News-Sentinel. Tennessee defenders swarm and arms seem to come from nowhere in search of the ball, which is in the protective custody of a Mississippi State player. The action occurred at a Southeastern Conference women's basketball game at Knoxville. Copyright ©1989, Albert P. Fuchs.

He Could've Been a Star

COLLEGE BASKETBALL

By *JOHN VALENTI*

Flora Adams spoke with a heavy heart, the kind you get when you are forced to watch your son make a shambles of his life. Once, she said, back when he was regarded as one of the better basketball players in New York City, she thought that someday he would play in the National Basketball Association. He was that good. "He had a future," she said.

She was in her apartment in the Andrew Jackson Projects near the Grand Concourse in the Bronx. It is a neighborhood where the landscape of burned-out tenements eerily mimics the tattered dreams of people who live there. A neighborhood where her son Richie first met his demise.

It started in junior high school, she said. Some wrong-minded friends. A mugging out on the Concourse. Later, it grew worse. Drugs. Muggings to support a habit. Stolen cars. Armed robberies.

"I don't understand," she said. "I raised four kids. I have two daughters and they were never in trouble, never did no drugs. My baby is 19 years old. I had no trouble with him.

"But in this building I'm in," she said, "mostly everybody is on crack. Everybody my other son hung out with is on crack. You know, he's not a bad child. If you knew him, you'd like him. Evidently he was just weak. He was a follower."

As Flora Adams spoke, her eldest son was across the East River in a jail cell on Rikers Island.

Once he was a player of no small renown at now-closed Benjamin Franklin High School, where teammates included Walter Berry, Gary Springer and Kenny Hutchinson; a player voted two-time Pacific Coast Athletic Association Player of the Year at Nevada-Las Vegas; a player good enough to be drafted by the Bullets. Now, Richie Adams, 26, awaits sentencing in New York State Supreme Court, First Judicial District, following his guilty plea on May 16 to a count of robbery, first degree, and two counts of grand larceny, fourth degree.

According to Colleen Roche, a spokesperson for the Manhattan District Attorney, Adams tried to get money "by placing a gun to the jaw of a woman at a cash machine" in Manhattan on September 25, 1988, and then on October 9, 1988, snatched a purse from a woman in an apartment building in Manhattan. While out on bail, Roche said, Adams was arrested for snatching a purse from a 68-year-old woman on April 30 in Grand Central Terminal.

As if to document how much of a wreck he has made of his life, Adams, who is 6-foot-9, 210 pounds and has no front teeth, grabbed the purse at 5:04 p.m. in the middle of a rush-hour crowd.

He was wearing a UNLV sweatshirt.

"He wasn't real difficult to identify," Roche said.

Now Adams faces 4½-9 years in the state penitentiary. His lawyer, David Breitbart, said neither he nor his client would comment before Adams is sentenced Tuesday.

"I told him," Flora Adams said, " 'You know, you are one of those people out there in the street that I'm afraid of.' He just sat there and gave me the strangest, saddest look. What could he say? I told him, 'That was somebody's mother you robbed.' "

★ ★ ★

Though a thinly built power forward/center, Richie Adams' play was indescribable around the basket. He could jump. He could intimidate. He could put fear in an opponent.

"It was a thrill to watch him play," said Sidney Green, the former Knick who played against Adams on the streets of New York City and, later, with him at Nevada-Las Vegas. "To just snatch shots out of the air the way he did, to dominate a game both offensively and defensively. Richie Adams was a smaller Bill Russell, that's the only comparison I can make. No problem, he could play in the NBA."

Adams was in 11th grade when he offered a glimpse of how good he might be. Gary Springer, then a senior and a two-time All-America at Franklin, got hurt before a game against Charles Evans Hughes, a team that featured Steve Burtt and Kevin Williams.

"Richie came in and had something like 42 points with 22 rebounds and 11 assists," said Stan Dinner, who coached Franklin. "It was, without a doubt, the greatest performance I've ever seen in high school; no, anywhere."

Springer said: "The ball would come off the rim and he just was going over everyone. Once, he threw it down so hard they had to stop the game until the rim stopped shaking."

That game gave Adams a reputation. And a nickname. They called him "The Animal." And with him, Franklin went on to be ranked second in the nation, losing only to an Adlai Stevenson team led by Ed Pinckney in overtime in the PSAL championship.

Adams failed to graduate, but earned his general equivalency diploma and attended Massachusetts Bay Community College for a year. Then he went to UNLV, where he twice was voted player of the year in the PCAA, leading the Runnin' Rebels to records of 29-6 and 28-4 as a junior and senior.

The Washington Bullets selected him in the fourth round of the 1985 NBA draft. But his behavior had already begun to set him back.

He was moody, laughing one minute and then not talking to anyone the next. He would act on a whim and often follow people with whom he should not have associated.

"I really believe that he was afraid of success," Flora Adams said. "The closer he got, the harder he made it on himself."

In high school, he "borrowed" a car that belonged to Dinner, who got a call from the local precinct just hours before a game asking him to identify half his team—all of whom had been found in the car, which had been reported stolen.

"When they saw we were Ben Franklin basketball players, they really didn't handcuff us," Springer said. "But they put us in a holding cell. We were like, 'Richie, didn't you tell Dinner you were taking the car?' He said he forgot."

Once, a girl in school told Adams she was hungry. "She was pregnant," Dinner said. "She said, 'Richie, I got nothing to eat.' Richie went out to the supermarket and loaded up just like that. He put it all under his coat and came back."

"He comes from a street area, real bad projects," Dinner said. "Despite that, Richie always was a nice kid, a polite kid who meant well even if he was self-destructive. He would give you the shirt off his back. . . . It's just the things you do at 14 that are funny, at 24 is a crime. When he took the food for that girl, it was funny. When he stuck up that woman, it wasn't funny anymore."

More serious problems surfaced at UNLV. Because the team had Sidney Green, then a senior who played the same position, Adams rarely played as a sophomore. "In his heart, Richie knew he was better than Sidney," said Joe Bostic, who runs a private school in Bedford-Stuyvesant and is a longtime friend of Adams'. "He started to act stupid."

Danny Tarkanian, the coach's son and a player on that team, was perhaps the closest to Adams then. In the book "Tark," Danny Tarkanian said: "More than once, he told me he was a manic-depressive. During some practices, he would just go sit in the corner and not talk to anyone. I mean, he wouldn't move. Guys would say things to him. Dad would try to get him on the floor. But Richie just sat there."

Then, after the season, Adams' grandmother died. Days later, so did the mother of his girlfriend. Adams refused to leave his room. He refused to return to school. By the time he did go back to UNLV, he had missed too many classes and had to sit out the year.

Adams had become so much of a problem, in fact, the coaching staff at UNLV did not want him back. Danny Tarkanian said he convinced his father to give Adams another chance. Jerry Tarkanian did. And Adams responded, not only on the court, where he averaged 15.8 points and 7.9 rebounds with 45 blocks as a senior, but off it, where he showed a remarkable ability to work with children.

"Richie just loved little kids," Danny Tarkanian said in "Tark." "After most games, there were 12 to 15 kids waiting for Richie. He walked from place to place in the gym, and little kids would follow him as if he was the Pied Piper. Other players went off with their girlfriends. Richie went to get ice cream with the children."

He briefly joined the Long Island Knights of the United States Basketball League to earn some money before the NBA draft. Hours after the draft, it was learned he had been arrested that morning in the Bronx—driving a stolen car to attend the draft.

"He had gone out to Long Island to pick up his paycheck," Flora Adams said. "He said the cab didn't wait for him and he didn't have cab fare to get back."

Adams went to rookie camp with the Bullets, but was eventually released. It seems no one looked highly on his sneaking out of camp each night and going home.

"Some friends came out to see him at the hotel," Springer said. "His get-high buddies. Richie climbed out the window, actually hung out the window, and went with his so-called friends."

Said Flora Adams: "Every night, his friends would go over and get Richard and every day the coaches from the team would come here, pick him up and bring him back."

Adams went on to play in Argentina on a team Springer also was supposed to join. "But," Springer said, "the guy mailed my plane ticket to Richie and Richie cashed it in—a $1,200 ticket. That's when I knew Richie was off the deep end."

★ ★ ★

Jerry Tarkanian sent Adams a plane ticket to Las Vegas, where he had a job in the recreation department lined up for him. Adams cashed the plane ticket.

Later, Bostic said, Tarkanian sent a non-refundable ticket. "I was supposed to meet Richie at 1 for a 4 o'clock flight," Bostic said. "All I had was a phone number of the place we were to meet. I called at 1. I called at 2. I called at 2:30. Finally, he showed up at the place and called me and said, 'Joe, come and get me now,' It was 3:15 and, of course, there was no way we could make it."

Dinner arranged for Adams to play in Yugoslavia.

"I called the representative of the team and said, 'I'll meet you tonight at 8 o'clock with Richie.' Richie met me at 11 a.m. and was with me all day. Around 7 p.m. he says, 'Coach, I'm hungry. Give me some money and I'll go get a sandwich.' I said, 'Great, Richie. Go get me a coffee, too.' I gave him a few bucks. I didn't see him again for four months."

Then came the muggings and robberies.

"To me," Bostic said, "it was his cry for help. Richie wants to change. But Richie does not have the internal strength to just pick up and put it behind him."

Still, it seems a lot of people like Richie Adams. "He is a soft-hearted, considerate person," Green said. "He would help you out in anything you'd ask him to do."

"He was a person who, if I could keep under my eye, I would be proud to have as a son," Bostic said. "Tomorrow, he could come and live in my house and I would not hide anything, I would not worry and he could be my babysitter and I would not worry. . . . He might not be allowed out after 11 p.m., but other than that, I would not worry."

"Nobody got hurt by Richie, did they?" Dinner said. "No. Richie would not hurt nobody, except maybe financially. He probably was more scared than they were when he did those robberies."

Said Flora Adams: "You know, when he first went to Rikers he would call and tell me to bring over all these clothes. I would bring him some and a few days later, he'd call me again. More clothes. I finally said, 'What are you doing with all these clothes? He was taking them and giving them to all the guys. 'Ma,' he said. 'But they don't have no clothes. They need them.' "

At 52, she wonders where it all went wrong. She has worked to make a better life for her children and grandchildren, two of whom, Richie Jr. and Richelle, are Richie's children by different girlfriends. She said she speaks with her son regularly, but always by phone. "I used to visit him," she said. "But I felt like the criminal, so I don't go no more."

The last time she saw her son, she said he looked better. His face, once drawn and gaunt from the self-abuse and drugs, had filled out. And even though he was still missing his front teeth, which she found in his jacket pocket while cleaning the other day, she said, "Richard always looks better when he is locked up. He looks healthier. He looks fatter. It's sad to say so, but I told him that he looked like my child again.

"I always ask myself, was there anything else differently I could have did? But I did the best I could for him. My children were never hungry. They never were dirty. They always had a roof over their head. I think I did good by these kids. It worked for three of them.

"See, I'm not blaming nobody. He has his own mind. But he is free-hearted. The people he thought was his friends really wasn't his friends. He never understood that. He thought everybody was his friend.

"Sometimes, I ask him, 'Richard, don't you wish you could start over again?' and he'll say, 'Yeah.'

"I still love him, but I am disappointed. If anyone could have made it, it could have been him."

The Tooz Couldn't Scare Away Death

PRO FOOTBALL

By *MIKE DOWNEY*

From the Los Angeles Times

Death should have feared John Matuszak. The other way around makes no sense. When the Grim Reaper came by to touch the Tooz on the shoulder Saturday night, the big guy should have sprung from his bed, ripped open his hospital gown from the neck down, roared like a primal beast and then poured the two of them a drink. He should have scared Death to death.

When you consider how many times John Matuszak teased eternity before, toying with alcohol and Quaaludes and guns the way he did, working hard and playing harder, it is a wonder that he lived as long as he did. Yet, that's the Tooz for you; he *was* a wonder. He was large and furry and ferocious, practically a centaur of a man, but there was a wonderful puppy dog playfulness about him, a wagging tail and an eager pant, that makes his passing all the sadder.

It was more than a decade ago that Coach Paul Wiggin of the Kansas City Chiefs had to pound on the Tooz's chest with his fists, had to watch this 6-foot-8, 300-pound man-child be strapped into a strait-jacket and hauled away in an ambulance after an overload of Valium and booze. In certain ways, John Matuszak was dying to die. His big old heart gave out because it just couldn't keep up with him.

Still, no way do you cut down a sequoia, and no way does it stand to reason that a man of John Matuszak's spirit and structure could be felled after only 38 years. The Tooz lived longer and stronger in his hitch on the mortal coil than many do in twice the time, and he seemed somehow indestructible, even though other men his age have continued to excel at athletics. If nothing else, at least we can now remember John Matuszak forever young.

The playing, the partying, the posturing, oh, the way this man lived. He liked to sneak up behind unsuspecting women and hoist them onto his shoulder, like an adagio dancer. One night in San Francisco, the Tooz literally picked up a pair, carried them toward a nearby bar—and forgot to measure the maximum headroom, knocking the poor things into the transom.

"You big dumbo! Couldn't you see we wouldn't fit?" one of the women yelled.

"I'm sorry," said the Tooz, "but, hey, you got to play with the small hurts, as Vince Lombardi used to say."

He would get away with stunts like that, because he could. No one scolded the Tooz, either because of that happy-go-lucky charm of his that guarantees forgiveness, or because it would have been like scolding Godzilla for stepping on all those trains. John Matuszak simply couldn't help himself. He was what he was. Either you accepted it, or you waited until he went away before breathing easy. All we can say is, if you knew him, you probably liked him.

Absolutely, the Tooz was out of control at times, no doubt about it. In college, at Tampa, Fla., he busted a fellow football player in the chops with an elbow during a game of pickup basketball, which eventually cost him $65,000 in medical and legal fees. Later, in that block-long Lincoln Continental of his that stored so many of his worldly goods, Matuszak occasionally stashed the machete or the Magnum handgun that he bought on whims.

One night outside Oakland, Kenny Stabler had to pay his roomie's bail, because the Tooz had been weaving all over the freeway, shooting at roadside signs. When the quarterback got to the jail, he found Matuszak standing outside a cell, wearing only three things: handcuffs, his Super Bowl ring and a pair of powder-blue, elephant-skin cowboy boots.

"That's my roommate," Stabler said. "I'd recognize him anywhere."

He was hell on wheels, the Tooz was. At the core of his astonishing physique and undeniable football-playing ability was the fire of rebellion. Coaches knew no way of controlling him. George Allen turned him loose in Washington after two weeks. Wiggin watched him nearly kill himself. John Madden fined him repeatedly for typical training-camp violations, like having a woman in his room, but, seeing as how these were the Raiders, generally the money went toward an end-of-the-year team party.

The most publicized infraction of the Tooz's playing career came before Super Bowl XV between Oakland and the Philadelphia Eagles at New Orleans. Soon as he hit town, Matuszak proclaimed himself gatekeeper and sergeant-at-arms. "I'm going to see that there's no funny business," he said. "I've had enough parties for 20 people's lifetimes. I've grown up. I'll keep our young fellows out of trouble. If any players want to stay, they gotta go through ol' Tooz."

Next night, ol' Tooz was dancing with another player's wife at 1 a.m., and two hours later, he was still as lit up as the entire French

Quarter. Come morning, Raider Coach Tom Flores slapped him with the obligatory $1,000 fine. Far more offended was the coach of the opposition, straight-arrow Dick Vermeil, who said in a huff: "If he was an Eagle, he'd be on a flight back to Philadelphia, right now!"

Matuszak nearly busted a gut, laughing.

"Why would anybody want to go to Philadelphia in the winter!" responded the Tooz.

Whatever it was that made John Matuszak whatever it is he was, he was one of a kind. He loved being with the Raiders, and they loved him. He was a hothead and a sweetheart and a born actor who might as well have been reading his epitaph when, in "North Dallas Forty," he screamed at one of his coaches that whenever he called it a business, they called it a game, but whenever he called it a game, they called it a business.

There is no logical explanation why a man of his proportions subsisted, for great periods of time, on bagels smeared with Cheez Whiz and triple shots of Crown Royal hooch, or why, when a female friend's pet poodles annoyed him with their barking, he fed them sleeping pills until they rolled over and played permanently dead.

That was John Matuszak. There is no explaining him, no excusing him. He was a one-ring circus, one no tent could contain. The man who terrorized patrons in saloons, who got sued for $1.5 million for football-tackling a male stripper on a San Francisco stage, was the same man whose parents taped an autographed photo on their refrigerator door, one that read: "Best Wishes to Mom and Dad. You're the Greatest."

John Matuszak has gone off now, either to steal the devil's pitchfork or to bend the bars of the pearly gates of heaven until somebody lets him in. We can see him now, lifting female angels onto his shoulder. They'd recognize him anywhere.

The Battle Is With Himself

BASEBALL

By *BRUCE BUSCHEL*

His white T-shirt and gray shorts strain to contain a muscle-beach body that has brought him power, speed and steroid speculation. His smoldering good looks complete the picture of intimidation. Jose Canseco must have discovered a Nautilus machine that pumps up not only deltoids but the chip that sits thereon.

One could say he is beside himself, but, upon closer inspection, it is actually his twin brother, Ozzie. They are not as identical as they once were, Ozzie looking more than four minutes younger, his hair cropped closer, a touch spiky. Their bodies, 24 years ago the same zygote, have retained their sameness; Ozzie has a bit less bulk and far less skulk—the former a result of fewer years in the gym, the latter, no time in the bigs, for Ozzie is still an Oakland farmhand. The Canseco twins dream of playing side by side, as they did in utero, in classrooms, on the diamond at Tamiami Park. The original Bash Brothers. Now, off the field, they are inseparable.

Twins don't have much need for other people.

Certainly not for this intruder, who had two strikes against him before arriving, being a reporter and an Anglo, two species of humanity Jose Canseco can usually duck here in Miami; stepping onto his home turf has evidently earned a called strike three. Though this meeting was arranged several months before, with Canseco's consent, he makes reaching first base as difficult as possible. No one ever said charm was essential to the art of powdering horsehides.

Cars pass by slowly, deliberately, their passengers gawking or yelling. The Canseco brothers are local heroes in the Westchester section of Miami, just west of Coral Gables. A sleek sports car trolls by with a blonde behind the wheel. The brothers know her, acknowledge her. "That's a man's car," snarls Jose disapprovingly. Machismo is not a word without meaning here in Miami, its mayor Cuban-born, more than half its population Hispanic, many of whom became millionaires without ever speaking English.

Canseco is appalled that people are still surprised by his unbroken English: "I'm an American, aren't I? I left Cuba before I was 1."

Jose Canseco Sr. moved his family—the twins, a daughter and his wife—from Havana to Opalocka in 1965. He says he taught his children more about baseball than politics but didn't hide his hatred of Communism. His sons confirm their decidedly nonpolitical upbringing. Still, they must know about the struggle, *la lucha;* most Cubans still long to reclaim their homeland. You don't grow up here—a country within a city—your ears filled with Castro and Kennedy, with *contras* and Mariel and Omega 7, and remain unpoliticized.

Canseco predicted he would lose Rookie of the Year honors in 1986 to California's Wally Joyner based solely on bigotry. ("Joyner? Talentwise, he can't carry my jock." The voters agreed.) He heard racist epithets at the Oakland Coliseum when no one else did. If some Hispanics allow their names to be Anglicized—Jorge Bell became George, Benito Santiago is Benny—no one dares call Canseco Joe. A 1988 Topps baseball card added the family name of Capas.

Jose Canseco Jr. can never really forget that, until *la revolucion,* he is the last Cuban superstar in America.

(He is unaware, however, that had Fidel Castro, a hard-throwing hurler scouted by the Senators, Giants and Pirates, accepted the $5,000 bonus offered by the Giants instead of completing law school, the Western Hemisphere might have shaped up differently. No, Fidel was not a lefty.)

A man in work clothes approaches Jose, asking in Spanish for an autograph while extracting an official American League baseball from its red-white-and-blue box. Jose says a couple of words in Spanish and signs the ball. Neither pain nor pleasure registers.

He paces his front lawn, pavonine. He says nothing. His head cocks suddenly to the right, twice, as if giving urgent directions, and he blinks a beat too long, a time too many. It's the image you carry from last season, when he'd enter the batter's box, all tics and twitches, his Adonis body nervously wiggling 36-ounce lumber like a plastic flyswatter, warning that any misguided insect that dared enter his zone might be rerouted to yonder bleachers. You don't forget No. 33 taking his studied lead off first, then breaking for second base with incongruous grace, black hair flowing from under his helmet, beating the tag and towering over the shortstop as he spanked the dirt from his tailored green-and-gold uniform.

If you saw him perform once, you had to see him again; if you read box scores, you were drawn to Oakland's, with special interest in the fine print detailing HRs and SBs; and if you owned him on a Rotisserie League team, you were nearly embarrassed by the daily riches. It is too depressing a thought, or too Hollywood hackneyed, that someone who provides so much pleasure can't pilfer a little for himself. Aren't baseball satisfactions transferable to real life?

His was the season of a million dreamers, a six-month joyride for which few men would not gleefully exchange a limb or more; in fiction, one dickers with the Devil for such a year. Hell, the mighty Babe might have called a single shot but Jose Canseco called a whole season! Predicted he would hit 40 homers and steal 40 bases and then did it, unaware it was a revolutionary act, a new standard for the sport. It wasn't some freaky numbers show either: His totals had depth—27 of his 42 home runs tied a game or put the A's ahead. Hitting .307, he amassed 124 RBIs and scored 120 runs and led the Athletics to the World Series and had fans singing his lyrical name, apolitically to be sure, in place of the first five words of the national anthem.

Some would bask in the afterglow of that for a lifetime; it doesn't seem to take Jose through an off-season. Dysphoria is his constant companion. You wish he were happier, as happy as you imagine you would be having lived every boy's fantasy.

A nasty narcissism may serve a slugger more than serenity. After all, Canseco won Most Valuable Player, not Mr. Congeniality.

★ ★ ★

The Babe Ruth Crown finds a new head today, this bitter Friday the 13th in January.

"I hope your questions are good," says the emcee at the noon press conference, "because there will be no answers. Jose Canseco is missing."

Laughter is laced with bile as the Slugger of the Year is compared to various body parts, with emphasis on orifices. "Selfish" is the adjective most often modifying the expletives. Few journalists are shocked by his evasion, for their relationship with the slugger in absentia has been rocky from the first. Here was fresh meat with all the fixings—the smarts, the fizz, talent to burn—and the writers wanted to embrace the swarthy new star. Jose was a tease, wouldn't put out. Rebuffed, the press took their revenge in unkind, if accurate, words. Canseco became more somber and abrasive.

To avoid the crush of reporters and Jose's offhand responses, the Athletics set up press conferences in many cities to somehow protect him. Their PR person has worked overtime on him and his lockerside manner. It has helped. Some.

"He might be like Ted Williams," muses Ed Beitiks, sports columnist for the *San Francisco Examiner.* "Williams always hated the press—and it didn't hurt him. If you saw Canseco as a rookie, you'd know how far he's progressed. 'Sophistication' is not a word you'd use to describe him. He's still acting off the same primal scream he did in high school. His success is not tied to the press; he'll make money without them. With no green stuff on the table, he's got no time."

Many point to Reggie Jackson as the source of Canseco's dilemma. Note how the self-ordained "Mr. 40/40" echoes "Mr. October."

The saturnine slugger was smitten with Reggie, the spiritual leader of the swingin' A's of the early 70s, whose carnival career featured a roller-coaster ride with the media and bumper cars with teammates, not to mention fireworks in the clutch. In the young right fielder with power, speed and ego, Reggie saw himself. Upon his return to Oakland in 1987, he taught Jose about the media. Which is akin to Robin Williams tutoring Sylvester Stallone—where Reggie has verbal intelligence and a yen for the limelight, Canseco is unable to undercut his arrogance with insight or anecdote. He pursues the postgame spotlight like a vampire seeks the sun.

"Reggie was a jerk," says one writer, "but he was a thinker and worth the extra effort. Jose has nothing to say. He was born to be in a clubhouse."

Still, no one imagines he will miss the big bash tonight, without warning: that has never happened, not in 33 years; not after 2,500 good citizens of Baltimore have paid $35 apiece to eat chicken and cheer the coronation. In the hometown of Babe Ruth, subjects are accustomed to an indulgent king, not a spiteful one.

Besides, Donald Fehr, head of the Players Association, has traveled from New York to talk with Canseco. Surely, he will show.

At the banquet, through speeches by Governor William Schaefer and Pete Rose and former Oriole Rick Dempsey, there is a group of kids in the balcony, lost bleacher bums, really, beer cans in hand, chanting, "Jo-se! Jo-se!"

By night's end, their two-note chant has been replaced by "No-show! No-show!"

"I feel like killing him," says mild-mannered Frank Sliwka, head of the Maryland Professional Baseball Players Association. "What a crude, irresponsible individual. And he still hasn't called, a week later. I heard his wife had the flu. I'm sorry, I don't buy it. I feel sorry for his agent. He flew here, with his pregnant wife, all the way from California, and he couldn't get through to his own client. 'Jose won't talk to me,' he kept saying. I played ball. I know the code of ethics, and this guy has lots of trouble ahead.

"He'll never see that crown. It's worth $3,500. I sent him two round-trip plane tickets for three different times, just in case, and he only returned two sets. Stuck me for $1,000. And the banquet was to raise money for kids with cancer. Can you imagine? You can't treat people this way. What's wrong with this guy?"

Canseco just said no.

★ ★ ★

Two cars pull into Canseco's driveway, the burgundy Corvette driven by his wife, the other by his sister-in-law. The chatter is about new acquisitions: gold chains and snakeskin boots and a Pet Shop Boys CD. Cousin David is cursed. Mrs. Canseco unlocks the wrought-iron gate and then the front door, and two white Maltese scurry and leap. They have missed their constitutional. Reminders of this oversight have been deposited on the floor. The newlyweds start sentences with "Your dogs. . ." and retort with "Oh, now they're my dogs?" The skittish canines, suffering from parallel identity crises, squawk, lick, nip, sniff and prove altogether amiable hosts.

The horse in the hallway is housebroken and silent. The golden statue of Pegasus stands in the foyer to announce that swiftness is valued in this home. "I don't want to be some sluggish power hitter," says Jose. "I thought 40/40 was realistic, and I don't see why 50/50 is not realistic. I don't place limits on myself. But I'm very down to earth about it. If I said I want to fly, that would be unrealistic." One can hear the faintest of whinnies from the hollow metal steed.

It is suggested that the coaches will not permit Jose to steal bases so regularly next season.

"Coaches? They couldn't stop me last year and they tried everything."

"He means the Oakland coaches," Ozzie corrects his brother. "Not your opponents."

"My own coaches?" Jose is flustered by the audacity of the thought. "No one tells me what to do."

"Stealing is not that dangerous," explains Ozzie, who swiped 16 bases in the minors, with 15 dingers, 80 ribbies and 114 strikeouts in 458 at-bats. "If you have good techniques, it's safe. Hitting a double is more dangerous, rounding first base full speed and you still have to slide into second." To the Cansecos, banging the ball out of the yard is the only truly safe strategy for a batsman.

It is becoming clear why some people at Jose's sports agency, to which he has just placed a call, are tempted to send Osvaldo on Jose's speaking engagements. Not only is he less petulant but he might accept. That accomplished, he might show up. Jose has turned down innumerable appearances, including *Carson* and *Letterman*. So tenacious was Letterman that he sent Jose a videotape of his interviews with athletes—reverential in nature—to ameliorate anxieties. Jose finally accepted—and then canceled the day of the show. Leading guesses as to the slugger's reluctance are shyness, torpidity and mortifying fear, the latter holding away.

"We are genetically the same," says Ozzie of his brother, "so people wonder why I can't hit as far as Jose or with as much consistency. The way I look at it, he has six years' experience on me. I pitched all the way through high school and three years in the Yankees system. The Yankees are very old-fashioned. Ruth and Mantle never lifted weights, so they figure it's not part of the game. If you're a pitcher, you pitch. I had five at-bats with them in two years. That's no way to treat a young player. I asked to be released, and Oakland picked me up three days later. As an outfielder. I'm much happier now."

It took him a long time to reach that realization. While pitching, he had been able to share his brother's profession without direct comparison. Ideal for twins: the same, yet different. All that has changed. If Ozzie can use Jose's head start to shield himself from negative contrast, Jose's guilt in outshining his twin is dimmed by his absolute certainty that Ozzie will join him in the majors, that they will wear identical Oakland uniforms, as they wore identical clothes until they were 15.

"I'm never jealous of Jose—he's my brother," says Ozzie sweetly. "Of course, when I walk down the street, most people say something about Jose Canseco's brother. That's if they know enough to tell us apart. All the attention given Jose either makes you mentally tough or you crack. I haven't cracked yet, so I guess I'm all right."

Canseco finally has his agent on the phone. The client complains about this reporter who wants too much time and then talks to his agent for nearly an hour: "Make sure it's a blood-red Corvette this time, not burgundy . . . if they need more commercials, maybe we could double them . . . I want a free Vette this time, not a loaner, the $55,000 one . . . yes, we'll ship the cars out west . . . how's the T-shirt deal going? Fuck them, no way . . . that's a free cruise, right? . . . for the four of us . . . great . . . hey, Ozzie, we're going on a cruise . . . I don't know where . . . where? . . . the Caribbean . . . about this instructional tape, if we cut out the middle man . . . if he's not reasonable, shut the door on him . . . we'll sell minimum 100,000 without him . . . damn, just like Jane Fonda! What check? . . . it was my bonus . . . the A's say I cashed it? . . . maybe my old man . . . he's so senile, maybe he put it through . . . I get $10,000 for MVP and $10,000 for playing 140 games . . . tell the Testarossa guy I'm 6-4 . . . he'll understand . . . he custom-made one for Dave Parker, he'll know how . . . just tell him I'm 6-4 . . ."

Jose Canseco earned $355,000 last year and will make $1.64 million this year. One cannot imagine him playing baseball for nothing. There's no kid in the kid. He never played Little League, never had posters or pennants over his bed, no portable radio under his pillow to listen to West Coast games. Maybe he doesn't understand the media because he never hungered for box scores and keen stories. He played soccer and basketball and didn't touch a baseball till he was 13 and never dreamed of playing in the bigs until he was a senior in high school. Jose Canseco's first pilgrimage to Cooperstown will be when he's inducted into the Hall.

"We can talk about a certain pitcher before a game," reports A's shortstop Walt Weiss, Canseco's closest teammate, "and invariably, he's never heard of the guy. Then he says he doesn't care, everybody has to throw a strike sooner or later. He doesn't really follow the game. Me? I know everything about every pitcher—I need to. I've spent many a sleepless night trying to figure out this game. Jose is the most nonchalant guy on the team. He takes a few hacks before a game and he's ready. After the game, he leaves the ballpark and never thinks about it again. He's not a fan. He never collected baseball cards."

He never collected baseball cards.

★ ★ ★

The 1986 Jose Canseco Donruss rated rookie card is worth $70.

If you get Jose Canseco to sign it, for $15, the value goes down. His signature is a defacement.

So maybe the kids who go to Steve Corbin's card shows are lucky. Corbin, stationed in Mechanicsville, Va., is the biggest card-show promoter on the East Coast. "I won't have Canseco," he vows. "I don't pay egos. This guy wants $15,000 for two hours or $20,000 for three hours. That's just silly. Kids have to pay $15 for an autograph not worth $8. Canseco's not alone, mind you, but he's the highest-priced active player now. He wants what Mickey Mantle gets and twice as much as Willie Mays. Dale Murphy won't do it, period. Pete Rose is the biggest asshole—stop him on the street and he'll ask for $10 just to say hello.

"Did you know Ozzie Canseco wants $1,500? Imagine, never played a game in the majors and he wants $1,500!"

The Canseco brothers do a half-dozen card shows in the off-season. Jose does about 20 a year. A close associate of Jose's wishes he wouldn't do any.

"I hate when he does those shows," he says. "I have a little brother, and I can't believe Jose charges so much money for his signature. He goes in for two or three hours, puts his head down, signs away and leaves with a pocketful of money. He doesn't even talk to the kids. The whole thing's obnoxious."

Canseco was to attend a show in Montgomery, Ala., in November. Two weeks before it, he threatened to cancel and renegotiated his price by $5,000. Then two days before, he wanted to cancel again.

"When I hear he's not showing up, I am devastated," says local promoter Jim Pitts, in fine southern drawl. "I'm just a small-town fella, but I have this contract that says he'll sign 1,500 autographs, and I've already had ads on radio stations, television stations and in baseball publications. I rented the Civic Center, and I arranged for the mayor to give Mr. Canseco the keys to the city. But he has another show that same day in Miami. Mr. Canseco says if I charter him a plane—for $3,625—he'll show up late in the afternoon.

"Mr. Canseco shows up at 5:15, and he signs 375 autographs and quits. Three hundred seventy-five! I had to refund almost $4,000 to people who had come from as far as three states away. Some of them slept in the parking lot overnight waiting for their hero.

"Backstage, we had some balls and photographs for him to sign, as part of the contract. Mr. Canseco took one look and said, 'I ain't signing all this shit.' He signed some, in a foul mood, all the while talking to his cousin David about this $13,000 deposit he just put down on a Ferrari. My fiancee is crying and I'm looking at bankruptcy and Mr. Canseco is talking about a Ferrari.

"I lost $11,000 on him. J.P. is still scrambling with his little ol' baseball-card shop in Montgomery, Alabama, but Mr. Canseco has lost a few fans in these parts. Let's put it this way. If he was on fire, no one would walk across the street to spit on him."

★ ★ ★

"It still feels funny signing 'Canseco,' " says Mrs. Canseco, who until November was Esther Haddad. She is signing papers brought over by a real-estate agent who's looking for a new home for the newlyweds, something bigger, closer to Coral Gables.

Though everyone calls her Cusy, her husband does not know the genesis of her nickname. (It was her brother's baby-talk version of "coochie-coochie.") About her nationality, he knows only "Arabian and Spanish." (Her father is Lebanese, her mother Spanish, and they met in Cuba.)

Cusy Canseco, 21, is petite except in those places a woman oughtn't be petite. In her stonewashed-denim outfit, matching skirt and jacket, with zippers up the front of each garment, she is obviously in great shape. She was Miss Miami 1986. There was no talent portion of the contest. As Jose continues to talk hardball on the phone, she talks to the realtor about her honeymoon and how the Hawaiian sun tans differently from the Florida sun, and she lifts her husband's shirt to prove it. She strokes his bronze stomach. They met in a health spa; she was working, she recalls, on her hamstrings when Jose introduced himself. They were sweaty. Before you could say gluteus maximus, they were living together in San Ramon.

She never saw or cared to see a baseball game until she met Jose. Last season, missing few home games, she got along famously with the baseball wives, a group distinguished, according to Jose, by their *esprit des bouches:* "They gossip a whole lot. Every time you see them, they're talking about this, talking about that. That's what women do when they get together—gossip."

The boys indulge in a little kibitzing of their own. It led to a $10,000 payday for Jose when he performed the startling feat of matrimony.

Standing around the batting cage during spring training, pitcher Dave Stewart heard Jose talking about getting married and laughed. He had heard it before. Canseco was quite the ladies' man. Not only shouldn't Jose get married, opined Stewart, but he wouldn't have the nerve to go through with it. A wager was proposed. Papers were drawn up and signed by both parties. Ballplayers love contracts.

What they don't love is losing money. Stewart has not yet made good on his bet. Canseco says he will pay. He will pay.

★ ★ ★

A print of *The Last Supper* hangs on the kitchen wall, flamingo-pink. You are apt to think it a joke, for Jose has a sardonic streak, until you notice the crucifix above the front entrance.

On the black marble table miniature Incas face off against miniature conquistadores. The armies gather dust, not prisoners of war. The Canseco brothers don't play chess too often.

The four young people inside the house—the twins and their women—plan vacations and compare furniture prices, and the atmosphere is reminiscent of rich kids at summer camp with unrestricted canteen privileges. Jose is clearly the bunk leader, his moods quickly detected and deferred to.

"It's a madhouse," he says. "This offseason is crazy. The phones won't stop. My number is private, not circulated, and I still get crank calls, all hours. I might have to change it every month now. People drive by at four in the morning screaming, 'Jose,' patching out in my yard, girls throw kisses, people want me all the time." He hears his words and stops to consider them. "Things are not out of control. I can control it to a certain point. Sometimes. Sometimes you just let it roll. I control it by letting the phone ring a hundred times. Is that control?"

His second phone line rings. It's Cousin David, who works with and/or for Jose. Or not at all. After listening to the reasons for David's disappearance, Jose explodes: "The next time, you're fired. Don't laugh, David. I don't care if you're a relative. You think I'm kidding, but I'm not."

He's not. He craves control. In a sport where so many things are beyond control—seven of 10 at-bats, sinking liners, games' outcomes—conflict is inevitable. On the field, Canseco shrugs off that which he cannot govern; an error is laughed at, a strikeout casually accepted. This unflappable pose, this cavalier mask, was adopted when dark passions worked against him: His mother died suddenly when he was 19. He grieved terribly. He has said, "It was the worst time I ever had . . . the only thing that comes close is I die. I'm dead." Facing mortality too abruptly and too young, he took life too seriously. Baseball included. To forget his mourning, or in testimony to it, he worked out six days a week, upper body one day, lower body the next, pumped enough iron to build a skyscraper, or a mausoleum, and added 20 pounds of serious muscle. Then 20 more.

As a rookie, he was prone to protracted slumps and depressions; he was "pissed off all the time" when coaches corrected his stance, his fielding, his two-strike stratagems; he was confused when teammates complained about his work ethic and selfishness, when the media carped about his taciturn nature.

Goodbye intensity. Hello insouciance. Now he puts on a show and puts up numbers and puts up with little else.

Now he doesn't care what anyone says.

★ ★ ★

"Ste-roids! Ste-roids!" bellowed the fans at Fenway Park during the playoffs. The visiting right fielder struck bodybuilder's poses and took bows, handling the crowd with customary cool. Inside, he was churning. He wanted to frappe the writer who started the rumors about Canseco Milk Shakes. Tom Boswell, the *Washington Post* columnist, had said on a late-night television show that Canseco had ingested steroids.

"Basically," says Canseco softly, "Thomas Boswell made some comments that were untrue, and, funny thing is, I've never spoken to the man about it. During the playoffs and World Series, he never approached me. All the other reporters did. I wanted to talk to him."

(Boswell replies: "I never spoke to him? Not true. Before the fifth game of the World Series, we spoke at length. He was cheerful and in a good mood. Of course this topic came up. Tony La Russa (the A's manager), one of my favorite people in baseball, had told me Canseco had taken steroids in the minors but not since. That's what I said on television. Tony later denied it, said there was a misunderstanding.")

A mucho-million-dollar misunderstanding, according to Canseco's agent, Dennis Gilbert.

"This guy Boswell cost us millions," he says. "The timing couldn't have been worse—during the playoffs. We had a seven-figure endorsement deal with Coke almost worked out and a big one with Colgate-Palmolive. They both backed out after the steroid thing. Burger King and Gillette put our deals on the back burner. Who wants their guy associated with steroids? The Coca-Cola deal, that was a home run! Sure, Jose wanted to sue and his father wanted to sue, but I advised them against it. Every day, fans would read 'CANSECO AND STEROIDS.' If Boswell could prove it, God bless him. But he can't. Jose will take a drug test if they want. I put in many calls to Boswell, and he's never returned any."

(Boswell replies: "He has never called me. Not once.")

Gilbert heads up the Beverly Hills Sports Council, which handles Danny Tartabull of the Royals and Bobby Bonilla of the Pirates and a dozen budding stars. He knows what he has in Canseco—a crossover dream, a bilingual heartthrob, Sexiest Athlete of 1988, according to *USA Today's* readers. Canseco got a 350 percent raise from Oakland this year, and he's headed for a fortune in endorsements. In addition to the usual baseball promotions, he has already done spots for American Express, Toyota, California eggs and a Bay Area Chevrolet dealer, in Spanish and in English. What Gilbert has landed is this country's premier Latino superstar, just as the Latin market is burgeoning.

America's 20 million Hispanics make up the 7th-largest Spanish-speaking population in the world. And the richest by far. By the next century, they will be the largest minority in the U.S. And Canseco, the Sensuous Bambino, could win another MVP award—Most Valuable Promoter.

Gilbert, a former minor leaguer himself, can get a bit exercised about his boy, even on his car phone from Beverly Hills.

"Fans don't pay money to see Mattingly or Brett—they do for Canseco. He's the best player in the game, the hottest thing going. Call it the Michael Jackson syndrome. Did you know they named a street after him in Miami? Here in Los Angeles, we have Martin Luther King Jr. Boulevard—in Miami, it's Jose Canseco Street."

Jose Canseco Street is that portion of S.W. 16th Street that runs from the Palmetto Expressway to S.W. 107th Avenue, not far from a street named for Jose Marti, the emancipator of Cuba. Call city hall and an Anglo says Canseco Street exists "because there is a Hispanic on the transportation board," then hurriedly passes the phone to an assumed expert on the subject, a Cuban, who admits to the existence of Jose Canseco Street but cannot place its honoree.

The client is not quite a Hispanic household name. Celebrity needs cultivation. Canseco will have to work on his image if he plans to exploit it.

"But Jose doesn't understand public relations or charities," his agent says. "I have him doing community service for the first time this year. His experience with reporters, well, they have been harmful to his teammates and to him. He's getting better. I don't honestly even know if he understands the difference between a newspaper and a magazine story."

Someone should tell him. He's going to need that information now that he's doing a weekly syndicated column (with a ghostwriter) and a book (with another writer). Agents want to have their cake and endorse it, too. They should counsel their clients, not kowtow to them. If Gilbert expects his boy to be a bonafide idol, he could start by enrolling Jose in finishing school.

And then hide his driver's license.

★ ★ ★

Dinner plans are made for tomorrow, away from the chaos. The athlete and the reporter have had this standing date for three nights already. After a day of house-hunting—ballplayers love to hunt in the off-season—the athlete will call the reporter. They shake hands on it. Like a pair of Greek goddesses.

The next day, the reporter, bolstered by shots of Cafe Bustelo and indefatigable faith, waits for the phone call. He watches the funeral of two policemen on television. Cops from all over the country are in attendance, their deep sadness that of an army that knows it will lose its war. Miami is a wicked place, perpetually crashing from different highs. Against a backdrop of shady deals and quick killings, race riots, cigarette boats and gun smugglers, marijuana millionaires and cocaine kings, steroids must seem a benign vice indeed. Round midnight, Mrs. Canseco calls to say her husband can't make it but will meet the reporter tomorrow at 11 a.m. sharp—Jose has an early plane to catch.

At 11 the next morning, the reporter is entertaining a pair of Maltese dogs on the first floor while the star is upstairs packing for a card show. Two phones ring. Two dogs yip. All four are ignored. Thirty minutes go by. The reporter's faith fatigues; he remembers reading how Cubans think Anglos are hung up on punctuality.

Eventually, at a Denny's restaurant, Canseco takes a quick look at the menu and orders a "Grand Slam." Oh, that it were so easy. The only one he's ever hit was in the first game of the '88 World Series, a titanic blast that could have set the tone for the contest had it not been for Kirk Gibson's gimpy, one-handed shot in the ninth. Oakland's bats entered the off-season five games too soon. Canseco went hitless the rest of the way, looking foolish against Orel Hershiser and nonchalant against other Dodger hurlers.

Critics argued he should have done something to break the Dodgers' trance: shortened his stroke, laid down a bunt, anything. He says his approach was unaltered by the magnitude of the clash. He had to consider it just another series, where the pressure is stultifying enough.

"The pressure is great! Everything is a state of mind. Unless you have played professional ball, you don't know. Some people say, 'I know exactly what you're going through, what you're feeling.' No, you don't. Don't talk to me about softball or Triple A. Until you feel it, you don't know. A player making a million dollars, a million and a half, he's expected to do everything. The burden put on his shoulders is awesome. And it's daily. Every single day. You're constantly reminded, you have to do this, or that, work on this, be consistent in this area, on and on. And then you have to be an example, on and off the field. It's tough. Very tough."

Don Baylor, eminence grise of the clubhouse, has said, "Before the fifth game of the World Series, Jose told reporters he could not be expected to carry the team. That's too bad. I would have switched positions with him for just one at-bat. . . . Jose's attitude is scarier than his potential. He can be one of the most selfish players I have ever seen."

Canseco will not permit anyone or any situation to put pressure on him. He has had enough of that. Generously, he calls his father a perfectionist. Jose Canseco Sr. owns a satellite dish and sees as many Oakland games as possible. He talks to his major-league son a couple of times a week. Gives him pointers. When Jose hit three home runs against Toronto one day, he called his father and heard, "What happened in the other at-bats?"

"I love my father," says Jose junior, "but if anybody puts pressure on me, it's him. He thinks he knows the game, but he doesn't. He was never a real fan. He tells me how I should hit a certain pitcher. Has my father ever played baseball? No. In the minors? In high school? No. How about street ball? No. If I strike out, I figure I have another opportunity. His attitude is always *right now*—you have to do everything now. That's not the way it is in the majors."

Or any other place.

At the end of every season, Jose senior pays his sons five bucks for every home run they've hit. It's a Canseco family tradition. Last year, Jose Canseco Sr. proudly shelled out $210 to Jose and $75 to Ozzie. Come October, when all the numbers are tallied, when the last pitch is pitched and the final out recorded, Jose junior will return to Miami to collect his due. He wants to pick up $250 from his old man this time around. It will mean a lot to him. Given a choice between getting his $1.6 million in salary or his father's 250 bucks, he'd rather . . . Nah. He'd take the million and a half.

3
4

End of an Era

by Dan Levine of the Dallas Times Herald. With the city of Dallas sprawling in the background and thousands of loyal Dallas Cowboys fans looking on, former coach Tom Landry delivers his farewell address. Landry, the only coach in the 29-year history of the franchise before the 1989 season, was honored by a Tom Landry Day parade through Dallas after his ouster by new Cowboys Owner Jerry Jones. Copyright ©1989, Dan Levine, Dallas Times Herald.

Child's Play

by Nicole Bengiveno of the New York Daily News. With a crooked, netless rim and dull backboard looming high above his head, a young member of the Brownsville Brooklyn Jets prepares for an upcoming game. He plays in a children's league that gives him brief respite from New York City's tough streets while offering hope for the future. Copyright ©1989, New York Daily News, Inc.

Walsh's Life Without a Team

PRO FOOTBALL

By *LOWELL COHN*

Squire Bill was out playing tennis. You used to know him as Bill Walsh, head coach of the San Francisco 49ers, but now he is Squire Bill, a man of leisure, except for weekends, when he provides analysis for National Football League games on NBC.

He's taken a small office in Menlo Park, where he watches film to prepare for upcoming games, and answers mail and chats on the phone. His secretary from the 49ers, Nicole Langerak, has moved to the new office with him, and seems refreshed by the regular 9-to-5 work day, one which actually includes a lunch break. In the past, she would work non-stop into the night, helping a manic Walsh get the week's game plan together.

On the walls of the office, Walsh has put up photos of his past life. There he is with his three great creations, quarterbacks Dan Fouts, Ken Anderson and, of course, Joe Montana. Another picture shows Montana handing off the ball to Roger Craig in last season's Super Bowl. And there's one modest, quaint, black-and-white shot of Bill and Dwight Clark, containing this inscription: "Bill, Thanks for giving me the opportunity and teaching me how to take advantage of it. Dwight."

★ ★ ★

At about 2:30 in the afternoon, Walsh returns to the office, his hair windblown, a tan on his face. He's in the bloom of health, a stark contrast to almost every other September of his adult life, when he would be pasty white and overstressed from studying too hard. Terry O'Neil, executive producer of NBC Sports, calls, and Walsh jokingly says to Nicole, "I'll take it on line 7." In fact, he has two lines, another indication of how his life has been simplified since he stepped away from coaching.

When he's done with O'Neil, Walsh pushes aside his new VCR, which he doesn't know how to attach to his TV set, and sits at a table and stares out the window. He's looking west across a golf course, toward Highway 280 and the Peninsula foothills. The word for the scene is bucolic. "When I first came to coach at Stanford, I lived in a condo between here and the freeway," he says, pointing to a development about 200 yards away. "It's like I went on a trip and came full circle."

Walsh stretches with a feeling of well being. Then he taps his fingers on the table and catches himself with an embarrassed smile. "I was tapping out a play," he says. "It's what I do this time of year, like the birds fly south. In June, I don't find myself doing that. When I catch myself, I laugh."

Walsh worked six preseason games for NBC. The broadcasts didn't make the airwaves. They were dry runs. In the last game, Walsh bumped into coaches Mike Ditka and Marty Schottenheimer. "They looked like death," he says. "It was the last preseason game. The season hadn't even started yet. I wanted to put my arms around them."

Walsh realized that the look of death he saw on Ditka and Schottenheimer used to be his look. That's why he quit. He didn't want to look like a corpse half the year and feel so pressured that he was afraid his brains might explode through his ears.

"It all took a toll," he admits. "During the season, if I could have just seen Half Moon Bay. But there was no time to see the ocean. I'm no different from any other coach—it's not like I had a Joan of Arc experience. I didn't feel I should continue. I had been successful, and I had the luxury of telling myself. 'This is enough.' "

For a while, Walsh became the head of football operations for the 49ers. He would sit in his office and make deals and put together the roster. "It was bland, very routine," Walsh says. "It wasn't a full-time job." He must have felt like extra baggage, like a failed executive who gets kicked upstairs. He also felt ambivalent about the players. "I was uncomfortable with the team," he says. "They weren't going to be mine. The team was George Seifert's and I was going to be a distraction."

Those feelings grew stronger during minicamps, when the players would be in meetings with their coaches or down on the practice field, and Walsh would be killing time in his office under a self-imposed house arrest. He felt self-conscious when a player would say hello. He even felt self-conscious when a player would glance at him. When NBC called, Walsh became excited. Here was a chance to feel alive again. It took Walsh three weeks to think things over, and then he told the 49ers he wanted out.

He feels happier now. "I've had my time," he says. "There was a time for me to coach, and I've coached. I have to understand that what happened is natural. It's not so much I don't belong, but there's a time to be there and a time to step away. It's not like death, but there is a tearing. There is a separation and a grieving and a melancholy. I'm leaving something that was my life. I'm leaving coaching, not just the 49ers. I had tears in my eyes at the Super Bowl during the warmups. I had to get myself back together for the team. I almost celebrate those moments. They're natural and real. There's no need to regret."

★ ★ ★

Perhaps he regrets his relations with certain players. At the beginning of this season, some players publicly criticized Walsh, and that hurt him. Looking out the window, he ponders the possibility that he was too distant from his players, that he was an unnecessarily complicated man who installed fear and uncertainty in the team.

"Was I too complicated?" he asks. "It depends on when. The players didn't say that early on. What was Bill Walsh like in '79 or '81 or '84? The Bill Walsh in 1981 was the same man the players at Stanford or the Bengals or the Chargers knew. Bill Walsh last year was under incredible stress. He was bitter. He was possibly more harsh on everybody.

"I may have become too complicated last year, but very few successful coaches are not complicated. The Good Guy Syndrome has no sustaining power. Good guys only win when they have all the right players. The great coaches like Vince Lombardi, Don Shula and Al Davis were not always good guys.

"I didn't want to be predictable as a coach. I was not going to be the same easy-going guy every day. I'd explode almost dramatically on occasion. But I would never explode at a player. I'd explode at a situation or a coach, and the coaches understood it. I'd tell a coach, 'I'm going to jump you,' and then at practice, I'd scream, 'Can't you get Paris to move quicker?' Then the player would feel bad because I attacked the coach.

"I knew when to release emotions and when not to. When I did, I was not fully in control. I was free with profanity at times. I did not use it at all other times. I created an atmosphere of expectancy. And especially, last season I had to grab that thing and shake it. The team was not going to make it."

★ ★ ★

Some people say Walsh as coach was a cold man who rarely praised or showed affection. He almost flinches at the words. "I kissed Joe Montana before the last five games we played together," Walsh says. "I kissed him on the cheek in the locker room. I told him, 'I love you, Joe.' "

Walsh is vague about what caused his bitterness and alienation last season. He admits his relations with the press deteriorated. He believes some writers wanted to revel in what he calls "the dying throes of a football coach." It is also likely that he felt removed from owner Ed DeBartolo Jr. After all, DeBartolo had stripped Walsh of the title of team president before last season began, and took the presidency for himself. That must have hurt Walsh, especially because it doesn't seem that DeBartolo took on any more responsibility with the title.

Understand, Walsh does not complain about DeBartolo. He only praises him. "Eddie is a generous man who does wonderful things for many people," is what Walsh says. But with strained relationships with the press and his owner, Walsh must have felt extremely alone. One player once said he looked up at Walsh's office and saw Bill staring out the window. "He reminded me of Howard Hughes looking out his window in Las Vegas," the player said. Told of that remark, Walsh smiles and says the comparison is apt. That's how lonely he became last year.

★ ★ ★

"That's why I resigned," he says. "I didn't want to become a coach who was removed from the team. I was losing the day-to-day interchange."

Walsh never visits the 49ers' headquarters in Santa Clara, although his office is only 20 minutes away. "I feel an urge not to go there," he says. "I'd be uncomfortable. There's an axiom I drove into the team. If a man steps aside because he's hurt or for whatever reason, we close ranks and move forward. If Joe Montana or Ronnie Lott or Dwight Clark gets hurt, we continue to play well. Over the years, we built an inner strength to fight adversity. It became our very nature as a team.

"The replacement player was expected to play as well. The team felt it like a surge of strength instead of a point of weakness. There was never any resignation when a man was injured. I would speak to the team in front of the injured man. It was tough when Keith Fahnhorst had to leave. We were talking about Harris Barton in Keith's presence. That separation is harsh.

"I explained to the team that we were like the British army in Burma. The elite troops were shot down first. The ones who won the final battle were almost the rejects. So the argument would be the best are cut down on occasion, but with inner confidence, you stride through that."

Walsh looks at the cars on 280. His voice is thick with emotion. "I prepared the 49ers to close ranks and play better," he continues. "Now I'm a victim of that. I step out. They close ranks and keep moving. I wave good-bye."

Back to Work

COLLEGE BASKETBALL

By *CURT HOLBREICH*

Norm Stewart wants to show that nothing has changed, that eight months after cancer surgery he is fit as ever, coaching the Missouri basketball team the way he has for 23 seasons.

In his nationally televised comeback in the Maui tournament last weekend, Stewart was at his fiery best, and so was his team.

The Tigers defeated Evansville, No. 11 Louisville and No. 17 North Carolina on the way to the tournament title and a No. 4 national ranking, and are 5-0 after beating Creighton, 86-79, Monday night. Through it all, Stewart played thinking coach and lively bench jockey.

"That's Norm," Missouri Athletic Director Dick Tamburo said. "In the heat of the game, he is his old self."

But, though Stewart acts as if nothing has changed, that he will remain the tenacious—some prefer belligerent—competitor he has been since his days as an All-American at Missouri in the mid-1950s, in his heart, he knows different.

Putting on his most convincing game face is more important now than ever—for himself, for his family, for his players and for Missouri basketball.

"One of the things about cancer, the doctors told us, is that you have to want to succeed," said Virginia Stewart, a former Missouri homecoming queen who married Stewart 33 years ago. "Getting back to work was very important to Norm."

If coaching is therapy, then, judging from appearances, the first treatment was a success.

For three games on three nights in the Lahaina Civic Center, a small gymnasium with no air-conditioning, in which temperatures reached 90 degrees, Stewart was electric.

He paced. He smiled. He screamed at players. He argued with officials. He yapped in mid-game with the Sacramento Kings' Bill Russell, seated near the end of the Missouri bench. He gestured in almost every conceivable way, to express his emotions and demonstrate to the officials a call or two they might have missed.

And with his Tigers on the way to an 80-73 championship victory over North Carolina, Stewart pulled the kind of showboat move that over the years has entertained his supporters and infuriated his detractors. He turned to a television camera, raised the thumb and pinky on his right hand and wiggled his wrist in a Hawaiian "hang-loose" gesture.

That bit of bench culture might have been lost on the landlocked folks watching back in Columbia, Mo., in the wee hours of Monday morning, but the rest of the act hit home.

His hair may be a little thinner, but Stewart, 54, demonstrated what he wants all to accept: The bleeding ulcers and the surgery for colon cancer and a diseased gall-bladder that forced him to miss Missouri's final 14 games last season will not drive him from coaching.

"At first we thought maybe it would be best he didn't come back," said sophomore guard Anthony Peeler, the Big Eight newcomer of the year last season. "Then we thought deep in our mind, and we knew that no matter what happened, he would want to be back. That is the way he is.

"But we wondered when he came back to practice what he would be like. We found out right away that he was the same coach."

That is what Stewart hopes everyone will conclude. He points out that the doctors have given him "a clean bill of health." But physical appearances are only part of the story. No matter how he acts on the basketball court, Stewart will never totally be the same.

Cancer changes everything.

★ ★ ★

In the days and hours away from the television glare, he will fight that reality. He will face the fear, the uncertainty and the anxiety of an examination every six months to tell him if the disease that cost him a third of his colon has reappeared.

Alone with his thoughts, he will contemplate mortality. He will recall a conversation with a nurse before he elected to undergo operational post-surgical cancer treatments. The brief exchange brought into the open words so hard to say.

" 'Norm, you have it figured out that life is fatal, haven't you?' " Stewart recalled the nurse asking him.

"Oh, yeah," was his simple reply; his thoughts were more complex.

"We all hear about mortality, and we are aware of it, but we don't think about it," Stewart said. "That is what happens with this. It is pushed straight up front to you, and you have to deal with it."

Stewart responded in the way that fits his confrontational image. He decided to attack his illness, regain his health and, if the doctors allowed, return to coaching as quickly as possible.

"Norm lives basketball; it has been his life," said Jack Lengyel, former Missouri athletic director who is now at Navy. "Knowing his competitive nature, I certainly expected that if there was any way he could, Norm would be back."

It was not the easy way out. Coaching is stressful anywhere, and the pressures at Missouri are particularly intense.

He has returned to a team deep in talent but troubled by joint investigations by the National Collegiate Athletic Association and an outside firm hired by the university to examine allegations of NCAA rule violations.

Stewart says those pressures might have contributed to the bleeding-ulcer attack that led to his passing out on a team flight to Oklahoma last February 9. Doctors discovered eight ulcers, seven in his stomach and one in his esophagus. Further tests revealed the cancer and gallbladder problems.

Although his team was ranked in the top 10 and was 20-3 when he fell ill, Stewart had been involved in a series of incidents. These reportedly ranged from exchanging obscenities with hecklers at Nebraska to allegedly threatening the year-old son of a St. Louis reporter. Stewart has denied making any threat.

The day before he blacked out, his assistant coach of 12 years, Bob Sundvold, was suspended after he admitted that he had violated NCAA rules by providing money for a round-trip plane ticket to P.J. Mays, an ineligible freshman recruit who has since left school. Sundvold has since been reinstated.

All that was going on at a time when Stewart was worried about his wife, who was recovering in the hospital after surgery that included the removal of a tumor that tests later determined was benign.

"There were a lot of things going on and I was trying to give my time to all of them," Stewart said. "I might have been a little stressed out."

★ ★ ★

Still, although he insists that he had no hint of his own health problems, he also said he might have been blinded by single-minded purpose.

"I went into last year with my mind really set on our ballclub," Stewart said. "I knew we had a good basketball team, and we had a good chance to go as far as we could. So I set myself aside from everything else. That was going to be it, and I zeroed in."

That all changed with his illness. Instead of trying to lead the Tigers to their first NCAA tournament victory since 1982, he wound up fighting for his health. He endured some difficult days. He developed complications after the surgery that he said kept him from eating for 16 days. He lost 30 pounds, to 185 over his 6-foot-5 frame.

"I was not in the best of shape," Stewart said. "I had a fever. I was getting into trouble."

Those who saw him were frightened.

"I visited him in the hospital when he was under sedation and he was in a different world," said Lee Coward, a senior point guard. "He told us not to worry. He said he would handle it, that he would do the right thing. But we knew emotionally he was holding a lot of things in.

"I'm just glad to have him back. It was a change when he was gone. It was a different atmosphere."

With Stewart out, the team was turned over to assistant coach Rich Daly, who is facing NCAA scrutiny over his admission that he brought in a player for a campus visit during a time when visits were not permitted.

Daly led the Tigers to the Big Eight tournament championship and the final 16 of the NCAA tournament, but it was a tumultuous time. Players said they rebelled under his authority and welcomed Stewart's return.

"He makes a difference," Coward said. "He has been on the sidelines 20-some years. He can put pressure on the officials. He can change the ballgame around. He is that type of person."

With the new season just under way and his team again near the top of the rankings, more attention has been brought on Stewart.

"I'd like to get it away from me as quickly as possible and get the focus on the players," Stewart said after his first Maui victory.

But to do that would be to ignore someone who has been one of college basketball's most confounding characters. Even before his illness, Stewart was a tough man to read. That has not changed.

Stewart reveals only pieces of what these recent months have brought to him and his family. He declines to discuss any significant details regarding his treatment after surgery. Tamburo, his athletic director, said that Stewart remained sketchy on his intentions to return until August.

Stewart is known to unleash his fury in an instant. His eyes can turn from inviting to steely cold. He can be profane, and he can hold a grudge.

He does this best with sportswriters. Stewart recalls an uncomplimentary article in his early days at Missouri that he said was the result of a recruiting battle with another school over a star Missouri player. He said the story caused him to end a working relationship with the reporter.

"I was not very nice, and I usually am not," Stewart said. "I said. 'It's just something you are going to have to handle,' and I hung up. To this day, when somebody does something like that, it's easy for me to eliminate him. I mean, he obviously needs me, and I don't need him. My wife will tell you I'm very severe when it comes to that."

Stewart says that reporters often tell just one side of the story, but even he allows that his side is not always becoming.

Take the incident near the end of an 89-72 victory at Nebraska last January 28. Stewart was overheard making a vulgar comment to fans seated behind the Missouri bench. Stewart said his response was in reaction to being called "a bush-leaguer, with some (obscene) adjectives in front of it," earlier in the game.

"I played baseball (in the Baltimore Orioles' farm system), and there's one word you don't call a baseball player, and that is a '*bush-leaguer,'* "Stewart said. "Well, my mistake was in replying to him."

Stewart can also be a polite, funny and engaging conversationalist, the type who will take the care to read name tags and call the personnel in a hotel coffee shop by their first names.

This is when Stewart is at his charming small-town best. This is the side of him those closest wish he could show more in public. They see the reports of Stewart's sometimes boorish public behavior and hope for a time when he can be understood as they know him.

★ ★ ★

"Norm has a great sense of humor, but not everyone gets the joke and that sometimes makes him look bad," Virginia Stewart said. "The words are so flat on paper. If only they could see the body language."

Then they should come to a Missouri game and watch Stewart's sideline pantomime. He has all the moves—the travel, the over-the-top, the hold, the three-point goal, the wave of the hand in disgust. It might play well at home, but try going into someone else's arena and doing that. No wonder he has become a magnet for hecklers.

Which raises an interesting question about what kind of reception Stewart will receive in arenas around the Big Eight. Will his fight back from cancer turn boos to cheers? Knowing Stewart, if they do, he would want them to turn out of respect, not sympathy.

He seeks respect not just for what he has overcome in the last eight months, but for what he has accomplished as an athlete and a coach. Stewart is sixth in victories among active coaches with a 526-267 record in 29 seasons at Northern Iowa and Missouri. He is the dean of Big Eight coaches and during his tenure has seen 26 other conference coaches come and go.

In his mind, that should have earned him respect that has nothing to do with sympathy.

He realizes that he is not likely to become a beloved coach to outsiders, but he wants respect. Maybe that is why he was so heartened by the community response to his illness.

He said he received thousands of get-well cards and letters. He said friends and strangers alike stopped by his home to offer home-cooked meals and help. He also learned that he is not alone with his disease.

"Any time we have a misfortune, people with that same misfortune contact you or you hear about them," Stewart said. "It has been so overwhelming because of the number of people that have cancer. The feeling there is for one another. I have really been impressed with that."

The outpouring could not have been more timely. With both husband and wife ill, they were unable to care for one another in a way their love said they should.

"Typically, I think a woman has a greater capacity for taking care of her man, than a man does a woman," Stewart said. "That is true in so many instances and I know it is in ours. It was hard for her to recuperate when you are mentally concerned about your mate.

"We kind of caught ourselves laughing because you are trying to take care of one another and you couldn't take care of yourself."

Virginia Stewart said: "I know it sounds funny but it drew us closer."

★ ★ ★

On the advice of Stewart's doctors, he and Virginia used some of their time together to take mini-vacations away from the pressures of Missouri. Only in August, after Stewart had completed his treatments and the doctors assured him there had been no recurrence of the cancer and he was free to go back to work, did he decide to return.

"If something happens, and I can't do it, then I'll have to make a decision," Stewart said. "But I have been doing this for 30-some years. For me, it is the same as someone going into an office to push paper or whatever he does.

"I don't mind turmoil."

But despite the tough words, some people around Stewart say they have seen a change in his manner. It struck Tamburo, the athletic director, a month ago as he watched Stewart conduct his first news conference since his return.

"I realized when I saw him at the press conference that his whole appearance is a little softer than it used to be," Tamburo said. "And he has told me there aren't going to be those 18-, 19-hour days, three or four days in a row. He is going to do his work, then go home for dinner."

That has not changed Stewart's intensity on the court or the demands he places on his players. He said he took them to task after a 65-53 first-round victory in Maui over Evansville for poor shot selection.

"I can't recall in the last 10 years having a team take more bad shots than that," Stewart said. "I have had teams hold the ball and have the 45-second clock run out, but at least they didn't take a bad shot. Taking a bad shot is kind of like giving up.

"I told my kids that after what I had just gone through, I was not going to tolerate that."

Leave it to Stewart to turn his experience as a cancer patient into a lesson in basketball. But that is far from all his players have learned about life and their coach over these difficult months.

Peeler, the sophomore guard, was on the plane when Stewart became sick. He saw the frantic activity to save Stewart and the fear around him.

"After we found out what it was, we never took anything for granted again in our lives," Peeler said. "Every day is a special day for each and every one of us. Any single moment of life is very important."

For Peeler, too, life will never be the same.

A Glimpse of the Phantom

PRO BASKETBALL

By *RICHARD O'CONNOR*

From PhillySport

Wasted talent in sports—especially pro basketball—is an old and sad story. How good could Marvin Barnes have been had he not self-destructed? And Micheal Ray Richardson could have rewritten the NBA record book—don't you think?—if it hadn't been for the nose candy.

Yet of all of the National Basketball Association tragedies, the saddest, and currently the strangest, is that of Raymond Lewis.

A 6-foot-1 guard out of Los Angeles, Lewis was a cult figure at Verbum Dei High School and a legend at California State-Los Angeles, where in his first season he beat out North Carolina State's David Thompson to lead the country in scoring with a 38.9 average. As a sophomore, he averaged 32.9 points and was so dazzling, so unstoppable, that the wise men of the game sat around and predicted he would become the best college player in the country by his junior year.

But at the end of his sophomore year, Lewis decided to leave college, declaring himself eligible for the 1973 NBA draft under the hardship rule. The 76ers, after naming Doug Collins as the team's (and the league's) No. 1 pick, selected Lewis as the last player of the first round. Lewis was just 20 years old, making him, at the time, the youngest player ever to be drafted into the NBA.

Still, expectations ran high. Said New York Knicks scout Dick McGuire: "Raymond Lewis has more raw basketball talent than any college player in the country—and that includes Bill Walton. He might be the best draft choice Philly has made since Billy Cunningham."

Lewis reported to the Sixers camp and bogarted everyone—including Collins. The *Daily News* bannered a headline: COLLINS TALKS A GOOD GAME, BUT RAYMOND LEWIS PLAYS IT. Another reported: LEWIS IS KIND OF YOUNG TO BE AN NBA LEGEND, BUT HE'S OFF TO A FAST START.

As it turned out, Raymond Lewis never became a legend in the NBA. Nor, for that matter, did he ever *play* in the NBA. Lewis ultimately walked away from pro basketball, disappearing one day into the mist, never to be heard from again. Over the years, ugly rumors about him periodically surfaced. He was a junkie, a pusher, a pimp. There were even reports that he was dead.

★ ★ ★

I had always been curious about Raymond Lewis, and a year ago I decided to track him down. For the longest time nobody seemed to know his whereabouts until, finally, a friend of a friend of a friend came up with a phone number. I called it. A man with a deep, gruff voice answered.

"Raymond Lewis, please," I said.

"Yeah."

I introduced myself and explained that I wanted to write a story about him.

He was silent for a long time. Then he said, "I don't know, man. There's been a lot of strange things happened and said 'bout me, so I don't know if I want to be speaking to no writer."

I pleaded my case.

"OK," he said, finally, "I'll give you five minutes."

"Where do you live?" I asked.

"Watts."

Watts does not appear to have recovered from the bloody riots of 1965. Buildings on that neighborhood's Central Avenue are boarded up; stores are burnt-out; garbage clogs the gutters and mangy dogs roam the streets. Men and women of all ages, wearing shabby clothes and ski caps, slump in doorways.

On this warm evening, I am driving around Watts, trying to find Raymond Lewis's house. I turn a corner and spot a group of teenagers. One is dribbling a basketball. I roll down the window.

"Excuse me," I say. "Can you tell me where I'd find 110th Street?"

Eyeballs slide. Surly looks are exchanged. Nobody speaks.

"Ah . . . well . . . actually," I manage, "I'm looking for Raymond Lewis."

The one dribbling the ball brightens. "What you want him for?" he asks.

I explain.

The kid says, "That man's the best, brother. He's better than most of the dudes playing in the NBA."

The chorus behind the kid grunts, "Yeah, baby, you tell him."

The kid gives me directions. I find the Lewis house. It is a tiny bungalow with a small dirt yard. Similar houses across the street are boarded up.

Men are drinking beer outside the house when I arrive. They quickly scatter—except for one. He is a stocky man, around 6'1", with a bloated face and drooping eyelids. He looks to be in his 50s. In fact, he is not yet 40.

He approaches me and says, "Did you find the place all right?"

I tell him about the kid and the kid's comments.

Raymond Lewis smiles triumphantly. "He's right, you know. I'm a legend around here." His smile quickly fades. He stares at me with piercing eyes. "As you can see," he says, "I'm still alive." He laughs crazily. "C'mon inside."

We start to walk into his house, but Lewis stops and points to a building in the distance. "That's where I went to high school," he says. "Verbum Dei."

The old-timers say that they never saw a basketball player at Verbum Dei the likes of young Raymond Lewis. As a freshman, he was so good he simply awed people. He wowed them with speed and quickness. With deft passing and fancy dribbling. But, most of all, he mesmerized them with his most lethal weapon—his jump shot. That was his gift, his art form. "He was so gifted offensively," says his former coach, George McQuarn, "it was frightening."

Indeed, his high school accomplishments speak for themselves. Three times his team won the California Interscholastic Federation divisional title, and twice Lewis was named the division's best player. "The bottom line on Lewis is that he's absolutely the best player ever to come out of California," McQuarn says.

Raymond Lewis's exploits were chronicled more closely than perhaps any other athlete in L.A.'s history. As a result, hundreds of college recruiters came to Watts and begged him to attend their school. When simple pleading didn't work, they tried seducing him with cars, clothes, money and women. Everyone thought he would go to Long Beach State, then coached by Jerry Tarkanian. But instead, Lewis chose California State.

Tark was crushed. "I never felt worse about losing a player," he said.

Why did Lewis choose tiny California State? No one knows for certain, but in his freshman year, he drove a new Corvette; by his sophomore year, he had a new Caddy, a new Pantera and a custom van.

Today, when asked how he could afford such luxury cars in college, he says, "Hey, I ain't getting into that, man. You're smart. You figure it out."

While Lewis won't discuss the school's recruiting practices, he will willingly talk about his basketball career at California State and is happy to recall the times he scored 30 points. Fifty points. Seventy points. And don't forget the game against Long Beach when he got 53 big ones and led his team to a double-overtime victory. Word had it Tark was so upset, he nearly swallowed his "biting towel."

"I played against Raymond Lewis in his first game as a sophomore," remembers Ray Vyzas, a former All-American at Sacred Heart University in Connecticut. "I couldn't believe how quick he was. And his shot? Oh, man, could he stick it. From all over the court." Vyzas shakes his head in amazement. "Let me tell you, Raymond Lewis could have won with Moe, Larry, Curly and Shemp as his teammates."

★ ★ ★

We enter the Lewis house now. It is small. Faded and torn yellow curtains over the doors and windows. The rug is frayed; the walls are bare. The room smells of cat urine. The only furnishings are a couch, a chair, a tape deck, speakers and a pile of albums.

When we both sit down, Lewis says, "OK, what is it you want to know?"

For starters, I say, I'd like to know what he's been doing the last few years. He hems and haws. Mentions a variety of menial jobs. Clerk, messenger, handyman for his grandfather, who owns the house he lives in and others in the vicinity.

"Who employs you *now?*" I ask.

"Nobody," he says. "Right now, I'm looking."

Suddenly, his face contorts into a scowl. He says in an angry voice, "Look, man, I know why you're here. You want to know if Raymond Lewis is strung out like people say. Well, he ain't. I'm live and I'm well." His voice drops, becomes confused. "All I am is a living example of someone who's been screwed by the NBA. I mean, I was blackballed by them suckers. They knew I could play. They just didn't want to pay me what I was worth." His hands knot into fists. Tendons bulge from his neck. His eyes are wild. "Look, man," he shouts, "when I look back at what happened to my pro career, all I can say is it was a nightmare."

★ ★ ★

Sixteen years later, the nightmare is still difficult to figure out. But here are the facts: Lewis says the Sixers promised him a $1 million-a-year contract to go hardship. Don DeJardin, then general manager of the Sixers, claims, "That's simply not true." Whatever the case, Lewis, who finally acted as his own agent, signed what he thought was a three-year guaranteed contract for $450,000. Truth was, the contract was for $190,000—a $25,000 signing bonus, $50,000 the first year, $55,000 the second and $60,000 the third. The remaining money was deferred.

"Raymond signed what was at the time a contract commensurate with other players drafted before and after him that year," says DeJardin, now a California businessman. "In fact, he received a fairly substantial bonus for the time."

Be that as it may, a Philadelphia reporter told *Sports Illustrated* that the contract was appropriate for "a third-round pick with terminal acne."

Angered, Lewis nevertheless reported to camp and so totally embarrassed Doug Collins that *SI* reported that 76ers coach Gene Shue "refused to allow Collins to guard Lewis, and that is when Lewis decided he needed some new and richer fine print in his contract."

When he didn't get it, he walked out of camp one day and flew home. He now says Shue called him and promised to renegotiate his contract if he would come back. Yet when he got to Philly, he claims Shue reneged on the deal. DeJardin, however, emphatically refutes that claim: "No way did we ever promise to renegotiate Raymond's contract. Look, he did play very well in preseason. But why would we have made any promises when he hadn't even played in a regular-season game?"

Whatever, Lewis once again walked out on the team, this time at halftime of an exhibition game. Shue sent assistant Jack McMahon to bring him back.

"The thing with Lewis was," Jack McMahon told me just before his death last spring, "he really felt that since he was outplaying Doug, he should have gotten more money. But I told him to be patient. For one thing, he had incentive clauses in his contract, whereby he could have made more money. But Raymond wouldn't listen. He was obsessed. But his contract was already signed." McMahon paused a second. "Let me say this about Raymond Lewis. The kid could really play. I mean, he could have been a star in the NBA. But he was always playing head games with others and himself."

Lewis sat out that first year. The following season, he came back to Philly but walked out again. Same reasons. He signed with the Utah Stars of the old American Basketball Association, but because he was still under contract to the Sixers he was pulled off the Stars' bench right in the middle of a game.

In 1975, new Sixers GM Pat Williams decided to give "the Phantom," as he was now called, another chance.

"When I was the GM with the Bulls in 1973, I went to see Lewis play against Northern Illinois," remembers Williams, now with the Orlando Magic. "When I left the gym that night, my body was tingling. I mean, here was a kid who had something special. Real star potential. So when I took the job with the Sixers, of course I wanted him."

The Sixers signed him and sent him to the Los Angeles Pro League. Lewis played well, but once, when he came down on a fastbreak and didn't get the ball, he continued running out of the gym.

He reappeared a few months later at Philadelphia International Airport, where he debarked a plane with Miss USA on one arm and a bible in the other.

At a press conference the next day, Lewis announced, "I'm ready to forget the past and just play basketball. I'd say it's about time to start my career."

But he didn't play well in camp. He blamed it on injuries. Others blamed it on the fact that rookie Lloyd Free upstaged him. Regardless, Lewis, as players like to say, "copped an attitude." He sulked, got lazy and then, one morning, as Pat Williams was walking into practice, Lewis was walking out. "I can't take it anymore," he said. "I'm going home."

"The truth is," says Williams, "Raymond was mentally tough enough to play in the league. He lacked inner strength."

Over the next few seasons, Lewis would have tryouts with the New York Knicks and the San Diego Clippers. But neither worked out. By then, his moves were slower, his jumper erratic and his once-burning desire for greatness was reduced to a mere pilot light.

★ ★ ★

Back in his living room, Lewis shifts in his chair and says, "I still don't know who the Sixers thought they were kidding. I would never have left school unless I thought I was going to get the millions, not a lousy few grand. It was bad enough they lied to me, but once I started cleaning Collins' clock, they should have reworked my deal. But, of course, Collins was the golden boy, while I was this uppity black kid."

Lewis goes on to say that his problems with the Sixers had racial overtones and that he was discriminated against. Yet even as he says this, his voice lacks conviction. "I'm just a victim of racism," he says softly.

As Lewis is speaking, a tall, pretty young girl bursts into the room. It's his daughter, Kamila, who is 13. She excitedly begins to ask her father a question.

"Wait a second," Lewis scolds, "can't you see I'm talking to someone? Now excuse yourself to my guest."

Kamila looks down at her shoetops. "Excuse me," she says sheepishly.

Raymond Lewis smiles. "That's good," he tells her. "Now what is it that's so important it can't wait?"

He puts his arm around his daughter's waist; she tells him about wanting to go see her grandmother.

Watching Lewis and his daughter, I am reminded of something he had told me earlier, when he said, "My family means everything to me." Indeed, he is—and always has been—extremely close to his grandparents. Even though his own mother and father are divorced, they both live nearby and he sees them regularly. As for himself, he's been married to the same woman, Sandra, for 16 years. Aside from Kamila, they also have a son, Rashad, who is nine.

Lewis and his daughter finish their conversation. He kisses her cheek. She leaves. For a moment, Lewis's eyes mist over. He sags in his seat. And just as I think he's going to get melancholy, he shoots upright in his chair. "What are you paying me for this story?" Stunned, I say magazines don't pay subjects for interviews. "Well, in that case," he says angrily, "you gotta go. No offense, man, 'cause I like you. But I just don't see why I should tell you my life story for nothing. I mean, it's unfair. Here your magazine's gonna use me to sell magazines and I don't get a penny of it." His eyes widen; his voice rises. "Bullshit!"

He falls silent. Takes a minute to compose himself. Then in a soft voice, he tells me how an actor he knows wants to do a movie about his life. He adds that if that doesn't work out, maybe he'll see about getting a tryout—with the Lakers.

I am incredulous. "You really think you could play for the Lakers?"

"Absolutely," he says. "Just ask anybody in the neighborhood. I can still do it."

He stands. I stand. We walk out of the bungalow into the fading daylight.

"Don't mean to throw you out," Lewis says. "But I ain't gonna be used by anyone so they can make money off me."

As I look at Raymond Lewis, I can't help but feel sad for him. He could have been one of the best, if not *the* best, basketball player ever to come out of L.A.

Yet unlike some ex-athletes, he has not descended into drugs and despair. Even though he lacks direction in his life, he still has a family who loves him. For that he should consider himself a lucky man. He shakes my hand goodbye. And then he turns toward the bungalow in pursuit of the rest of his life.

PRIZE-WINNING WRITERS IN BEST SPORTS STORIES 1990

Mitch Albom (Mark Messner) is the lead sports columnist for the *Detroit Free Press.* The 31-year-old Philadelphia native was graduated from Brandeis University with a sociology degree and then earned master's degrees in journalism and business administration from Columbia University. Albom has been named the Associated Press Sports Editors top columnist for the last three years after finishing second in 1985. He is the only writer to win the prestigious award three times.

Thomas Boswell (Curse of Modern Sports: Me-Itis) is a sports columnist for the *Washington Post* and a contributing editor and monthly columnist for *Golf* magazine. The 1969 Amherst College graduate is one of the most respected baseball writers in the country and has written three books on the sport: *How Life Imitates the World Series, Time Begins on Opening Day* and *The Heart of the Order.* Boswell has won numerous sportswriting awards and now is a four-time winner in *Best Sports Stories* competition. He is making his 11th appearance in the anthology.

Angelo Cataldi (co-author of Team Doctors: A Crisis in Ethics) is a sports special projects writer for the *Philadelphia Inquirer.* The 38-year-old Cataldi, who joined the Inquirer sports staff in 1983, previously had worked at the *Narragansett Times* and the *Providence Journal-Bulletin* in his home state of Rhode Island. Upon his arrival in Philadelphia, Cataldi covered the hockey Flyers before moving over to the football Eagles. His coverage of the Eagles' first season under Coach Buddy Ryan earned him recognition as a finalist in the 1987 Pulitzer Prize for special subject reporting. Cataldi owns a bachelor degree in journalism from the University of Rhode Island and a master's degree in journalism from Columbia University.

Pat Jordan (War of the Roses) is a free-lance writer and author who works out of Fort Lauderdale, Fla. His work has appeared in such magazines as *Sports Illustrated, Inside Sports* and *Gentlemen's Quarterly*, for which he wrote the magazine winner that appears in *Best Sports Stories 1990.* Jordan, a former professional baseball pitcher who spent most of his three years in the Atlanta Braves organization, is a graduate of Fairfield University in Fairfield, Conn. He has authored nine books, including the acclaimed baseball memoir *A False Spring.*

Glen Macnow (co-author of Team Doctors: A Crisis in Ethics) has been with the *Philadelphia Inquirer* since 1986, writing primarily about the financial, legal and marketing aspects of sports. The 34-year-old Buffalo, N.Y., native had previously handled the same kind of writing for the *Detroit Free Press* after stints in Florida with the *Fort Lauderdale News* and *Sun-Sentinel* and *Florida Today.* The Boston University graduate is making his second consecutive appearance in *Best Sports Stories.*

OTHER WRITERS IN BEST SPORTS STORIES 1990

Paul Attner (Kareem: Leaving Legacy of Consistency) has been a national correspondent for *The Sporting News* since 1984. The former *Washington Post* sportswriter, a 1969 graduate of California State University at Fullerton, was selected Alumnus of the Year by the university's School of Communications in 1986. Attner, the author of three books, has won numerous sportswriting awards, including three first places in the annual Pro Football Writers Association of America writing contests and a first-place award in the U.S. Pro Basketball Writers Association annual contest. He is making his third appearance in *Best Sports Stories.*

Thomas Bonk (Boy Wonder) is a sports feature writer for the *Los Angeles Times* who specializes in college basketball and professional tennis. The 1971 North Texas State University graduate also has covered college football and golf during his seven-plus years in Los Angeles. Bonk began his professional career with the *Houston Post*, working 11 years for the publication in different capacities ranging from sports columnist and assistant sports editor to assistant news editor. The Denton, Tex., native is married and has a 2-year-old son.

Ron Borges (Rooted in Tradition: The Raiders' Art Shell), a sportswriter for the *Boston Globe,* has spent the last 14 years in pursuit of professional athletes from coast to coast. He began his career at one of the smallest weekly newspapers in Massachusetts, the now-defunct *Martha's Vineyard Grapevine.* He worked for the *Sacramento Union*, the *Oakland Tribune* and the *Baltimore News-American* before joining the Globe staff in 1983. A former features award winner in the Associated Press Sports Editors annual competition, Borges' column on boxer Mike Tyson captured the commentary award in *Best Sports Stories 1989.* He is making his sixth appearance in the anthology.

Mark Bradley (Last Week's Miracle, This Week's Tragedy) is the lead columnist for the *Atlanta Journal-Constitution.* The 1977 University of Kentucky graduate began his career at the *Lexington Herald-Leader* in 1978 and worked there until his move to Atlanta in 1984. One of his 1985 columns captured first place in the annual Associated Press Sports Editors competition and he has been honored eight times by the U.S. Basketball Writers Association. Bradley is making his second appearance in *Best Sports Stories.*

Bruce Buschel (The Battle Is With Himself) is a free-lance writer who works out of New York. He is a former staff writer for the Sunday magazine of the *Philadelphia Inquirer* and *Philadelphia* magazine. He currently contributes to such publications as *PhillySport* and *Atlantic City* magazine and maintains a close tie with *Gentlemen's Quarterly,* for which he served as a senior writer for three years. The former winner of the Golden Quill sportswriting award is hard at work on his first novel.

Lowell Cohn (Walsh's Life Without a Team) has been a sportswriter and columnist for the *San Francisco Chronicle* since 1979. The Brooklyn native attended Lafayette College in Easton, Pa., before heading west and earning a Ph.D. in English from Stanford University. Cohn worked as a free-lance writer for several years after graduation, contributing frequently to *Sports Illustrated.* He currently lives in Oakland with his wife and two sons.

Mike Downey (The Tooz Couldn't Scare Away Death) is a nationally syndicated sports columnist for the *Los Angeles Times* who also writes a weekly column for *The Sporting News.* The 38-year-old Steger, Ill., native began his career as a sportswriter in Chicago for both the *Chicago Daily News* and *Chicago Sun-Times*. He also wrote about show-business personalities for the entertainment pages and authored a one-hour NBC-TV special on Comiskey Park and Wrigley Field. He became a columnist for the *Detroit Free Press* in 1982 and was twice honored as Michigan Sportswriter of the Year by the National Sportscasters and Sportswriters Association. Downey, who is making his third appearance in *Best Sports Stories*, was honored in 1988 by the Association as California Sportswriter of the Year.

Dave Dye (The Mouth That Roars) has been writing about sports for the *Detroit News* for the last four years. He moved to Detroit after spending less than a year in Florida with the *St. Petersburg Times*. Since joining the News, Dye has covered the Detroit Pistons of the National Basketball Association and Michigan State University athletics. He currently works as the paper's national baseball writer. Dye, who earned his bachelor's degree in journalism from Michigan State in 1984, was an all-state honorable mention hockey player while attending high school in Ann Arbor, Mich.

Lewis Freedman (Iditarod Rescue Is Sweeter Than Victory) is sports editor of the *Anchorage Daily News*. The 1973 graduate of the Boston University School of Public Communication recently completed his master's degree in international affairs at Alaska Pacific University in Anchorage. Freedman worked for the *Philadelphia Inquirer, Florida Times-Union* and *Syracuse Herald-Journal* before joining the Daily News six years ago. He has authored a book on mountain climbing, *Dangerous Steps*, that will be published in 1990 and he is making his third appearance in *Best Sports Stories*.

Tom Friend (Manley: Crisis After Crisis) is a sportswriter for the *Washington Post*. The Washington, D.C., native went on a journalistic journey that covered more than 6,000 miles before returning to the Washington area in 1987. He was graduated with a degree in journalism from the University of Missouri in 1983 and worked briefly with the *Kansas City Star-Times* before moving to the *San Jose Mercury-News* and then the *Los Angeles Times* in a two-year period. He spent two years with the Times before heading back east. Friend has covered such teams as the Kansas City Kings and Golden State Warriors of the National Basketball Association, baseball's San Diego Padres and the National Football League's Washington Redskins.

John Hawkins (The Dean) has spent the last three years writing for the *Washington Times*, where he has covered college sports, the National Football League and major league baseball. He spent 3½ years with the *Baltimore News American* before joining the Times sports staff. The Towson State University graduate has done numerous free-lance articles that have appeared in such magazines as *Insight, Off the Glass* and the *Blue Ribbon Basketball Yearbook*. Hawkins is single and lives in Burtonsville, Md.

Tom Hawthorn (Brophy's Last Brawl) is a 29-year-old free-lance reporter based in Vancouver, British Columbia. He began his journalism career in 1979 with the now-defunct *Vancouver Daily Courier* and later worked for the *Canadian University Press*, the *Vancouver Sun*, the *Mexico City Daily News* and the *Toronto Globe and Mail*. As a free-lancer, Hawthorn's work has appeared in such publications as *Toronto Life, West, Montreal* and the *Financial Times of Canada*. His report titled *The Return of the Battle of the Monster Trucks* was included in the 1989 edition of *Best Canadian Essays*, an annual anthology.

Phil Hersh (In End, Rose Not Bigger Than Baseball) covers international sports, including the Olympics, for the *Chicago Tribune*, the publication for which he has worked since 1984. Prior to that, he worked for the *Chicago Sun-Times*, the

Chicago Daily News, the *Baltimore Evening Sun* and the *Gloucester* (Mass.) *Daily Times.* Hersh, a 1968 graduate of Yale University with a bachelor's degree in French, has won several awards in the Associated Press Sports Editors annual competition and has been nominated for a Pulitzer Prize. The 1986 winner in the commentary category of *Best Sports Stories*, Hersh is making his seventh appearance in the anthology.

Curt Holbreich (Back to Work) covers San Diego State University sports for the *Los Angeles Times.* The 31-year-old Holbreich is a graduate of Wesleyan University and the Columbia University School of Journalism. Prior to joining the Times, he worked for the *Pittsburgh Press, USA Today* and the *Camden* (N.J.) *Courier-Post.* Holbreich is making his third appearance in *Best Sports Stories.*

Jan Hubbard (Coming to America) has covered professional basketball for Long Island-based *Newsday* since April 1989. Prior to that, he covered the National Basketball Association and the Dallas Mavericks for nine years, first for the *Fort Worth Star-Telegram,* then for the *Dallas Morning News.* The 1975 Southern Methodist University graduate also has worked for the *Fort Worth Press* and the *Beaumont* (Tex.) *Enterprise.* Hubbard, who has written a weekly NBA column for *The Sporting News* for eight years, is making his second appearance in *Best Sports Stories.*

Bruce Jenkins (Knowing Billy Was a Privilege) is the lead sports columnist for the *San Francisco Chronicle.* He joined the newspaper in 1973 after his graduation from the University of California at Berkeley and worked as a full-time baseball writer (switching between the Giants and Oakland Athletics) from 1978 through '86. Jenkins has covered the last 11 World Series and the last three Wimbledon tennis championships. He has been honored in several sportswriting competitions and wrote a book, *Life After Saberhagen*, which was published in 1986. Jenkins currently is nursing three different book projects in his spare time.

Mark Kram (A Sore Subject) has been writing about sports for the *Philadelphia Daily News* since 1987. Before coming to Philadelphia, the Baltimore native worked as a sportswriter for the *Detroit Free Press* and the *Baltimore News-American.* Kram, who lives in Haddonfield, N.J., with his wife and daughter, is making his third consecutive appearance in *Best Sports Stories.*

Mike Lopresti (Ryan Strikes Milestone) is a national sports correspondent-columnist for Gannett News Service, which serves 88 newspapers in the Gannett Group. He operates out of Richmond, Ind., where he worked several years at the *Palladium-Item* newspaper before joining GNS. Lopresti has covered a wide spectrum of sports, ranging from high schools to the World Series, the Super Bowl and the Olympics. Lopresti is married and has two children.

Barry Lorge (The Legacy of Chris Evert) is sports editor and columnist for the *San Diego Union* and a contributing editor to *Tennis* magazine. The 1970 Harvard graduate moved to San Diego in 1981 after five years as a staff writer for the *Washington Post.* Lorge, who has covered sports stories in more than 20 countries on five continents, is making his eighth appearance in *Best Sports Stories.*

John Meyer (Field of Freedom) has been a staff writer for the *Rocky Mountain News* since 1981. Before coming to Denver, he worked as a sportswriter for the *St. Petersburg* (Fla.) *Independent*, the *Dallas Times-Herald* and the *Fort Lauderdale Sun-Sentinel.* In 1985, Meyer was part of a Denver-based expedition that climbed Mount Everest. He climbed with the team, reaching an altitude of 24,000 feet on Everest's West Ridge, filed weekly stories and produced an eight-part series upon his return. He currently covers golf, skiing and other general assignments.

William Nack (The Longest Ride), a senior writer for *Sports Illustrated*, is considered one of the top horseracing writers in the country. Nack, a native of Chicago and a graduate of the University of Illinois, served two years in the Army (part of his tour in Vietnam) before becoming a columnist for Long Island-based *Newsday*. He joined the SI staff in 1979. Nack, the author of *Secretariat: The Making of a Champion*, is a resident of Washington, D.C. He has four children ranging in age from 18 to 23.

Glenn Nelson (Inner Strength: Steve Largent's Farewell) has been covering sports for the *Seattle Times* for the last eight years. His assignments have included the National Basketball Association's Seattle SuperSonics, the National Football League's Seattle Seahawks and the 1988 Olympic Games in Seoul, South Korea. The 31-year-old Nelson was born in Japan and raised in Seattle. He earned a journalism degree from Seattle University and a master's degree in political science from Columbia University.

Richard O'Connor (A Glimpse of the Phantom), a former college basketball star at Duke and Fairfield universities, is Editor and part owner of *SportsTravel* magazine. O'Connor, born in New Jersey, was a high school basketball All-America who received a scholarship to Duke. After helping the Blue Devils reach the NIT in 1972, he transferred to Fairfield, where he later served as the team's co-captain while leading it in scoring. After a brief stint with the San Diego Conquistadors of the American Basketball Association, he turned to freelance sportswriting in 1977. His stories have appeared in such publications as *Gentlemen's Quarterly, Playboy, Sports Illustrated, Sport, TV Guide, PhillySport* and *People*. O'Connor, who resides in Glen Ridge, N.J., was Editor and part owner of *Sports Wise Magazine* in New York from 1980-85.

Mark Purdy (After 10 Days of Pain, Let's Resume Series Gracefully) has been sports editor of the *San Jose Mercury News* since 1984. A graduate of Northwestern University, he also has worked at the *Los Angeles Times*, the *Cincinnati Enquirer*, the *Dayton Journal Herald* and his hometown newspaper, the *Celina* (O.) *Daily Standard*. Purdy is making his third appearance in *Best Sports Stories*.

Ron Rapoport (Thompson's Attack on Prop 48 is Wrong) is a sports columnist for the *Los Angeles Daily News*. A Stanford University product who did graduate work at the Columbia University School of Journalism, Rapoport served earlier stints with the *Minneapolis Star*, the *Associated Press*, the *Los Angeles Times* and the *Chicago Sun-Times*. He was the 1984 winner of the National Headliner Award for "consistently outstanding sports columns," and his work also has been honored by the Associated Press Sports Editors Association. Rapoport is making his eighth appearance in *Best Sports Stories*.

Scott Reid (Is Perfection Good Enough?) is a general assignments reporter in the sports department of the *Dallas Times Herald*. He has covered racial and drug-related issues in college and high school sports and he has written a series of articles examining the financial status of the Major Indoor Soccer League. Before coming to Dallas, Reid attended the University of Washington where he earned academic honors as a History of the Americas major. He also competed for the Washington cross country and track and field teams. He is making his first appearance in *Best Sports Stories*.

Jeff Rude (Lamarr Mondane: Uncovering the Legend) has been deputy sports editor of the *Chicago Sun-Times* since 1986. A 1976 University of Missouri graduate, Rude began his journalism career as an intern for the *Richmond* (Va.) *News Leader*. He went on to work as a sportswriter for the *Shreveport* (La.) *Journal* and *Jacksonville Journal*, a sports editor/columnist for *Today* in Cocoa, Fla., a deputy sports editor for the *Pittsburgh Post-Gazette* and assistant sports editor for the *Dallas Morning News*.

Mark Shelton (Stroke of Genius) is associate editor of *Ohio Magazine* and author of *Working In A Very Small Place*, a book about neurosurgeon Peter J. Jannetta. A native of Chicago, Shelton has been published widely in magazines, newspapers and literary journals, including *Pittsburgh* magazine and the *Pittsburgh Post-Gazette*. He resides in Athens, O.

Teri Thompson (Tennessee Revives Bad Memories) is a sports columnist for the *Rocky Mountain News*, where she has been working in various capacities since 1978. Her duties have included basketball, football and general assignment reporting. A native of Clarksville, Ark., and a graduate of the University of Arkansas, Thompson worked two years with the *Arkansas Democrat* and two years with the *Colorado Springs Gazette-Telegraph* before joining the News. She won a first-place award in the Sigma Delta Chi annual journalism contest for best sports commentary in 1988 and her work has been cited by the annual Associated Press Sports Editors judges. She is making her second appearance in *Best Sports Stories*.

Joseph Tintle (The Bayonne Bleeder's Bloodiest Brawl) is associate editor of *The Ring* and *KO* magazines. A graduate of Fairleigh Dickinson University and a former sportswriter for *Newsday*, Tintle has covered the boxing scene for several New Jersey dailies and recently completed a book, *Behind This Face*, which tells the story of former heavyweight contender Chuck Wepner, actor Sylvester Stallone's inspiration for his portrayal of Rocky Balboa in the "Rocky" movies. Tintle currently lives in Union, N.J., with his wife and son.

Mike Tulumello (Frank Kush) is a sports reporter for the *Tribune Newspapers* of Arizona (Mesa, Tempe and Chandler). Although he currently covers the National Basketball Association's Phoenix Suns, Tulumello specializes in news-oriented sports stories, such as tracking the graduation rates of Arizona collegiate athletes. The 1978 Arizona State graduate began his career covering sports for the *New Times*, a Phoenix-area weekly. He also worked for the *Associated Press* and the *Memphis Press-Scimitar*.

John Valenti (He Could Have Been a Star) covers sports for Long Island-based *Newsday's* New York edition. The Hofstra University graduate began working for *Newsday* in 1981 and spent four years taking the results of high school games over the telephone. Promoted to full-time status in 1985, Valenti now covers local New York colleges, Seton Hall University basketball and the National Basketball Association's New Jersey Nets. Valenti lives on Long Island with his wife and son.

Jay Weiner (A Struggling Hero: Killebrew Hits Hard Times) is a sports feature writer for the *Minneapolis Star Tribune*. Born in Philadelphia in 1954, Weiner attended Oberlin College and was graduated from Temple University. He interned and later worked full-time for Long Island-based *Newsday* before joining the Star-Tribune's staff in 1980. His assignments have included the Minnesota Twins, the 1984 and 1988 Winter and Summer Olympic Games, the role of intercollegiate athletics in higher education and the business aspects of sports, from high schools to the major leagues. Weiner, a consistent winner in state and national writing contests, also is a weekly commentator for Minnesota Public Radio.

Alexander Wolff (The Coach and His Champion) is a senior writer for *Sports Illustrated*, the publication for which he has worked since 1980. His primary focus has been college basketball, but Wolff also has covered such sports as tennis and college football. A Wilmington, Del., native who earned a history degree from Princeton University in 1980, Wolff lives in New York City. He is the author of three books, *The In-Your-Face Basketball Book*, co-authored with Chuck Wielgus, it's sequel, *Back-In-Your-Face Guide to Pickup Basketball* and *From A-Train to Yogi*, a book about nicknames.

PRIZE-WINNING PHOTOGRAPHERS IN BEST SPORTS STORIES 1990

Bernard Brault (Speed!) is a staff photographer at *La Presse* newspaper who also does free-lance work out of Canada. Brault, who lives in Longueuil, Quebec, began his career in 1976 as a staff photographer at a local newspaper before taking the free-lance route four years later. His work has appeared in several Quebec sports magazines and he has contributed to such wire services as *United Press Canada, Reuters* and *Canadian Press.* Brault, who began contributing to *La Presse* in 1984, has earned numerous citations for his work and gives seminars on sports photography a couple times a year. The 1989 winner for Best Action photo in *Best Sports Stories* competition, Brault is making his fifth consecutive appearance in the anthology.

Stephen Morton (A Bunch of Bull) has been a staff photographer at the *Gainesville* (Fla.) *Sun* since 1986. He attended high school in Key West, Fla., and later attended Florida Keys Community College and the University of Florida. Morton was a stringer at the *Sun* for one year before landing an entry-level position with the paper.

Greg Trott (Ump Grump) is a staff photographer at the *Vacaville* (Calif.) *Reporter.* A 1981 Fresno State University graduate with a degree in photojournalism, Trott worked as an intern for two years at the *Redding* (Calif.) *Record-Searchlight* before joining the *Reporter.* Trott, who has sold some of his work to *The Sporting News* and the National Football League, is making his second consecutive appearance in *Best Sports Stories.*

OTHER PHOTOGRAPHERS IN BEST SPORTS STORIES 1990

Tracy Baker (Anybody's Ball) is a 1970 University of Michigan graduate who worked as both a staff photographer and graphics editor at a chain of 18 semi-weekly newspapers in suburban Detroit from 1971-77. He worked free-lance in Detroit for the next few years before moving to Hamburg, West Germany, in 1983 to free-lance for American and German clients. Baker worked as a staff photographer at *The European Stars and Stripes*, a daily newspaper published by the U.S. Department of Defense, in 1985. Baker, who has received more than 30 foreign and domestic photography awards, is making his first appearance in *Best Sports Stories.*

Nicole Bengiveno (Child's Play) has been a staff photographer at the *New York Daily News* since 1986. She previously had been a staff photographer at the *San Francisco Examiner* for eight years and was named Bay Area Press Photographer of the Year in 1979. Bengiveno won first-place awards in features competition from the New York Associated Press in 1987 and 1989. She is making her first appearance in *Best Sports Stories.*

Louis DeLuca (Follow the Bouncing Balls) has been a staff photographer at the *Dallas Times Herald* for the past six years. He began his career with the *Shreveport* (La.) *Journal,* moved to the *Chicago Sun-Times* in 1983 and to Dallas a year later. DeLuca has won in *Best Sports Stories* competition on four occasions: in 1987 and 1988 for best black and white feature photo, and in 1984 and 1986 for best black and white action photo. He was the 1982 Photographer of the Year in Louisiana, Texas and New Mexico and was runner-up for that honor in 1985 and 1987.

Albert P. Fuchs (Web of Arms) has been a general assignment photographer at the *Knoxville News-Sentinel* since August 1987. Prior to joining the *News-Sentinel*, the 1983 Bowling Green State University graduate worked at both the *Orange County* (Calif.) *Register* and the *Kettering-Oakwood* (O.) *Times*. The Cleveland native is making his first appearance in *Best Sports Stories*.

Richard B. Gentile (Bush League) is a free-lance sports photographer in the Washington D.C.-Baltimore area. His work has been published in many of this country's leading sports publications, including *The Sporting News* and *Baseball Digest*. Much of Gentile's work is in association with the National Football League.

G. Loie Grossman (A Big Divot) has been a staff photographer at the *Philadelphia Daily News* since 1983. The 1976 Penn State graduate has won numerous awards for her work, including New Jersey Photographer of the Year awards in 1984 and 1988 and a first-place prize in the news-picture story category of the Pictures of the Year competition in 1984. Grossman is making her first appearance in *Best Sports Stories*.

Elizabeth Karnazes (Sweet Victory) is a San Francisco-based free-lance photojournalist whose work primarily has appeared in *United Press International* since 1988. The Boulder, Colo., native covers a wide variety of assignments—including professional sports—and is making her first appearance in *Best Sports Stories*.

Dan Levine (End of an Era) has been a staff photographer at the *Dallas Times-Herald* since May 1984 and is also responsible for a variety of editorial assignments at the paper. The 30-year-old Levine has been a Christian for four years and is a member of Christians In Photojournalism, a nationwide group that seeks to promote Christian values in the newspaper workplace. The 1983 Ohio University graduate is making his first appearance in *Best Sports Stories*.

Andrea Mihalik (Yakety-Yak) has been a staff photographer at the *Philadelphia Daily News* for the last 1½ years. She graduated from Philadelphia's Tyler School of Art in 1987 and worked for a small daily in West Chester, Pa., before joining the *Daily News*. Mihalik, who won two Associated Press Managing Editors awards while in college, is making her first appearance in *Best Sports Stories*.

Brian Peterson (Man Down) has been a staff photographer at the *Minneapolis Star Tribune* since April 1987. Prior to joining the *Star Tribune*, the 30-year-old Peterson worked at the *St. Paul Pioneer Press Dispatch*, the *Colorado Springs Sun* and the *Faribault* (Minn.) *Daily News*. He is a four-time recipient of the Minnesota Press Photographer of the Year award. A 1981 Bemidji State (Minn.) University graduate, Peterson has won awards from the Baseball and Football Halls of Fame and is making his second straight appearance in *Best Sports Stories*.

Tom Reese (A Real Yawner) has been a staff photographer at the *Seattle Times* for the last 2½ years. The 31-year-old St. Louis native previously worked at the *Everett* (Wash.) *Herald*, the *Columbia* (Mo.) *Daily Tribune* and the *Kansas City Times*. Reese is making his first appearance in *Best Sports Stories*.

Christopher Smith (The Chase) has worked in the photography department at the *Brantford* (Ont.) *Expositor* for the past three years. A graduate of McMaster

University in Hamilton, Ont., Smith began working at the newspaper as head proofreader in 1971 before moving into the composing room for a 10-year stay. He is making his second straight appearance in *Best Sports Stories.*

Billy Weeks (The Big Splash) has been a staff photographer at the *Chattanooga Times* since April 1984. He worked two years at the University of Tennessee at Chattanooga while attending that school and currently teaches photojournalism part-time at a local college. Weeks, who enjoys photographing nature and wildlife as well as sporting events, is making his third appearance in *Best Sports Stories.*

Diane Weiss (Airborne) has been a staff photographer at the *Detroit News* since June 1989. Before joining the *News*, she was a contract photographer for the *Philadelphia Inquirer* for six years and also did free-lance work for *United Press International* in Philadelphia from 1987-89. The 33-year-old Philadelphia native covered the Eagles, Phillies, 76ers and Flyers during her time at her hometown paper and currently covers the Detroit Red Wings hockey team for the *News.* Weiss is making her first appearance in *Best Sports Stories.*

THE PANEL OF JUDGES FOR BEST SPORTS STORIES 1990

James D. Atwater was dean of the School of Journalism at the University of Missouri-Columbia from 1983 to 1989 and now teaches magazine writing there. Before moving to Missouri, he was a writer and senior editor for the *Saturday Evening Post* and spent 21 years with *Time* as a correspondent, writer and senior editor.

Brian Brooks is an associate professor of journalism at the University of Missouri and coordinator of the school's editing programs. The former reporter and editor at the *Memphis Press-Scimitar* and *Columbia Missourian* managing editor is co-author of *News Reporting and Writing, The Art of Editing* and *Working With Words.*

George Kennedy is managing editor of the *Columbia Missourian* at the University of Missouri School of Journalism. Before moving to Columbia, Kennedy spent 7½ years as a reporter and editor with the *Miami Herald* and two summers as a writing coach for the *San Jose Mercury.* He is co-author of *News Reporting and Writing* and *The Writing Book,* two college and professional textbooks.

Bill Kuykendall is an associate professor and director of the photojournalism sequence at the University of Missouri School of Journalism. He formerly was director of photography at the *Seattle Times* and a frequent speaker on photojournalism and photo department management. Kuykendall also directs the international Pictures of the Year competition.

Daryl Moen is a professor at the University of Missouri and director of Professional Programs at the university's School of Journalism. He is a former managing editor of the *Columbia Missourian* and two other dailies. Moen also is co-author of *News Reporting and Writing* and *The Writing Book* and author of *Newspaper Layout and Design.*